Objectives in

Soil and Water Conservation Engineering

For JRF, SRF, NET, ARS,
IARI Ph.D., State Exams. etc.

Pawan Jeet
Prem

Published by :
New Vishal Publication
E/153, West Patel Nagar, New Delhi - 08
E-mail : *nvpbooks@hotmail.com*
Website : www.newvishal.weebly.com

First Edition : August, 2016
Second Edition : September, 2017
Third Edition : February, 2024

Price : Rs. 360.00
Rupees Three Hundred and Sixty Only

Published by :
NEW VISHAL PUBLICATION
E-153, West Patel Nagar, New Delhi – 110008
Ph. : 9811251105
E-mail : nvpbooks@hotmail.com
Website : www.newvishal.weebly.com

Available in Delhi at :
Pusa Agricultural Books Service
29, Shishir Hostel, IARI, Delhi-12
Ph. : 011-25841048, 9868827628
E-mail : pusa.agri@gmail.com

Graphics and laser typesetting by :
Oberoi Graphics, New Delhi

Printed at :
Narula Printers,
Jhilmil Industrial Area, Delhi

PREFACE

This objective book is intended to be used by students of Soil and Water Conservation Engineering, Land and Water Management Engineering, Irrigation & Drainage Engineering/Irrigation & Water Management Engineering and agricultural engineering/agricultural students of different colleges of Indian Universities. The purpose of the book is to make students excel in different exams like Agricultural Research Service (ARS), National Eligibility Test (NET), PhD entrance exam of different Agricultural Universities etc. Chapters have been identified according to the ARS pattern. Some useful information regarding SI units, measurements, mathematical equations, related formulas, different dimensionless numbers etc. have been included for ready reference for users of this book.

Few questions from instrumentation and basic mathematics which are being asked in IARI PhD Exam have also been included in various chapters. The authors would feel obliged if the readers points out both grammatical and technical error if any, in the book for rectifying in the successive editions.

We would like to sincere thanks Mr. Deepak Singh, Mr. Sujeet Desai, Man Mohan, Ravindra (Scientist, ICAR) for providing their valuable suggestions to us throughout the preparation of this book.

We would also like to extend our heartfelt gratitude to Manoj, Veerana, Manish, Abhinav, Bikram, Jaya, Laulina, Ajita, Vikash, Aarti, Aniket, Om, Ankit, Sumeet and Sushil (students of distinguish division of IARI) for their most valuable help rendered in relation to planning and preparation of this book.

We owe a debt of gratitude to distinguish scientists of Division of Agricultural Engineering, IARI for their help and blessings.

New Delhi

Pawan Jeet and Prem

CONTENTS

Books list for ICAR-JRF/NET/ARS/ SRF Examination Preparation

Soil and Water Conservation Engineering / Land and Water Management Engineering

Hydrology

- Engineering Hydrology: K Sbramanyam
- Hydrology: Principles, Analysis and Design: H. M. Raghunath

Soil and water conservation Engineering

- Soil and water conservation Engineering.: R. Suresh
- Land and Water Management Engineering: V.V.N. Murthy and Madan K. Jha
- Principles Of Agricultural Engineering (Vol II): A. M. Michael and T. P. Ojha,
- Soil and Water Conservation Engineering: Glenn O. Schwab; Delmer D. Fangmeier; William J. Elliot and Richard K. Frevert (Published by Wiley)

Irrigation

- Irrigation Theory and Practice: A.M. Michael
- Land and Water Management Engineering: V.V.N. Murthy and Madan K. Jha
- Handbook of Agri. Engineering: ICAR

Drainage

- Land and Water Management Engineering: V.V.N. Murthy and Madan K. Jha
- Handbook of Agri. Engineering: ICAR

Watershed Development and Management

- Soil and water conservation Engineering.: R. Suresh

- Water Harvesting and Recycling: Indian Experiences: V N Sharda; Sikka and Shamra
- Hydrology and Soil Conservation Engineering: Including Watershed Management: Ghanshyam Das

Wells and Pumps & Groundwater hydrology

- Groundwater Hydrology: D.K.Todd
- Water Wells and Pumps: S D Khepar; A M Michael and M S K Sondhi
- Applied Hydrology: V. T. Chow

Fluid mechanics

- Fluid mechanics: R. K. Bansal
- Open-Channel Hydraulics: V. T. Chow

Objectives in SWCE

- Objectives in Soil and Water Conservation Engineering: Pawan Jeet and Prem
- Question Bank on Agriculture & Food Engineering : Garg and Pritam Chandra
- Agricultural Engineering Question Bank (Dapoli QB): Jain brothers
- Question bank on Agricultural Engineering: Rawat and Nikhade

Numerical practices

- A Numerical Approach in Agricultural Engineering with Objective: Sanjay Kumar
- Numerical Problems in Agricultural Engineering: Nikhade, Rawat and Victor
- Agricultural Engineering through Objectives: Radhey Lal

Agriculture Research Scientists (ARS) Syllabus

Discipline: Land and Water Management Engineering

Unit 1: Groundwater Development, Wells and Pumps

Water resources of India. Irrigation potential and contribution of groundwater, utilizable groundwater resources and level of groundwater development in the country, scope of groundwater development. Aquifer types and parameters. Principles of groundwater flow, interaction between surface and groundwater, natural and artificial groundwater recharge. Hydraulics of fully and partially penetrating wells. Design, construction and development of irrigation wells. Water lifts, pumps and prime movers, well and pumps characteristics, performance evaluation and selection of pumps. Energy requirement in groundwater pumping. Design of centrifugal pumps. Groundwater pollution. Salt water intrusion in inland and coastal aquifers. Application of groundwater models for groundwater development and management. Conjunctive use of surface and groundwater.

Unit 2: Open Channel Hydraulics

Hydraulics of open channel flow, energy and momentum principles, specific energy, Hydraulic jump and its classification. Design of different types of irrigation channels. Irrigation water measurement: using velocity area method, water meters, weirs, notches, flumes, orifices etc. Water conveyance and control. Conveyance losses and lining of irrigation channels. Irrigation water delivery and distribution.

Unit 3: Soil, Plant, Water and Atmosphere Relationship

Soil and water as vital resources for agricultural production. Water retention by soil, soil moisture characteristics, field capacity, permanent wilting point, plant available water and extractable water. Soil irrigability classifications, factors affecting profile water storage. Determination of soil water content, computation of soil water depletion, soil water potential and its components, hydraulic head. Field water budget water gains and water losses from soil, deep percolation beyond root zone, capillary rise. Evapotranspiration (ET) and irrigation requirement, critical stages of crop growth in relation to irrigation. Irrigation scheduling. Plant water relations, concept of plant water potential, significance of osmotic adjustment, leaf diffusive resistance, canopy temperature, canopy temperature depression (CTD).Water movement through soil plant atmosphere system. Uptake and transport of water by roots. Development of crop water deficit, crop adaptation to water deficit, morpho physiological effect of water deficit. Drought tolerance, mechanisms of drought tolerance, potential drought tolerance traits and their measurements. Management strategies to improve crop productivity under limited water supplies. Contingent crop plans and other strategies for aberrant weather conditions. Cropping patterns, alternate land use and crop diversification in rain fed regions.

Unit 4: Hydrology and Soil and Water Conservation

Hydrologic cycle, precipitation, infiltration and surface runoff. Measurement and analysis of hydrologic data. Application of statistics in hydrology. Probability concepts. Distributions and application. Intensity duration frequency analysis. Hortonian and saturation overland flow theories, partial source area concept of surface runoff generation. Rainfall and run off relationships, stream gauging and runoff measurement. Different methods of surface runoff estimation, hydrographs, S-hydrograph, IUH, unit hydrograph theory and its application, Flood routing methods and calculations. Soil erosion and types of erosion. Soil loss measurement and estimation. Universal soil loss equation and subsequent its modifications, soil and water conservation structures and their design. Gully control structures and their design. Design and construction of farm pond and reservoir. Seepage theory. Design of earthen dams and retaining walls, stability analysis of slopes. Mathematical models and simulation of hydrologic processes. Application of GIS in soil and water conservation.

Unit 5: Watershed Management

Watershed concept, Identification and characterization of watersheds. Hydrological and geomorphological characteristics of watersheds. Land capability and irritability classification and soil maps. Principles of watershed management. Development of watershed management plans, its feasibility and economic evaluation. Land levelling and grading, machineries and equipments for land levelling.

Unit 6: Irrigation Water Management

History of irrigation in India. Management of irrigation water. Major irrigation projects in India. Crop water requirements. Soil water depletion, plant indices and climatic parameters. Crop modeling, water production function. Methods of irrigation, surface methods, overhead methods, Pressurized irrigation system such as drip and sprinkler irrigation. Merits and demerits of various methods. Hydraulics of furrow, check basin and border irrigation, Hydraulics and design of pressurized irrigation systems. Irrigation efficiency and economics of different irrigation systems. Application and distribution efficiencies. Agronomic considerations in the design and operation of irrigation projects, characteristics of irrigation and farming systems affecting irrigation management. Irrigation legislation. Irrigation strategies under different situation of water availability, optimum crop plans and cropping patterns in canal command areas. Quality of irrigation water and irrigation with poor quality water. On farm water management, socio-economic aspects of on farm water management. Scope for economizing the use of water.

Unit 7: Management of Degraded, Waterlogged and Other Problematic Soils and Water

Problem soils and their distribution in India. Water quality criteria and use of brackish waters in agriculture. Excess salt and salt tolerant crops. Hydrological imbalances and their corrective measures. Concept of critical water table depths for crop growth. Contribution of shallow water table to crop water requirements.

Management strategies for flood prone areas and crop calendar for flood affected areas. Crop production and alternate use of problematic soils and fish production. Agricultural field drainage and theory of flow in saturated soil. Flow net theory and its application. Drainage investigations. Drainage characteristics of various type of soils. Water table contour maps and isobaths maps. Drainage coefficient. Design and installation of surface and subsurface drainage system. Interceptor and relief drains and their design. Drain pipe and accessories. Pumped drainage. Drainage requirements of crops. Drainage in relation to salinity and water table control. Reclamation of ravine, waterlogged, swampy areas and polders. Salt-affected soils and their reclamation. Command area development organizational structures and activities. River valley projects, interstate disputes. Water rights and legal aspects. Irrigation water user's association concept and responsibilities. Environmental considerations in land and water resources management.

ICAR-JRF/SRF Syllabus

MAJOR SUBJECT GROUP - AGRICULTURAL ENGINEERING AND TECHNOLOGY

(**Subjects**: Soil & Water Conservation Engg., Irrigation & Drainage Engg./Irrigation& Water Management Engineering)

UNIT-I: Elementary Statistics and theory of probability, differential and integral calculus, linear algebra and Fourier series, differential equations, vector algebra & vector calculus, elementary numerical analysis.

UNIT-II: Surveying and leveling; hydrology, water resources in India; efficiency in water use; irrigation system and equipment; water conveyances and associated efficiency; soil-plant-water relationship; estimation of evaporation and water requirements of crop; water harvesting and use, farm ponds and reservoirs, command area development, land use capability classification, ground water development, wells and pumping equipment, soil erosion and its control, land shaping and grading equipment and practices, hydraulic structures, drainage of irrigated and humid areas; salt balance and reclamation of saline and alkaline soils.

IARI-PhD Entrance Syllabus

Basic concepts in calculus, trigonometry, analytical geometry, linear algebra and algebra of real and complex numbers; instrumentation for measurement of forces, torque, temperature, moisture, fluid flow; basic principles of simulation; methods of statics, dynamics and mechanics of materials; common distributions of random variables and methods of statistical inference; energy sources - their utilisation and efficiencies on the farm; uses and application of computers.

Soil and Water Conservation Engineering

Principles of fluid mechanics; theory of ground water recharge, collection, analysis and interpretation of hydrological data; principles and practices of irrigation and drainage, soil erosion; types, measurement and control; stream gauging and sediment monitoring; soil conservation practices, command area development; watershed management; open channel flows; design and operation of water lifting devices; consumptive use of water; estimation of evapotranspiration; irrigation water distribution methods; water harvesting; lining of waterways and canals; modelling of soil-plant-water relationships; stability of slopes and design of earthen dams.

1 Open Channel Hydraulics / Fluid Mechanics

1. **Measurement and analysis of water is a science - deals with** **[NET - 2013]**
   (a) Hydrometry (b) Hydrology
   (c) Limnology (d) Hydrometeorology

2. **Any channel which is supplied with water from canal and is maintained by farmers not the government is** **[NET - 2013]**
   (a) Watercourse (b) Chak
   (c) Module (d) Distributary

3. **The structures in which discharge is constant and fixed within limits, irrespective of the fluctuations of the water levels of either the distributary or of the water course or both are called** **[NET - 2013]**
   (a) Rigid modules (b) Flexible modules
   (c) Non - modular modules (d) None

4. **Warabandi or Osrabandi systems distribute the water to farmers with main objective and requirement is** **[NET - 2013]**
   (a) Demand (b) Supply
   (c) Continuous (d) Equity

Answers	1. (a) 3. (a) 2. (a) 4. (d)

5. **The kinematic viscosity of water at 20°C is almost [NET-2013, ARS-2014]**

(a) 10^{-6} m²/s (b) 10^{-4} m²/s

(c) 10^{-2} m²/s (d) 10^{-5} m²/s

6. **Darcy's law is valid in a porous flow media if Reynolds number is [NET-2013, IARI PhD 2013, NET-2014]**

(a) > 1 (b) < 1

(c) > 2000 (d) < 2000

7. **A sheet of water, which overflows a weir is called as [NET-2013]**

(a) Head (b) Nappe

(c) Crest (d) Notch

8. **Venturimeter works on the principle of [NET-2013]**

(a) Darcy (b) Bernoulli

(c) Hooghoudt (d) Chezy

9. **The size of the Parshall flume is specified by [NET-2013]**

(a) Head in diverging section

(b) Head in converging section

(c) Throat width

(d) None of the above

10. **The unit of Manning's roughness coefficient is [NET - 2013]**

(a) $L^{-1/6}T$ (b) $L^{-1/3}T$

(c) $L^{1/6}T$ (d) $L^{1/3}T$

11. **The dimensions of intrinsic permeability is [ICAR JRF-2011, 2012, BHU-2012, NET-2013]**

(a) L (b) T

(c) LT^{-1} (d) L^2

Answers	
	5. (a) 7. (b) 9. (c) 11. (d)
	6. (b) 8. (b) 10. (b)

12. At critical flow condition, the specific energy is minimum and discharge is [IARI PhD-2011, BHU-2012, NET-2013]

(a) Maximum (b) Minimum

(c) Alter (d) No change

13. The ratio of inertia force to gravitational force is called as [IARI PhD-2011, NET-2013, ARS-14]

(a) Froude number (b) Weber number

(c) Reynolds number (d) Pressure coefficient

14. For the same head, the discharge in contracted weir with two end contractions is [NET-2013]

(a) Less than suppressed weir

(b) More than suppressed weir

(c) Equal to suppressed weir

(d) None of the above

15. Weir under no ventilation condition comes under [NET - 2013]

(a) Suppressed (b) Submerged

(c) Contracted (d) Free

16. Most efficient hydraulic channel cross - section is [NET-2013, ARS-2014,2015]

(a) Trapezoidal (b) Circular

(c) Rectangular (d) Semi-circular

17. For a shallow wide rectangular channel, the ratio of wetted perimeter to hydraulic radius is [NET-2013]

(a) Less (b) More

(c) Equal (d) None of the above

18. The length of hydraulic jump is calculated with sequential depths (y1 and y2) is [NET-2013]

(a) Capacity (b) L = 6.9 (y1-y2)

(c) Spacing (d) None of the above

Answers	12. (a)	14. (a)	16. (d)	18. (b)
	13. (a)	15. (a)	17. (a)	

19. **The Froude number for an triangular section with side slope m : 1 (H : V) is [NET-2013]**

(a) $\frac{mV}{\sqrt{gd}}$ (b) $\frac{V\sqrt{2}}{\sqrt{gy}}$

(c) $\frac{V}{\sqrt{mgd}}$ (d) None of the above

20. **Hydraulic jump is an example of the flow type is [NET-2013]**

(a) Steady and non-uniform

(b) Unsteady and non-uniform

(c) Steady

(d) Unsteady

21. **If bulk and particle density of soil are 1.35 and 2.7 respectively. The void ratio is [BHU-2012, NET-2013]**

(a) 1 (b) 0.25

(c) 0.50 (d) 0.44

22. **If saturation soil moisture content is 35% and bulk density of soil is 1.2 g/cc. Then the porosity is [NET-2013]**

(a) 0.35 (b) 0.25

(c) 0.65 (d) 0.20

23. **The Energy line equal to gradient lines in which flow through [NET - 2013]**

(a) Pipelines (b) Open channel

(c) Both a) and b) (d) None of the above

24. **Bernoulli's principle is based on the conservation of [BHU-2010, ICAR JRF-2012, IARI PhD 2013]**

(a) Mass (b) Momentum

(c) Energy (d) Both a) and c)

Answers	**19. (a)**	**21. (a)**	**23. (b)**
	20. (a)	**22. (a)**	**24. (c)**

25. The Co-efficient of discharge of orifice is **[ICAR JRF - 2012]**

(a) 0.62 (b) 0.99

(c) 0.95 (d) Both b) and c)

26. The current meter is used to measure **[ICAR JRF-2012]**

(a) Velocity (b) Head

(c) Discharge (d) Pressure

27. How many water columns (cm) in 1 bar pressure ? **[ICAR JRF-2012]**

(a) 1019.72 (b) 1034

(c) Both a) and b) (d) None of the above

28. What is the unit of bulk density ? **[ICAR SRF-2013]**

(a) g/cc (b) Kg/cc

(c) Both a) and b) (d) None of the above

29. A flowmeter that is independent of fluid density is **[ICAR SRF-2013]**

(a) Rotameter (b) Orifice meter

(c) Electromagnetic flow meter (d) None of the above

30. At critical flow condition in the channel the value of Froude number is **[BHU-2010 & 2012, ARS-2014]**

(a) Greater than 1 (b) Less than 1

(c) Equal to 1 (d) None of the above

31. A Parshall flume is based on the concept of **[IARI PhD 2013, ARS-2014]**

(a) Hydraulic jump (b) Hydraulic drop

(c) Uniform flow (d) Turbulent flow

32. At alternate depth 1m and 1m, the value of Froude number is **[ARS-2014]**

(a) Greater than 1 (b) Less than 1

(c) Equal to 1 (d) None of the above

Answers	**25. (a)**	**27. (a)**	**29. (a)**	**31. (a)**
	26. (a)	**28. (c)**	**30. (c)**	**32. (c)**

33. **Discharge through porous material is directly proportional to the .... power of radius of porous materials.**
[ARS-2014]

(a) 2nd (b) 6th
(c) 5th (d) 4th

34. **The Bulk density is ...... than the particle density.**
[ARS-2014]

(a) Less (b) More
(c) Equal (d) All of the above

35. **The Cipoletti weir is contracted trapezoidal weir having side slope [JRF-2011, IARI PhD-2011, ARS-2014]**

(a) 2 : 1 (b) 1 : 2
(c) 4 : 1 (d) 1 : 4

36. **Casgrande apparatus is used in measuring**
[BHU-2012, ARS-2014]

(a) Plastic limit (b) Liquid limit
(c) Solid limit (d) All of the above

37. **Reynolds number is defined as the ratio of**
[BHU-2010, IARI PhD-2013, SRF-2013]

(a) Inertia to gravity force (b) Inertia to elastic force
(c) Inertia to viscous force (d) Viscous to inertia force

38. **For a given fluid the dynamic viscosity is 0.06 poise, density is 0.9 g/cc, the kinematic viscosity (in stokes) is**

(a) 0.04 (b) 0.054
(c) 0.067 (d) 0.4

39. **The discharge coefficient of an orifice meter is**

(a) Greater than the venturimeter
(b) Smaller than the venturimeter
(c) Equal to the venturimeter
(d) Greater than one

Answers	33. (d)	35. (d)	37. (c)	39. (b)
	34. (a)	36. (b)	38. (c)	

40. In a static fluid, the pressure or intensity of pressure is same in all directions, the fluid is

(a) Real fluid (b) Newtonian fluid

(c) Non - Newtonian fluid (d) Ideal fluid

41. Gauge pressure = absolute pressure – .... [JRF-2011]

(a) Vacuum pressure (b) Atmospheric pressure

(c) Hydrostatic pressure (d) None of the above

42. Stokes law is used to find out [JRF-2011]

(a) Terminal velocity (b) Drag coefficient

(c) Surface tension (d) Viscosity

43. An imaginary lines connecting points of equal atmospheric pressures is called as [JRF-2011, ARS-2013]

(a) Isobar (b) Isobath

(c) Isochor (d) Isopleth

44. Fluid flow in circular pipe is said to be laminar if Reynolds number is [JRF-2011, ARS-2013]

(a) < 1 (b) $= 1$

(c) < 2000 (d) > 4000

45. Find the hydraulic mean depth (m) of lined canal water course rectangular in section with a bottom width of 50cm and depth of flow of 25 cm [JRF-2011]

(a) 0.125 (b) 0.126

(c) 0.127 (d) 0.128

46. A soil sample of porosity of 40 %, its void ratio is [JRF-2011]

(a) 0.06 (b) 0.28

(c) 0.40 (d) 0.66

Answers	**40. (d)**	**42. (a)**	**44. (c)**	**46. (d)**
	41. (b)	**43. (a)**	**45. (a)**	

47. If the Froude number of flow in an open channel is more than 1, then the flow is said to be

[IARI PhD-2011, JRF-2011]

(a) Critical (b) Sub - critical

(c) Super - critical (d) None of the above

48. The wetted perimeter (m) of a rectangular open channel of bottom width = 1.2 m and depth of flow = 0.8 m is

(a) 0.68 (b) 1.74

(c) 1.36 (d) 2.80

49. Hygrometer is used to measure

(a) Specific gravity (b) Humidity

(c) Viscosity (d) Wind speed

50. Void ratio is defined as the ratio of **[BHU-2010]**

(a) Volume of void to total volume

(b) Volume of void to volume of solid

(c) Volume of void to volume of water

(d) None of the above

51. In the design of an agitator vessel with model volume V_1 and prototype volume V_2, the scale-up ratio is given by

[GATE-2015]

(a) V_1/V_2 (b) V_2/V_1

(c) $(V_2/V_1)^{1/2}$ (d) $(V_2/V_1)^{1/3}$

52. For a fully developed laminar flow through a smooth pipe, the relationship between friction factor (f) and Reynolds number (Re) is **[GATE-2014]**

(a) $f \propto (Re)$ (b) $f \propto (Re)^{-1}$

(c) $f \propto (Re)^2$ (d) $f \propto (Re)^{-2}$

Answers	**47. (c)**	**49. (b)**	**51. (d)**
	48. (d)	**50. (b)**	**52. (b)**

53. A soil has a void ratio of 0.75 and a specific gravity of 2.66. The value of critical hydraulic gradient at which quick sand condition will occur is [GATE-2013]

(a) 0.95 (b) 1.05

(c) 2.09 (d) 6.64

54. If the density of a fluid changes from point to point in a flow region, the flow is called [GATE-2011]

(a) Steady flow

(b) Unsteady flow

(c) Non - uniform flow

(d) Compressible flow

55. The viscosity of a Newtonian fluid depends primarily on X and to a lesser degree on Y. X and Y are [GATE-2011]

(a) X = temperature, Y = flow velocity

(b) X = flow velocity, Y = pressure

(c) X = temperature, Y = pressure

(d) X = roughness of the surface across which the fluid flows, Y = flow velocity

56. A completely saturated clay soil has particle density of 2600 kg m^{-3} and bulk density of 1400 kg m^{-3}. It has a moisture fraction of 40% on volume basis. The porosity of the soil is [GATE-2011]

(a) 0.46 (b) 0.54

(c) 0.74 (d) 0.86

57. While deriving the Chezy formula for uniform flow, it is assumed that there is a balance between [GATE-2010]

(a) Gravity and Inertial forces

(b) Inertial and Viscous forces

(c) Frictional and Gravity forces

(d) Frictional and Inertial forces

Answers	**53. (a)**	**55. (c)**	**57. (c)**
	54. (d)	**56. (a)**	

58. The Co-efficient of discharge of Cipoletti weir is [ARS-2013]

(a) 0.629 (b) 0.99
(c) 0.95 (d) Both b) and c)

59. If bulk density of a particulate material is 600 kg m^{-3} and true density is 1000 kg m^{-3}. The porosity of the material is [GATE - 2010]

(a) 20% (b) 40%
(c) 60% (d) 80%

60. A fluid in which shear stress is more than the yield value and proportional to the rateof shear strain is called [GATE-2007]

(a) Newtonian fluid (b) Ideal plastic fluid
(c) Non - Newtonian fluid (d) Real fluid

61. The discharge (m^3/s) through a 90° V-notch for a head of 0.5 m and coefficient of discharge of 0.6 is [GATE-2007]

(a) 0.25 (b) 0.50
(c) 0.65 (d) 0.75

62. A saturated soil sample has 42.2 % water content and unit weight 2.69. The void ratio of the soil sample will be [BHU - 2015]

(a) 0.784 (b) 0.478
(c) 0.874 (d) 0.087

63. The velocity head in the case of fluid flow is the [BHU-2012, ARS 2015]

(a) Kinetic energy per unit area
(b) Kinetic energy per unit flow area
(c) Kinetic energy per unit weight
(d) Kinetic energy per unit time

Answers	58. (a)	60. (b)	62. (a)
	59. (b)	61. (c)	63. (c)

64. If the diameter of a pipe is halved flow of water in it experiences the increase inthe head loss due to friction **[BHU - 2012]**

(a) Two times (b) Four times
(c) Ten times (d) Sixteen times

65. A dimensionless number representing the ratio of inertial forces to viscous forces in fluid flow is better known as **[BHU - 2010]**

(a) Stantan number (b) Prandtl number
(c) Froude number (d) Reynolds' number

66. The head over a V notch at the end of channel is 75 cm, if an error of 0.15 cm is possible in the measurement of head, then the percentage error in computing the discharge will be **[BHU - 2010]**

(a) 0.3 (b) 0.5
(c) 1.0 (d) 1.5

67. If discharges in two circular orifices O_1 and O_2 placed at depths of 20 cm and 80 cm below a constant level of water in a tank are equal, the ratio of the diameters of the orifices O_1 and O_2 is **[BHU-2010]**

(a) 1 : 2 (b) 2 : 1
(c) 1.414 : 1 (d) 1 : 1.414

68. The time taken for a tank (filled to height 'h' above its flat base) to empty through an orifice in the base varies as the following power of 'h' **[BHU-2010]**

(a) 1 (b) 1/2
(c) -1/2 (d) -1

69. At sub - critical state of flow, the ratio of gravitational and inertial force is **[BHU-2010]**

(a) More than 1 (b) Less than 1
(c) Equal to 1 (d) None of the above

Answers			
	64. (a)	66. (b)	68. (b)
	65. (d)	67. (c)	69. (b)

70. **Under open channel flow conditions, the hydraulic jump is formed when the Froude number is [BHU-2010]**

(a) Equal to one (b) More than one
(c) Less than one (d) None of the above

71. **The equipment which continuously records the water level of the flowing stream is called as [BHU - 2010]**

(a) Current meter
(b) Parshall flume
(c) Discharge recorder
(d) Stage level recorder

72. **If the viscous forces are so strong, relative to the inertial forces, that viscosity plays a significant part in determining flow behaviour then now in the channel will be [BHU-2010]**

(a) Turbulent (b) Laminar
(c) Discontinuous flow (d) None of the above

73. **Archimedes' principle is used in determining the [IARI PhD-2013]**

(a) Shape of a solid
(b) Surface area of an irregular solid
(c) Centre of gravity of a floating body
(d) Volume of an irregular solid

74. **If the value of dy/dx = 0 in the dynamic equation of gradually varied flow, then the flow is [IARI PhD-2013]**

(a) Steady (b) Uniform
(c) Laminar (d) Non - uniform

75. **The velocity distribution across a pipe flowing full is [IARI PhD-2013]**

(a) Uniform (b) Triangular
(c) Parabolic (d) Semi - circular

Answers	70. (b)	72. (a)	74. (b)
	71. (d)	73. (c)	75. (c)

76. A rectangular channel 40 cm wide is carrying a discharge of 0.1 m^3/s at a depth of 20 cm. State whether the flow is [IARI PhD - 2013]

(a) Critical (b) Subcritical
(c) Supercritical (d) None of the above

77. If the saturated hydraulic conductivity of a soil is 1 m/day, the rate of water transmission across a rectangular area 100 m long and 1 m height under a unit hydraulic gradient will be [IARI PhD - 2013]

(a) 1 m^3/day (b) 10 m^3/day
(c) 100 m^3/day (d) 1000 m^3/day

78. Local atmospheric pressure is measured by [IARI PhD - 2013]

(a) Hydrometer (b) Hygrometer
(c) Barometer (d) Altimeter

79. Chezy formula assumes that [IARI PhD-2013]

(a) The force resisting the flow per unit area of the stream bed is proportional to the velocity
(b) The effective component of the gravity force causing the flow is equal to the total force of resistance
(c) The force resisting the flow per unit area of the stream bed is inversely proportional to the velocity
(d) None of the above

80. The correct conditions for which the hydraulically efficient rectangular channel will deliver maximum discharge are P – depth of water is equal to half the breadth of channel [GATE-2016]

Q – depth of water is equal to breadth of channel
R – depth of water is equal to twice the breadth of channel
S – hydraulic radius is equal to half the depth of water

(a) P and R (b) P and Q
(c) P and S (d) R and S

Answers	76. (b) 77. (c)	78. (c) 79. (a)	80. (c)

81. **A soil has bulk density and particle density of 1.48 Mg m^{-3} and 2.64 Mg m^{-3}, respectively. The saturated volumetric moisture content of soil is 36%. The porosity and void ratio of the soil are [GATE-2016]**

(a) 0.36 and 0.56 (b) 0.44 and 0.79

(c) 0.79 and 0.44 (d) 0.56 and 0.36

82. **An ideal fluid has**

(a) Zero surface tension and is incompressible

(b) Zero shear stress and behaves as a perfect gas

(c) Constant density of viscosity

(d) Zero viscosity and is incompressible

83. **The drag coefficient as predicted by the Stokes' law**

(a) Increases with the Reynolds's number

(b) Decreases with the Reynolds's number

(c) Is independent of the Reynolds's number

(d) Depends upon the energy of the falling object

84. **The most economical channel section for irrigation is [NET/ARS-2016]**

(a) Parabolic (b) Rectangular

(c) Semi - circular (d) None

85. **The specific energy at critical flow condition is [NET/ARS-2016]**

(a) Minimum (b) Maximum

(c) Mean value (d) None

86. **If the void ratio of a soil column is 0.43, the soil porosity is [GATE-2018]**

(a) 0.30 (b) 0.40

(c) 0.70 (d) 0.75

Answers	81. (b) 82. (d)	83. (b) 84. (c)	85. (a) 86. (a)

87. **A soil sample has a porosity of 40%. Void ratio of the soil sample is [GATE-2019]**

(a) 0.367 (b) 0.467

(c) 0.567 (d) 0.667

88. **Water is flowing at a velocity of 1.6 m s^{-1} in a pipe of diameter 8 cm and length 100 m. Assuming the value of coefficient of friction for pipe, f = 0.005 and acceleration due to gravity, g = 9.81 m s^{-2}, the head loss (in meter) due to friction in the pipe is [GATE-2019]**

(a) 1.28 (b) 2.28

(c) 2.78 (d) 3.26

89. **A sample of wet sandy-clay loam soil of mass 135 kg is collected for laboratory tests. The wet density, water content (weight basis) and specific gravity of solids of this soil sample are 1.8 g.cm^{-3}, 18%, and 2.7, respectively. The dry density (in g.cm^{-3}) and porosity (in percent) of the soil sample, respectively, are [GATE-2021]**

(a) 1.53 and 43.50 (b) 1.53 and 77.00

(c) 1.65 and 43.50 (d) 1.65 and 77.00

90. **The ratio of inertial forces to viscous forces is knows as .... [GATE-2022]**

(a) Froude number

(b) Reynolds number

(c) Power number

(d) Biot number

91. **A sample of 90% saturated clay soil has void ratio and specific gravity of 0.8 and 2.7, respectively. The bulk unit weight of soil in N m^{-3} is ____________. [GATE-2022]**

(a) 10594.80 (b) 18639.00

(c) 18.64 (d) 10.60

Answers	**87. (d)**	**89. (a)**	**91. (b)**
	88. (d)	**90. (b)**	

92. **The pressure drop through a well-designed constriction is to be used for measuringthe velocity of flow through a circular pipe. If the pressure drop from a 0.1 mdiameter section to a 0.05 m diameter section of the pipe is 7.5 kPa, the velocity inm s^{-1} in the 0.1 m diameter section of the pipe is .... [GATE-2022]**

(a) 0.5 (b) 1.0

(c) 1.5 (d) 2.0

OOOOO

Answers	92. (b)

2 Irrigation Water Management

1. **Upper Bari Doab canal is constructed on the river** **[ARS - 2014]**

   (a) Beas (b) Indus
   (c) Ravi (d) Chenab

2. **The empirical method for computing the consumptive use of a crop using the mean monthly temperature and day light hours is** **[GATE-2010, ARS-2014, 2015]**

   (a) Thornthwaite (b) Hargreaves
   (c) Blaney Criddle (d) Lowry Johnson

3. **Tolerable limit of water spreading for cotton crop to dispose water from field is** **[ARS-2014]**

   (a) 7 days (b) 1 days
   (c) 2 days (d) 3 days

4. **.................. refers to the difference between field capacity and permanent wilting point.** **[ARS-2014]**

   (a) Available water (b) Hygroscopic water
   (c) Wilting point (d) None of the above

5. **................. equation is the alternative of the FAO Penman Monteith equation.** **[ARS-2014]**

   (a) Thorntwaite (b) Hargreaves
   (c) Blaney Criddle (d) both a) and c)

Answers	1. (c) 3. (d) 5. (b) 2. (c) 4. (a)

6. **Penman Monteith equation is the latest formula for estimation of** **[ARS-2014]**
   (a) Reference ET (b) PET
   (c) Evaporation (d) None of the above

7. **The size of stream in border irrigation depends on** **[ARS-2014]**
   (a) Width of border (b) Wetted areas
   (c) Both a) and b) (d) Discharge

8. **The uniformity coefficient of sprinkler irrigation is (as per BIS)** **[JRF - 2011, NET - 2013, ARS - 2014]**
   (a) 85% (b) 75%
   (c) 70% (d) 95%

9. **If irrigation water diverted to field is 10m, and runoff and other losses is 2 m and 1 m respectively. The application efficiency is** **[NET-2013, ARS-2014]**
   (a) 80% (b) 60%
   (c) 70% (d) 100%

10. **The uniform distribution of water application is achieved by** **[JRF-2012, NET-2013, ARS-2014]**
    (a) Water distribution efficiency
    (b) Water application efficiency
    (c) Conveyance efficiency
    (d) None of the above

11. **Stewart - Hagan - Pruitt and Jensen models is used for the estimation of** **[ARS-2014]**
    (a) Crop production (b) Water balance
    (c) ET (d) All

12. **The water spreading to the field is signified by** **[ARS-2014]**
    (a) Infiltration rate (b) Runoff
    (c) Evaporation (d) All

Answers	6. (a)	8. (a)	10. (a)	12. (a)
	7. (c)	9. (c)	11. (a)	

13. .... formula is used for measuring discharge through sprinkler nozzle [ARS-2014]

(a) Torricelli (b) Cavazza
(c) Darcy (d) Tanda

14. In unsaturated condition, the pressure head measuring instrument is [ARS-2014]

(a) Tensiometer (b) Resistance block
(c) Gypsum block (d) All

15. The pressure head of sand media filter is [NET-2013, ARS-2014]

(a) 8 m (b) 6 m
(c) 4 m (d) 2 m

16. If sprinkler spacing is 10m then the catch spacing will be .... interval. [ARS-2014]

(a) 2 m (b) 4 m
(c) 10 m (d) None of the above

17. National Water Policy was adopted in the year [SRF-2013]

(a) 2012 (b) 1987
(c) 1989 (d) 2002

18. Conjunctive use refers to the application of water [SRF-2013]

(a) By augment (b) In time
(c) In space (d) All

19. Which irrigation method is most suitable for Rice crop [IARI PhD-2011, SRF-2013, NET-2013]

(a) Border (b) Basin
(c) Furrow (d) Surge

Answers				
	13. (a)	15. (d)	17. (b)	19. (b)
	14. (a)	16. (a)	18. (d)	

20. Tensiometer reading indicates to
[IARI PhD-2011, SRF-2013, NET-2014]

(a) Soil moisture content (b) Soil moisture potential
(c) Soil moisture tension (d) None of the above

21. Which state of India having highest areas is irrigated by canal ? **[JPSC-2011, SRF-2013]**

(a) Punjab (b) Bihar
(c) Haryana (d) UP

22. The pressure plate apparatus is used for measuring
[SRF-2013]

(a) Field capacity (b) Wilting point
(c) Pressure (d) Available water

23. The delta for a crop when its duty is 864 hectares/cumec in the field with base period of crop 120 days is
[JRF-2012, NET-2013]

(a) 12 cm (b) 1.20 cm
(c) 120 cm (d) None of the above

24. The Major irrigation project having catchment areas is (ha) .... **[JRF-2012,BHU-2012]**

(a) Less than 2000 (b) 2000 - 10000
(c) More than 10000 (d) None of the above

25. Time domain reflectometer (TDR) is used to measure
[IARI PhD-2011, NET-2013]

(a) Soil moisture (b) Salinity
(c) Pressure (d) Capillary tension

26. Gypsum block is used to measure **[NET-2013]**

(a) Soil moisture (b) Salinity
(c) Velocity (d) Capillary tension

Answers	20. (c)	22. (a)	24. (c)	26. (a)
	21. (d)	23. (c)	25. (a)	

27. **Operating pressure (kg/cm^2) of low to medium sprinkler is [NET-2013]**

(a) 1.4 - 4.2 (b) Less than 0.5

(c) More than 4.2 (d) 0.5 - 1.2

28. **Surge flow irrigation is [NET-2013]**

(a) The completion of irrigation in the second cycle using reduced stream size

(b) Continuous irrigation

(c) Corrugation irrigation

(d) Spate irrigation

29. **Net irrigation requirement with an exclusive of precipitation carry over soil moisture or ground water contribution or the gains in soil moisture is [NET-2013]**

(a) Consumptive use (Cu)

(b) Cu – Effective rainfall

(c) (Cu – Effective rainfall) / efficiency

(d) Effective rainfall

30. **Unit of water productivity is [NET-2013]**

(a) Kg/ha-cm (b) Kg/ha

(c) ha-cm/Kg (d) Kg/cm

31. **The flow when water starts disappear at head end until it eventually recedes from whole field after cut off flow [NET-2013]**

(a) Recession flow (b) Advance flow

(c) Ponding time (d) Depletion flow

32. **Total amount of losses takes place due to drip irrigation for the application of water from source to field [NET-2013]**

(a) 10% (b) 20%

(c) 10 - 20% (d) More than 20%

Answers	27. (a)	29. (a)	31. (a)
	28. (a)	30. (a)	32. (a)

33. Tolerable limit of water spreading for vegetable crops to dispose water from field is [NET-2013]

(a) 2 days (b) 1 day
(c) 7 days (d) 3 days

34. The irrigation channel is mostly designed on the principal of [ARS-2014]

(a) Laceys' (b) Darcy
(c) Mannings' (d) Hooghoudts'

35. "Super passage" in canal irrigation system refers to [SRF-2013]

(a) Irrigation channel passes over drainage channel
(b) Drainage channel passes over irrigation channel
(c) Both a) and b)
(d) None of the above

36. The check gate is used to [ARS-2013, 2014]

(a) Maintain water level (b) Divert water to channel
(c) Both a) and b) (d) Neither a) nor b)

37. Hydrant is a type of [ARS-2013, 2014]

(a) Riser valve (b) Suction valve
(c) Discharge valve (d) All of the above

38. The water crosses across the stream in the natural area/ surface is called [JRF-2012, ARS-2013]

(a) Culvert (b) Flume
(c) Sluice (d) Syphon

39. Velocity measured using current meter based on two points at depth [NET-2013]

(a) 0.2 d and 0.8 d (b) 0.3 d and 0.6 d
(c) 0.3 d and 0.8 d (d) 0.1 d and 0.5 d

Answers	33. (b)	35. (b)	37. (a)	39. (a)
	34. (a)	36. (c)	38. (b)	

40. **Device placed over riser valve outlets as a means of connecting portable gated pipes to the pipeline.** **[NET-2013]**

(a) Hydrant (b) Gated pipes
(c) Coupler (d) Air vent

41. **Total depth of irrigation to a crop is known as**

(a) Delta (b) Base
(c) Duty (d) Irrigation intensity

42. **The area irrigated through any source once in a year for a particular crop is known as**

(a) Gross irrigated area
(b) Net irrigated area
(c) Gross net un-irrigated area
(d) None of the above

43. **Pitot tube is used for measurement of** **[ARS-2013]**

(a) Pressure (b) Acceleration
(c) Discharge (d) Velocity at a point

44. **Darcy's law is mostly applicable for**

(a) Turbulent flow
(b) Steady flow
(c) Unsteady flow
(d) Laminar flow

45. **Water storage efficiency is defined as** **[BHU-2010]**

(a) (Water stored in root zone)/(Water delivered to the field)
(b) (Water stored in the root zone during irrigation)/(Water needed in the root zone prior to irrigation)
(c) (Water stored in the field)/(Water applied in the field)
(d) None of the above

Answers	**40. (a)**	**42. (b)**	**44. (d)**
	41. (a)	**43. (d)**	**45. (b)**

46. **A layer is designated as imperious if its hydraulic conductivity is**
    (a) 1/5 to 1/10 of hydraulic conductivity of upper layer
    (b) 50% hydraulic conductivity of upper layer
    (c) 40% hydraulic conductivity of upper layer
    (d) None of the above

47. **In a semi-modular outlet, the discharge is [GATE-2012]**
    (a) Independent of water levels in the distributary and the water course
    (b) Depends upon the water levels of both distributary and water course
    (c) Depends upon the water level in the distributary
    (d) Depends upon the water level in the water course

48. **Pan evaporation data recorded at a certain location over a period of one week are 4.0, 4.3, 4.6, 4.9, 5.12, 5.18, and 6.21 mm. If irrigation scheduling based on ratio of irrigation water (IW) to cumulative pan evaporation (CPE) is practiced, the depth of irrigation at an interval of a week for IW/CPE = 0.9 is [GATE-2013]**
    (a) 3.60 (b) 4.41
    (c) 5.59 (d) 30.88

49. **Several identical sprinkler nozzles, each having discharge Q (litre per min.), are spaced in a grid of size L (metre) × S (metre). The application rate in mm/h is [GATE-2014]**
    (a) $(60\,Q/LS)$ (b) $(3600\,Q/LS)$
    (c) $(LS/60\,Q)$ (d) $(LS/3600\,Q)$

50. **A crop has effective root zone depth of 1200 mm and monthly (30 days) crop evapotranspiration of 260 mm. The effective rainfall during 30 days period is 20 mm. The field capacity and permissible soil moisture depletion (volume basis) are 16% and 8%, respectively. The irrigation interval in days for the crop will be [GATE-2014]**
    (a) 30 (b) 18
    (c) 12 (d) 8

Answers	**46. (a)**	**48. (d)**	**50. (c)**
	47. (c)	**49. (a)**	

51. In a citrus orchard, planting is done at a spacing of 5 m × 5 m. The daily pan evaporation of the orchard is 6 mm. The pan coefficient, wetting factor (crop canopy factor) and crop coefficient are 0.8, 0.6 and 0.6, respectively. Four drippers each of 4 L h^{-1} discharge are used to irrigate each plant. The time of operation of drip irrigation system in hours will be [GATE-2014]

(a) 2.7 (b) 4.5

(c) 16.2 (d) 19.8

52. Discharge through an irrigation outlet is independent of the water levels in the distributary and water courses in case of [GATE-2015]

(a) Non - modular outlet (b) Semi - modular outlet

(c) Kennedy's gauge outlet (d) Gibb's module outlet

53. Two irrigation channels are designed in the same type of alluvial soil having the channel bed slopes of 1.52×10^{-4} and 1.6×10^{-4}, respectively. If the design discharge of the first channel, using Lacey's regime theory, is 30 m^3s^{-1}, then the design discharge of the second channel in m^3 s^{-1} will be [GATE-2015]

(a) 22.05 (b) 29.74

(c) 30.26 (d) 40.81

54. A Cipolletti weir has the crest length of 1.2 m and a crest water level of 0.5 m. The average approach velocity of water in m s^{-1} on the crest is [GATE-2015]

(a) 0.49 (b) 1.18

(c) 1.19 (d) 1.32

55. A 10 ha field has 1.2 m deep layer of sandy loam soil underlain by sandy soil up to a depth of 5 m. A pre-irrigation rainfall brings moisture content of the top 0.3 m layer to its field capacity. The moisture content of rest of the sandy loam layer remains at permanent wilting point. The volumetric moisture content at field capacity and

Answers	51. (a) 53. (a) 52. (d) 54. (b)

permanent wilting point are 32 and 16%, respectively for the sandy loam soil. The field is irrigated with a stream size of 240 L s^{-1} for 24 hours. Considering the drainage from the sandy loam soil as deep percolation, application efficiency and deep percolation ratio in percent respectively are [GATE-2013]

(a) 56.40 and 43.60 (b) 69.44 and 30.56

(c) 75.18 and 24.82 (d) 92.60 and 7.40

56. A regime channel carrying a discharge of 25 m^3 s^{-1} is designed using Lacey's regime theory. The side slope of the channel is ½ H : 1 V, and Lacey's silt factor is unity. The bottom width and depth of flow in the channel in m respectively are [GATE-2012]

(a) 20.26, 1.38 (b) 20.26, 1.56

(c) 23.75, 1.56 (d) 32.78, 1.56

57. For a channel cross section and discharge the specific energy in a channel section is a function of [IARI PhD-2013]

(a) Velocity only (b) Depth of flow and velocity

(c) Depth of flow only (d) None of the above

58. A trapezoidal canal, having a bottom width of 5.0 m and a side slope of 1 H : 1 V, is carrying a discharge of 20 m^3 s^{-1}. The critical depth in m is [GATE-2012]

(a) 1.09 (b) 1.18

(c) 2.12 (d) 2.62

59. A cross regulator is usually provided [GATE-2010]

(a) At the head of the off-taking channel

(b) In the main channel upstream of the Off-taking channel

(c) In the main channel downstream of the off-taking channel

(d) In the watercourse to regulate the outlet

Answers	**55. (b)**	**57. (c)**	**59. (b)**
	56. (b)	**58. (a)**	

60. **The Medium irrigation project having catchment areas (ha)** **[ARS-2013]**

(a) Less than 2000 (b) 2000 - 10000
(c) More than 10000 (d) None of the above

61. **Upper Bari Doab canal is constructed on the river Ravi in the state** **[ARS-2013]**

(a) Uttar Pradesh (b) Punjab
(c) Andhra Pradesh (d) Maharashtra

62. **An instrument used for measurement of saturated hydraulic conductivity of soils is** **[BHU-2015]**

(a) Permeameter (b) Hydrometer
(c) Conductivity meter (d) Manometer

63. **Part of water loss from a short green grass cover which is never short of water is known as** **[BHU-2015]**

(a) Consumptive use
(b) Evapotranspiration
(c) Potential evapotranspiration
(d) Transpiration

64. **USWB Class A pan evaporimeter has diameter of about** **[BHU-2015]**

(a) 100 cm (b) 120 cm
(c) 150 cm (d) 175 cm

65. **Overall project irrigation efficiency in Govt. owned irrigation projects in India is about** **[IARI PhD-2011, BHU-2015]**

(a) 5% (b) 30%
(c) 70% (d) 80%

66. **In normal condition water loss from surface irrigation varies from** **[BHU-2015]**

(a) 30 - 45% (b) 25 - 30%
(c) 10 - 15% (d) 15 - 20%

Answers	60. (b)	62. (a)	64. (b)	66. (a)
	61. (b)	63. (c)	65. (b)	

67. **Canal lining is essential to check the [BHU-2010 & 2015]**
(a) Seepage losses (b) Evaporation losses
(c) Growth of weeds (d) Flow rate of canal

68. **PIM refers to [ARS-2013, BHU-2015]**
(a) Program of Integrated Management
(b) Participatory Irrigation Management
(c) Pressure Irrigation Management
(d) Private Irrigation Management

69. **Water meter is used for measuring the [BHU-2015]**
(a) Stream current (b) Pipe flow
(c) Runoff (d) Channel flow

70. **Which of following is not related to irrigation ? [BHU-2015]**
(a) Check gate (b) Water course
(c) Turnout (d) Coshocton wheel

71. **Authority for efficient canal water management at field level is known as [BHU-2012, ARS-2014]**
(a) Central water commission
(b) National water policy authority
(c) Command area development authority
(d) Central board of irrigation and power

72. **In drip irrigation design, the design criteria is generally based on an emitter flow variation of [BHU-2012]**
(a) < 20% (b) > 20%
(c) < 5% (d) < 10%

73. **In standard design of drip irrigation system, the maximum allowed pressure variation within the entire network is [BHU-2012, ARS-2015]**
(a) 5% (b) 10%
(c) 15% (d) 20%

Answers	67. (a) 68. (b)	69. (b) 70. (d)	71. (c) 72. (a)	73. (b)

74. Application rate in sprinkler irrigation should be [BHU-2012]

(a) More than infiltration rate

(b) Equal to infiltration rate

(c) Lesser than infiltration rate

(d) Irrespective of infiltration rate

75. Operating pressure for drip irrigation system is normally kept between [BHU-2012]

(a) 0 - 1 Kg / cm^2

(b) 5 - 10 Kg / cm^2

(c) 1 - 5 Kg / cm^2

(d) More than 10 Kg / cm^2

76. "Classical tail enders problem" means [BHU-2012]

(a) Farmers having their land holdings at tail of a canal are problematic

(b) Lesser availability of water at tail end of canal

(c) Smaller land holdings are located at the tail end of canal

(d) There is nothing called a tail enders problem

77. A pressure compensating emitter [BHU-2012]

(a) Maintains constant pressure all along the laterals

(b) Maintains constant discharge along the lateral

(c) Maintains constant discharge of an emitter

(d) Maintains pressure and discharge in permissible range

78. Normally the root zone depth considered to be kept free from groundwater level below [BHU-2010]

(a) 0.5 m (b) 1.5 m

(c) 3 m (d) 4 m

Answers	**74. (a)** **75. (a)** **76. (a)** **77. (c)** **78. (b)**

79. A steady state flow condition exists when [BHU-2010]

(a) The water level in the wells ceases to decline

(b) The water level responds to changes in atmospheric pressure

(c) The water level drops as the pumping is continuer

(d) None of the above

80. With increase in supplied irrigation water, the yield of the crops [BHU-2010]

(a) Increases continuously

(b) Decreases continuously

(c) Increases up to a certain limit and then becomes constant

(d) Increases up to a certain limit and then decreases

81. The discharge rate of drip irrigation usually ranges from [BHU-2010]

(a) 2-10 lit/day (b) 2-10 lit/min

(c) 2-10 lit/hr (d) 2-l0 lit/sec

82. For irrigating orchards, the most suitable method is [BHU-2010]

(a) Border irrigation method

(b) Basin irrigation method

(c) Sprinkler irrigation method

(d) Drip irrigation method

83. The ratio expressed in percentage of irrigation water stored in root zone and available for crop production to that delivered at the head of the field is known as [BHU-2010]

(a) Irrigation efficiency

(b) Project efficiency

(c) Farm irrigation efficiency

(d) Field irrigation efficiency

Answers	79. (a) 81. (c) 83. (a) 80. (d) 82. (d)

84. Fixing of irrigation for each shareholder of an outlet on the basis of his size of holding under the Culturable command area of the outlet is referred to as [BHU-2010]

(a) Warabandi

(b) Irrigation scheduling

(c) Intensity of irrigation

(d) Irrigation share

85. Inflow rate in surface irrigation should be [BHU-2010]

(a) < infiltration rate (b) ~ infiltration rate

(c) > infiltration rate (d) Not related to above

86. The period in days for which water is supplied to a crop in a canal command is called [BHU-2010]

(a) Duty (b) Delta

(c) Base period (d) None of the above

87. Water application efficiency in drip irrigation is usually [BHU-2010]

(a) 60% (b) 70%

(c) 90% (d) 50%

88. The secondary salinization in an irrigation command is caused by [IARI PhD-2013]

(a) Heavy rainfall

(b) Application of chemical fertilizer

(c) Excessive irrigation leading to water-logging

(d) Lack of irrigation

89. Under irrigated conditions, the flow towards sub-surface drain is [IARI PhD-2013]

(a) Gradually varied (b) Spatially varied

(c) Uniform (d) Non - steady

Answers	**84. (a)**	**86. (c)**	**88. (c)**
	85. (c)	**87. (c)**	**89. (b)**

90. A trapezoidal channel has a bottom width of 1 m, side slope 1:1 and depth 1 m. Its cross-sectional area will be [IARI PhD-2013]

(a) 1 m^2 (b) 2 m^2
(c) 1.414 m^2 (d) 4 m^2

91. Along the direction of flow, the base of a Parshall flume at the throat is [IARI PhD-2013]

(a) Sloping downwards (b) Sloping upwards
(c) Narrowed (d) Broadened

92. Distribution of irrigation water for a fixed duration and in proportion to the holding size is called [IARI PhD-2013]

(a) Shejpali (b) Warabandi
(c) Block system (d) Zonal system

93. In surge irrigation, water is applied [IARI PhD-2013]

(a) Under pressure (b) Intermittently
(c) Through pipes (d) In small plots

94. When ground water flows into a stream to augment its discharge, the stream is called [IARI PhD-2013]

(a) An influent stream (b) An effluent stream
(c) A perennial stream (d) An ephemeral stream

95. A current meter is used to measure [IARI PhD-2013]

(a) Alternating current
(b) Direct current
(c) Flow velocity in a canal
(d) Discharge of water in a pipe

96. An electric analog model utilizes the similarity between [IARI PhD-2013]

(a) The Darcy's law and the Kirchoff's law
(b) The Darcy's law and the Ohm's law
(c) The Darcy's law and the Coulomb's law
(d) The Darcy's law and the Laplace's equation

Answers	
	90. (b) 92. (b) 94. (b) 96. (b)
	91. (a) 93. (b) 95. (c)

97. **First irrigation commission in India was constituted during the period**

(a) 1898 - 1900 (b) 1901 - 1903

(c) 1905 - 1907 (d) 1910 - 1912

98. **Bhakra project is a**

(a) Major irrigation project

(b) Minor irrigation project

(c) Medium irrigation project

(d) Major hydroelectric and irrigation project

99. **The fundamental equation describing saturated flow in a porous media is attributed to**

(a) Darcy (b) Navier-Stokes

(c) Dupuit - Forechheimer (d) Kozeny

100. **Thc most critical stage for wheat[NET/ARS-2016]**

(a) Milking stage (b) CRI

(c) 3 leaf stage (d) None

101. **The discharge from a sprinkler nozzle depends on [GATE-2018]**

(a) operating pressure and nozzle geometry

(b) operating pressure and distribution pattern

(c) application rate and nozzle angle

(d) operating pressure and application rate

102. **Tensiometer installed in the soil measures [GATE-2019]**

(a) osmotic suction of soil moisture

(b) soil permeability

(c) soil moisture content

(d) capillary potential of the soil

OOOOO

Answers			
	97. (b)	99. (a)	101. (a)
	98. (d)	100. (b)	102. (d)

3 Watershed Management

1. **The performance of various ongoing projects / programmes of watershed development are based on the [ARS-2014]**
   (a) Common Guidelines for Watershed Development Projects based on Haryali guidelines
   (b) Haryali guidelines
   (c) DPAP
   (d) IWDP

2. **DEM is similar to the model [ARS-2014]**
   (a) Digital Terrain Model (DTM)
   (b) RUSLE Model
   (c) SWAT Model
   (d) All

3. **The longitudinal slope of loamy (medium) soil is [SRF-2013, ARS-2014]**
   (a) 0.05 - 0.20 (b) 0.20 - 0.40
   (c) 0.40 - 0.65 (d) None of the above

4. **When 2nd order channel joined with 3rd order channel, the order of channel formed [ARS-2014]**
   (a) 2nd (b) 3rd
   (c) 4th (d) None of the above

Answers	1. (a) 3. (b) 2. (a) 4. (b)

5. **PRA stands for** **[NET-2013, ARS-2014, ARS-2015]**
   (a) Participatory Rural Appraisal
   (b) Participatory Rural Approval
   (c) Participatory Rural Agriculture
   (d) Participatory Rainfed Agriculture

6. **If depth of contours are more at higher altitudes and is gradually decreases downwards, looks as** **[NET-2013, ARS-2014]**
   (a) Hillocks (b) Ridge
   (c) Valley (d) Cliff

7. **Watershed refers to draining water to a** **[ARS-2014]**
   (a) Single outlet (b) Two outlet
   (c) No outlet (d) All of the above

8. **In land grading, the ratio of cut-fill should be** **[NET-2013, ARS-2014]**
   (a) Less than 1 (b) 1.2 - 1.6
   (c) More than 2 (d) 1.8 - 2.2

9. **Which class of LUCC is most suitable for forestry practices?** **[SRF-2013]**
   (a) V (b) VI
   (c) VII (d) VIII

10. **The most common method of land leveling design is** **[JRF-2012, ARS-2013 & 2015, SRF-2013]**
    (a) Plan inspection method
    (b) Contour adjustment method
    (c) Plane method
    (d) Profile method

11. **The size (lakh hectare) of Micro watershed is [SRF-2013]**
    (a) 0.0001 - 0.001 (b) 0.001 - 0.01
    (c) 0.10 - 0.50 (d) 2 - 10

Answers	**5. (a)**	**7. (a)**	**9. (c)**	**11. (a)**
	6. (c)	**8. (b)**	**10. (c)**	

12. The number of first order stream and second order stream is 16 and 4 respectively. The bifurcation ratio is [SRF-2013, NET-2013]

(a) 4 (b) 0.25
(c) 64 (d) 16

13. Contour line never crosses each other except in [JRF-2012]

(a) Ridge (b) Overhanging cliff
(c) Hillocks (d) Valley

14. The earth is also known as [NET-2013]

(a) Yellow planet (b) Blue planet
(c) Green planet (d) Brown planet

15. Laser grading equipment are used mainly for[NET-2013]

(a) Reduce soil disturbance (b) More earth moving
(c) Reduce cost (d) All of the above

16. Small watersheds are dominated by [NET-2013]

(a) Surface runoff (b) Overland flow
(c) Base flow (d) Floods

17. The land capability classification has how many classes [IARI PhD-2011, NET-2013]

(a) 2 (b) 4
(c) 8 (d) 5

18. Two watersheds A and B with same area having number of channels of A more than B. Therefore A will have more than B [NET-2013]

(a) Stream frequency
(b) Compaction coefficient
(c) Drainage density
(d) Form factor

Answers	12. (a)	14. (b)	16. (b)	18. (a)
	13. (b)	15. (d)	17. (c)	

19. Hypsometric curve shows the relationship between [NET-2013]

(a) Relative height vs relative area

(b) Relative elevation vs relative area

(c) Relative relief vs relative height

(d) Both (a) and (b)

20. Land grading is beneficially in un-irrigated areas for [ARS - 2014]

(a) Moisture conservation

(b) Soil erosion reduction

(c) Safe disposal of runoff

(d) All of the above

21. Elongation ratio is calculated by [NET-2013]

(a) $1.128 \frac{A^{0.5}}{l}$ (b) $1.128 \frac{A^{-0.5}}{D}$

(c) $1.128 \frac{A^{0.5}}{D}$ (d) $11.28 \frac{A^{0.5}}{D}$

22. Drainage density is defined as the ratio of [IARI PhD-2011]

(a) Length of individual stream to area

(b) Total length of stream to total area

(c) Area of stream to length of stream

(d) None of the above

23. During land leveling of agricultural land for irrigation and drainage purposes, the acceptable deviation in elevation from the design value in meter is [ARS-2013, GATE-2015]

(a) 0.015 (b) 0.025

(c) 0.055 (d) 0.150

Answers	19. (d) 20. (d)	21. (a) 22. (b)	23. (a)

24. The process of determining the elevation of different points in a vertical plane is known as [GATE-2014]

(a) Leveling (b) Surveying
(c) Contouring (d) Tacheometry

25. A circular shaped watershed has a Form Factor of [BHU-2012]

(a) 0.78 (b) 1.57
(c) 1 (d) 3.14

26. If a watershed has high drainage density then the peak of its hydrograph compared to that of a low drainage density, when all other factors remain the same, will be [BHU-2010]

(a) Sharp crested (b) Hat crested
(c) Wide crested (d) Double crested

27. Watershed shape is evaluated by [BHU-2010]

(a) Form factor
(b) Compactness factor
(c) Form factor and compactness factor
(d) Stream density

28. If the size of a watershed increases, the runoff [BHU-2010]

(a) Volumes and rates decrease
(b) Volumes and rates increase
(c) Volume decreases but the rate increases
(d) Volume increases but the rate decreases

29. The exact method of computing volume of earthwork in land levelling is [BHU-2010]

(a) Four point method (b) End area method
(c) Prismoidal formula (d) None of the above

Answers	24. (a)	26. (a)	28. (d)
	25. (a)	27. (c)	29. (c)

30. **The water harvesting scheme is recommended for** **[IARI PhD-2013]**
    (a) Sandy soil having infiltration rate higher than rainfall intensity
    (b) Water - logged area
    (c) Area with relatively low slope with adequate provision of water storage
    (d) None of the above

31. **The instrument used to measure the area of a map is known as** **[IARI PhD-2011, 2013]**
    (a) Dumpy level
    (b) Theodolite
    (c) Planimeter
    (d) Current meter

32. **Geometric similarity among watersheds is described by** **[IARI PhD - 2013]**
    (a) Comparing the land use pattern in watersheds
    (b) Comparing the slope and soil type in watersheds
    (c) Time of concentration for watersheds located in same region
    (d) Quantitative study of land forms in watersheds

33. **Which new programme to give impetus to watershed development in the country ?**
    (a) Hariyali (b) Neeranchal
    (c) IWDP (d) DPAP

34. **At present, Total degraded land (Mha) in India is (Ministry of agriculture annual report 2013-14)**
    (a) 175 (b) 145
    (c) 120 (d) None of the above

Answers	30. (c)	32. (d)	34. (c)
	31. (c)	33. (b)	

35. What is the extent of water and wind eroded areas in India ? (Mha)

(a) 24, 9 (b) 24, 15

(c) 15, 24 (d) 9, 24

36. Which of the following is not a feature of watershed ? [IARI PhD 2013]

(a) Hydrological unit

(b) Biophysical unit

(c) Socio - economic unit

(d) Production unit

37. A watershed area of 1851 hectare has maximum distance of 7.12 km from the outlet to the farthest point on the divide line. The form factor of the watershed is [GATE-2016]

(a) 2.60 (b) 2.73

(c) 0.365 (d) 0.385

38. If the departure and latitude of a line during Theodolite survey are 70.03 m and -100 m, respectively, the whole circle bearing of this line in degree is [GATE-2018]

(a) 55 (b) 125

(c) 135 (d) 145

39. The hydrologic reservoir routing methods use [GATE-2021]

(a) Bernoulli's equation only

(b) Hydrologic continuity equation only

(c) Muskingum equation only

(d) Both the hydraulic momentum and hydrologic continuity equations

OOOOO

Answers	35. (a)	37. (c)	39. (b)
	36. (d)	38. (d)	

4 Hydrology and Soil & Water Conservation

1. **The hydraulic method of flood routing is based on [NET - 2013, ARS - 2014]**
   - (a) Equation of continuity
   - (b) Equation of momentum
   - (c) Both (a) and (b)
   - (d) Equation of energy

2. **If 5 year 1 day rainfall is 300 mm then 5 year 2 day rainfall at same location will be [ARS-2014]**
   - (a) 300 - 350 mm
   - (b) 200 - 250 mm
   - (c) 250 - 300 mm
   - (d) Less than 200 mm

3. **A direct runoff hydrograph due to a storm was found to be triangular in shape with a peak of 150 m^3 / s, time for start of effective storm to peak of 24 h and a total time base of 72 h. the duration of the storm in this case was [ARS - 2014]**
   - (a) Less than 24 h
   - (b) More than 24 h
   - (c) Less than 72 h
   - (d) None of the above

4. **The key trench of Homogeneous dam is [ARS-2014, NET-2014]**
   - (a) Composite kind of material
   - (b) Single kind of material
   - (c) Both (a) and (b)
   - (d) None of the above

Answers	1. (c) 3. (a) 2. (a) 4. (b)

5. **In earthen dam, the drain trench material is**

(a) Concrete (b) Plastic

(c) Clay (d) None of the above

6. **The .... distribution is used to model the distribution of the maximum of a number of samples of various distributions [ARS-2014]**

(a) Gumbel (b) Logarithmic - Pearson

(c) Normal (d) Skew - Pearson

7. **The maximum recharge of Ground water lakes place when [ARS-2014]**

(a) Lower rainfall intensity

(b) High rainfall intensity

(c) High runoff

(d) High runoff

8. **Hydraulic jump takes place when flow enters from [NET - 2013, ARS - 2014, ARS - 2015]**

(a) Supercritical to critical

(b) Critical to sub critical

(c) Subcritical to super critical

(d) Supercritical to sub critical {or steep to low slope}

9. **The manning's coefficient of grassed waterways varies [ARS-2014]**

(a) 0.01 - 0.02 (b) 0.02 - 0.04

(c) 0.03 - 0.05 (d) Less than 0.01

10. **The velocity of flow in poor grassed diversion is [ARS-2013]**

(a) 0.9 - 1.2 m/s (b) 1.5 - 2 m/s

(c) 2 - 2.5 m/s (d) 0.5 m/s

Answers	5. (c)	7. (a)	9. (b)
	6. (a)	8. (d)	10. (a)

11. The float block in spillway is provided for [ARS-2014]

(a) Flow measurement

(b) Energy dissipation

(c) Erosion control

(d) All of the above

12. Isohyet is a line joining of equal [ARS-2014]

(a) Depth of rainfall (b) ET

(c) Time of travel (d) Depth of water table

13. D_{15} (Earth and Rock-Fill Dams) denotes to [ARS-2014]

(a) Grain size for the protected (or base) material

(b) Grain size for the filter material

(c) Depth of water table at 15 cm

(d) None of the above

14. The contour cultivation is most effective on slope [ARS-2014]

(a) Less than 2% (b) 10 - 15%

(c) 15 - 20% (d) 2 - 7%.

15. Sloping inward terrace is applicable in areas of [ARS - 2014]

(a) Deep soils (b) Shallow soils

(c) Both (a) and (b) (d) None of the above

16. Chemical most suitable for evaporation inhabitation is [NET - 2013, ARS - 2014]

(a) Cetyal alcohol (b) Steryl alcohol

(c) Ethyl alcohol (d) Methyl alcohol

17. The availability of iron in Ground Water is tested by [ARS - 2014]

(a) Boiling (b) Distilled

(c) Expose in air (d) Heating in sun

Answers				
	11. (b)	13. (b)	15. (a)	17. (c)
	12. (a)	14. (d)	16. (a)	

18. NRCS curve number method is used for the estimation in watershed [ARS-2014, 2015]

(a) Peak runoff (b) Direct runoff

(c) Rainfall (d) Base flow

19. The drought is called as 'severe' if seasonal rainfall deficiency compared to normal value is [NET - 2013, ARS - 2014]

(a) More than 50% (b) Less than 25%

(c) 25 - 49% (d) 75%

20. The value of curve number (CN) in NRCS curve method is [IARI PhD-2011, ARS-2014]

(a) 100 - 0 (b) 0 - 100

(c) More than 100 (d) -100 to 100

21. The Coshocton wheel is used for [IARI PhD-2011, ARS-2014]

(a) Sediment sampling (b) Runoff estimation

(c) Rainfall measurement (d) All of the above

22. Under normal conditions which is used [ARS-2014]

(a) AMC - I (b) AMC - II

(c) AMC - III (d) All of the above

23. Initially, used for runoff estimation is [ARS-2014]

(a) AMC - I (b) AMC - II

(c) AMC - III (d) All of the above

24. In Check against sliding criteria of dam design [ARS-2014]

(a) Horizontal force is less than friction resistance force

(b) Horizontal force is more than friction resistance force

(c) Friction resistance force is less than friction resistance force

(d) Horizontal force is equal to friction resistance force

Answers				
	18. (b)	20. (b)	22. (b)	24. (a)
	19. (a)	21. (a)	23. (d)	

25. In flood routing, inflow hydrograph related with **[ARS-2014]**

(a) Outflow hydrograph
(b) Storage
(c) Both (a) and (b)
(d) None of the above

26. The formula [T= (N+1)/m], in which T is the time period, N is recurrence interval and m is number of successive year of occurrence of rainfall, represent **[ARS-2014]**

(a) Weibull's (b) Tyler's
(c) Henderson's (d) Gumbell's

27. Hyetograph refers to the ratio **[IARI PhD-2011, BHU-2012, SRF-2013]**

(a) Rainfall intensity vs time
(b) Discharge vs time
(c) Rainfall depth vs time
(d) Accumulated rainfall vs time

28. For an annual series arranged in decreasing order of magnitude, the return period for a magnitude listed at position m in a total of N entries is **[SRF-2013]**

(a) m/N (b) m/(N+1)
(c) (N+1)/m (d) N/m

29. What is the value of light rainfall intensity (cm/h) ? **[JRF - 2012]**

(a) Less than 2.5 (b) 2.5 - 7.5
(c) Greater than 7.5 (d) None

30. Drop spillway is applicable for the drop height of **[BHU - 2010, JRF - 2012]**

(a) Less than 3 m (b) More than 3 m
(c) Upto 6 m (d) 3 - 10 m

Answers	25. (c)	27. (a)	29. (a)
	26. (a)	28. (c)	30. (a)

31. **Erosion is more sensitive in the flow condition** **[JRF-2012]**

(a) Laminar (b) Turbulent
(c) Uniform (d) Steady

32. **Middle third rule is safeguarding against** **[JRF-2012]**

(a) Sliding (b) Overturning
(c) Crushing (d) Shearing

33. **From total geographical area in Mha and average annual rainfall of India, the generated runoff volume (Mha) is** **[NET - 2013]**

(a) 100 - 150 (b) 150 - 200
(c) 200 - 300 (d) 350 - 400

34. **In drizzle the size of droplet is about** **[NET-2013]**

(a) More than 0.5 m (b) Equal to 0.5 m
(c) Equal to 1 (d) Less than 0.5

35. **For checking the inconsistency of rainfall data which method is used** **[NET-2013]**

(a) Double mass curve (b) Mass curve
(c) Both (a) and (b) (d) None of the above

36. **At laminar wind flow soil erosion is** **[NET-2013]**

(a) Zero (b) Less
(c) More (d) Not depends

37. **The area under hyetograph represents** **[NET-2013]**

(a) Total rainfall intensity
(b) Total rainfall amount
(c) Direct runoff
(d) Effective rainfall

Answers	**31. (a)**	**33. (d)**	**35. (a)**	**37. (b)**
	32. (a)	**34. (d)**	**36. (a)**	

38. **Distance of protection due to wind erosion is maximum at an angle** **[NET-2013]**

(a) 0° (b) 30°
(c) 45° (d) 90°

39. **Hill type bench terrace is used for which type of soil** **[NET - 2013]**

(a) Deep (b) Shallow
(c) Medium (d) None of the above

40. **The sediment collected at the downstream section of stream should be** **[NET-2013]**

(a) Less than gross erosion
(b) Same as gross erosion
(c) More than gross erosion
(d) None of the above

41. **The ratio of total amount of rainfall received to the excess rainfall time period is** **[NET-2013]**

(a) Φ - index (b) A & B
(c) w - index (d) None

42. **For the base flow separation fixed slope method used is** **[NET-2013]**

(a) $N = 0.83A^{0.2}$ (b) $N = 0.83A^{-0.2}$
(c) $N = 0.83A^{0.3}$ (d) $N = 0.2A^{0.83}$

43. **Return period of temporary vegetated grassed waterways and diversion ditch are** **[ARS-2013, 2015, NET-2013, BHU-2015]**

(a) 10 yrs (b) 25 yrs
(c) 20 yrs (d) 50 yrs

44. **For 100 year return period PMF what would be the probability of flood occurring at least once in 10 successive years** **[NET-2013]**

(a) 0.64 (b) 1
(c) 0.36 (d) 0

Answers	
Answers	**38. (a) 40. (a) 42. (a) 44. (a)** **39. (d) 41. (a) 43. (a)**

45. **Kirpich's formula is used for computation of [NET-2013]**
    (a) Time of concentration (b) Direct runoff
    (c) w-index (d) Peak discharge

46. **Which of the following probability distribution in not applicable in flood flows due to higher skewness [NET-2013]**
    (a) Normal (b) Log Pearson
    (c) Gumbel (d) Log Normal

47. **Which of the following is not a sediment transportation phenomenon in wind erosion ? [NET-2013]**
    (a) Transulation (b) Surface creep
    (c) Saltation (d) Suspension

48. **Mulching is used for [IARI PhD-2011, NET-2013]**
    (a) Conserving soil moisture
    (b) Preventing soil compaction
    (c) Protecting crop from insects
    (d) Ensuring good germination

49. **The thin film of soil layer eroded due to flowing water is called as [NET - 2013]**
    (a) Sheet erosion (b) Flow erosion
    (c) Splash erosion (d) None of the above

50. **Time-area histogram diagram used in which model [ARS-2013, NET-2013]**
    (a) Clark (b) Nash
    (c) Both (a) & (b) (d) None of the above

51. **Which type of equation is used in both prism and wedge storage [NET-2013]**
    (a) Muskingum (b) Modified pulse
    (c) Pulse (d) None of the above

Answers	
	45. (a) 47. (a) 49. (a) 51. (a) 46. (a) 48. (a) 50. (a)

52. Unit hydrograph with 1 cm excess rainfall generates peak runoff of 120m³/s. The peak runoff (m³/s) of same UH for 3 cm excess rainfall [NET-2013]

(a) 360 (b) 60
(c) 40 (d) 120

53. The DRH (m³/s) generated by flood hydrograph of 1800 m³/s with base flow 200 m³/s is [NET-2013]

(a) 1600 (b) 2000
(c) 2200 (d) 9

54. In India daily rainfall readings are collecting during which time of the day ? [NET-2013, 2014]

(a) 8.30 a.m. (b) 9.30 a.m.
(c) 11.30 a.m. (d) 04.00 p.m.

55. A strong jump having Froude number greater than 9, the energy dissipation [ARS-2014]

(a) Less than 5% (b) 5 - 15 %
(c) 75 - 85% (d) 15 - 45%

56. The most wind erosion prone state in the country is [IARI PhD-2011, ARS-2014]

(a) Gujarat (b) Punjab
(c) UP (d) Rajasthan

57. What is the maximum permissible length (m) of graded terrace ? [SRF-2013]

(a) 40 - 50 (b) 300 - 500
(c) 1200 - 1400 (d) 1500 - 2000

58. The Froude number of steady flow in permanent structure is [SRF-2013, NET-2014]

(a) 1 - 1.7 (b) 1.7 - 2.5
(c) 2.5 - 4.5 (d) 4.5 - 9

Answers	52. (a)	54. (a)	56. (d)	58. (d)
	53. (a)	55. (c)	57. (b)	

59. Hydrograph is a plot of **[JRF-2012]**

(a) Rainfall intensity vs time

(b) Discharge vs time

(c) Cumulative Runoff vs time

(d) Cumulative discharge vs time

60. Hill type bench terrace is used for which type of soil **[NET-2013]**

(a) Deep (b) Shallow

(c) Medium (d) None of the above

61. The sediment collected at the downstream section of stream should be **[NET-2013]**

(a) Less than gross erosion

(b) Same as gross erosion

(c) More than gross erosion

(d) None of the above

62. The movement of soil particles having sizes in the range of 0.05 to 0.5 mm through a series of benches is known as **[NET-2014]**

(a) Saltation (b) Suspension

(c) Surface creep (d) All of the above

63. Location of permanent gully control structure is decided on the basis of **[JRF-2011]**

(a) Gully depth (b) Gully width

(c) Gully bed slope (d) All of the above

64. Permanent gully control structures are designed in respect of **[JRF-2011]**

(a) Hydrologic (b) Hydraulic

(c) Structural (d) All of the above

Answers	59. (b)	61. (a)	63. (c)
	60. (a)	62. (a)	64. (d)

65. Engineering measures to control erosion are more effective, when land slope [JRF-2011]

(a) Exceeds 10% (b) Exceeds 2%
(c) Exceeds 5% (d) None of the above

66. A structure will not fail against tension, when [JRF-2011]

(a) Eccentricity (e) not greater than b/6
(b) Eccentricity is greater than b/6
(c) Eccentricity is equal to b/6
(d) None of the above

67. Berms are provided, when [JRF-2011]

(a) Embankment height exceeds 15 m
(b) Embankment height exceeds 10 m
(c) Embankment height exceeds 20 m
(d) All of the above

68. A forms of precipitation having size of fine drops is less than 0.5 mm and intensity is less than 1mm / h is called as [JRF - 2011]

(a) Rainfall (b) Drizzle
(c) Glaze (d) Snow

69. Free board is provided to accommodate the embankment height against

(a) Overtopping (b) Overturning
(c) Sliding (d) All of the above

70. The Rational method is used to estimate [GATE-2013, ARS-2015]

(a) Runoff volume (b) Peak runoff rate
(c) Runoff depth (d) Direct surface runoff

71. Chute spillway is suitable in [ARS-2013]

(a) Low slope (b) Steep slope
(c) Moderate slope (d) None of the above

Answers				
	65. (b)	67. (b)	69. (a)	71. (b)
	66. (a)	68. (b)	70. (b)	

72. **Terracing is constructed in the area of**
   (a) High rainfall
   (b) Low rainfall
   (c) Moderate to high rainfall
   (d) None of the above

73. **Hydrological flood routing methods use [ARS-2015]**
   (a) Equation of continuity only
   (b) Both momentum and continuity equation
   (c) Energy equation only
   (d) Equation of motion only

74. **Effective rainfall refers to**
   (a) Rainfall which percolates into groundwater
   (b) Total amount of rainfall
   (c) Amount of rainfall used by the plants
   (d) Amount left in the field after runoff

75. **A 16 m high wind break is constructed to protect soil from wind erosion due to wind velocity of 18 m/s at 15 m height. The minimum wind velocity at 15 m height capable of moving the soil fraction is 8 m/s. The angle of deviation of prevailing wind direction from the perpendicular to the wind break is 30°. The distance of full protection from the wind break in m is [GATE-2013]**
   (a) 60.44 (b) 104.69
   (c) 306.00 (d) 530.01

76. **An imaginary surface obtained by joining the water levels in several observation wells driven in a confined aquifer is known as [IARI PhD-2011, GATE-2014]**
   (a) Phreatic surface (b) Piezometric surface
   (c) Capillary fringe (d) Water table

Answers	72. (c)	74. (c)	76. (b)
	73. (a)	75. (b)	

77. **A 100 ha watershed received rainfall at a rate of 5 cm/h for 2 hours. If the runoff generated by the storm was at the rate of 1 m^3/s for 10 hours, the runoff coefficient for the watershed would be [GATE-2013]**

(a) 3.6×10^{-3} (b) 6.0×10^{-2}

(c) 0.36 (d) 36

78. **A watershed, with an area of 360 km^2, has a triangular shaped 4-h unit hydrograph with a base of 50 hours. The peak discharge of direct runoff hydrograph due to 3 cm of rainfall-excess in 4 hours from the watershed in m^3/s is [GATE-2013]**

(a) 13.33 (b) 40.00

(c) 120.00 (d) 160.00

79. **Bench terraces are to be constructed on a 15% hill slope. The batter slope is 1 : 1 and vertical interval is 2.5 m. The earth work in cutting is equal to filling. The quantum of earthwork in m^3/ha will be [GATE-2014]**

(a) 2656 (b) 2818

(c) 4248 (d) 5312

80. **If x be the highest mean monthly precipitation and y be the mean annual precipitation, then the 'rainfall aggressiveness' to soil erosion is [GATE-2015]**

(a) (x^2/y) (b) (y^2/x)

(c) (y^2/x^2) (d) (x^2/y^2)

81. **An unsteady time - drawdown pumping test was conducted in a confined aquifer and the drawdown was measured with time in an observation well located at a certain distance away from the pumping well. Using these time-drawdown data, we can determine [GATE-2015]**

(a) Transmissivity only (b) Storage coefficient only

(c) Specific storage only (d) Both (a) & (b)

Answers	**77. (c)**	**79. (a)**	**81. (d)**
	78. (c)	**80. (a)**	

82. The soil erodibility factor needs to be determined for use in the universal soil loss equation. The length, in m and slope, in % of the experimental plot to be used for this purpose, respectively are [GATE-2012]

(a) 19, 12 (b) 21, 11
(c) 22, 9 (d) 23, 8

83. A trapezoidal grassed waterway is constructed along a longitudinal gradient of 4%. If the cross-sectional area of flow is 1.52 m^2, wetted perimeter is 12.5 m and Manning's n for the waterway is 0.04 $m^{-1/3}$ s, the flow through the waterway in $m^3\ s^{-1}$ is [GATE-2012]

(a) 1.9 (b) 2.1
(c) 2.3 (d) 2.5

84. In the USLE A = RKLSCP, K stands for [JPSC-2011]

(a) Slope length (b) Runoff - rainfall factor
(c) Soil erodibility (d) Cover and management

85. The incorrect statement from the following is [GATE-2015]

(a) The peak runoff from an agricultural watershed is generally less than that from an urban Watershed of the same area
(b) The horizontal hydraulic conductivity of soil is less than its vertical hydraulic conductivity
(c) The magnitude of a 75 - year flood is less than that of a 100 - year flood
(d) The rating curve due to an unsteady flood event forms a loop

86. A steady discharge of 60 $m^3\ s^{-1}$ is passing through a trapezoidal irrigation channel with a bottom width of 5 m, bed slope of 0.01% and Manning's roughness coefficient of 0.025. The conveyance of the channel in $m^3\ s^{-1}$ is [GATE-2015]

(a) 2000 (b) 200
(c) 6000 (d) 600

Answers	82. (c) 83. (a) 84. (c) 85. (b) 86. (c)

87. A catchment of 720 ha area has 25-year mean rainfall intensity of 100 mm h^{-1} occurring for duration equal to its time of concentration. During a storm event, the catchment received a total of 7.5 cm design rainfall for 6 hours. Assuming φ - index of 0.25 cm h^{-1} and runoff coefficient of 0.6, the peak ordinate of the 6 - h unit hydrograph in m^3s^{-1} will be [GATE-2015]

(a) 10 (b) 20

(c) 30 (d) 40

88. A triangular 5-hour unit hydrograph (UH1) of a catchment area of 400 km^2 has a peak discharge of 60 m^3s^{-1}. Another triangular 5-hour unit hydrograph (UH2) having the same base width as UH1 has a peak flow of 90 m^3 s^{-1}. The catchment area corresponding to UH2 in km^2 is [GATE-2014]

(a) 267 (b) 600

(c) 750 (d) 867

89. The relationship between outflow Q in m^3 s^{-1} and storage S in m^3 for an emergency spillway in a reservoir is Q = S/ 4000. Inflow, outflow and storage are assumed to be zero at time t = 0. If the inflow rate is 300 m^3 s^{-1} at the end of t = 3 hours, the outflow rate in m^3 s^{-1} is [GATE-2012]

(a) 152.84 (b) 164.84

(c) 172.34 (d) 184.84

90. It is proposed to construct bench terraces on a 10% hill slope. If the batter slope is ½ H : 1 V, the percentage area that will be lost for cultivation due to bench terracing is [GATE - 2012]

(a) 4.68 (b) 5.47

(c) 6.25 (d) 6.78

91. The wedge storage in a river reach during the passage of a flood wave is [GATE-2011]

(a) Positive during rising phase

(b) Negative during rising phase

Answers	**87. (b)**	**89. (c)**	**91. (a)**
	88. (b)	**90. (b)**	

(c) Positive during falling phase
(d) Constant

92. For a catchment with an area of 400 km², the equivalent discharge of the S-curve obtained by summation of 4-h unit hydrograph in $m^3 s^{-1}$ is [GATE-2011]

(a) 100 (b) 139
(c) 200 (d) 278

93. A 100 ha reservoir receives 2500 mm of rain fall during a period of 2 years. During this period the mean inflow to the stream is 1.0 $m^3 s^{-1}$. The mean outflow from the stream is 0.8 $m^3 s^{-1}$ and the increase in the storage is 500 ha-m. Assuming that there is no seepage loss, the total evaporation during the period in m is [GATE-2011]

(a) 1.011 (b) 10.11
(c) 101.1 (d) 1011

94. In India, one rain gauge station is for every [NET-2013]

(a) 520 km^2 (b) 690 km^2
(c) 260 km^2 (d) 130 km^2

95. The drainage density of any catchment varies inversely with [ARS-2013]

(a) Area of the basin (b) Drainage frequency
(c) Length of basin (d) None of the above

96. Normal range of velocity of vertical axis current meter is [ARS-2013]

(a) 0.15 - 1 m/s (b) 2 - 4 m/s
(c) 0.15 - 4 m/s (d) 3 - 6 m/s

97. The apron length in masonry dam should [ARS-2013]

(a) Not less than 1.5 times the dam height
(b) Less than 1.5 times the dam height
(c) Equal to 1.5 m the dam height
(d) ¾ of dam height

Answers	92. (d)	94. (a)	96. (c)
	93. (b)	95. (a)	97. (a)

98. The thickness of apron/stilling basin is decided based on [NET-2013]

(a) Uplift pressure (b) Eccentricity

(c) Frictional forces (d) None of the above

99. Contour bounding is a method of soil conservation used in [UPSC-2013]

(a) Desert margins, liable to strong wind action

(b) Low flat plain, close to stream courses, liable to flooding

(c) Scrublands, liable to spread of weed growth

(d) None of the above

100. The rainfall on five successive days in a catchment was measured as 3, 8, 12, 6, and 2 cm. If the total runoff at the outlet from the catchment was 15 cm, the value of the φ-index (in mm/hour) is

(a) 0.0 (b) 1.04

(c) 1.53 (d) 2.79

101. The direct runoff hydrograph of a storm obtained from a catchment is triangular in shape and has a base period of 80 hours. The peak flow rate is 30 m^3/s and catchment area is 86.4 km^2. The rainfall excess that has resulted the above hydrograph is

(a) 5 cm (b) 8 cm

(c) 10 cm (d) 16 cm

102. The annual precipitation data of a city is normally distributed with mean and standard deviation as 1000 mm and 200 mm, respectively. The probability that the annual precipitation will be more than 1200 mm is

(a) Less than 50% (b) 50%

(c) 75% (d) More than 75%

Answers	98. (a)	100. (c)	102. (a)
	99. (d)	101. (a)	

103. **The formation which contains sufficient amount of water but has very small quantity to transfer the water is called** **[BHU-2015]**

(a) Aquifuse (b) Acquiclude
(c) Aquitard (d) Blind aquifer

104. **The limit of slope length at which soil erosion begins is called as** **[BHU-2015]**

(a) Optimum slope length
(b) Critical slope length
(c) Allowable slope length
(d) None of the above

105. **Transportation of soil particles under splash erosion will be greater on** **[BHU-2015]**

(a) Level land surface
(b) Uniform sloppy land surface
(c) Irregular surface
(d) Level land without cover

106. **Soil detachment by raindrop is independent of** **[BHU-2015]**

(a) Land slope (b) Soil colour
(c) Soil depth (d) Soil texture

107. **Rill erosion is also known as** **[BHU-2015]**

(a) Gully erosion (b) Micro channel erosion
(c) Micro erosion (d) Path erosion

108. **Sheet flow is generated when** **[BHU-2015]**

(a) Land slope is steep
(b) Land surface is rough
(c) Land surface is smooth with uniform slope
(d) Both (a) & (b)

Answers	**103. (b)**	**105. (b)**	**107. (b)**
	104. (b)	**106. (b)**	**108. (c)**

109. Rill erosion usually begins in the [BHU-2015]

(a) Lower part of land slope
(b) Upper part of land slope
(c) Middle of land slope
(d) Entire length of land slope

110. Sediment yield will be higher from the watershed dominated by [BHU-2015]

(a) Splash or raindrop erosion
(b) Sheet erosion
(c) Rill erosion
(d) Both (a) & (b)

111. Soil detachment in raindrop erosion takes place due to [BHU-2015]

(a) K.E of raindrop (b) Running flow
(c) P.E. of raindrop (d) Land slope

112. Detachment of soil particle by flowing water varies as [BHU-2015]

(a) Square of its velocity
(b) Fifth power of its velocity
(c) Square root of its velocity
(d) Fourth power of its velocity

113. Organic erosion occurs in the form of [BHU-2015]

(a) Phytogenic erosion (b) Zoogenic erosion
(c) Attrition (d) Both (a) & (b)

114. Erosion under shifting cultivation, deforestation cultivation on steep slopes without protective measures is associated with [BHU-2015]

(a) Anthropogenic erosion (b) Phytogenic erosion
(c) Zoogenic erosion (d) Extraction

Answers			
	109. (a)	111. (a)	113. (d)
	110. (c)	112. (a)	114. (a)

115. Bed width of medium gully is **[BHU-2015]**

(a) More than 50 m (b) Not less than 18 m

(c) 20 m (d) 4 - 8 m

116. The flow velocity of runoff at which washing of soil particle takes place is called as **[BHU-2011, 2015]**

(a) Maximum velocity (b) Permissible velocity

(c) Critical velocity (d) Design velocity

117. Area under a hydrograph represents **[BHU-2012]**

(a) Volume of runoff (b) Area of watershed

(c) Watershed feature (d) Stream flow feature

118. Curve number represents **[IARI PhD-2011, BHU-2012]**

(a) Rainfall property (b) Runoff trend

(c) Watershed feature (d) Stream flow feature

119. A practical method of reducing sheet erosion from sloping lands is **[BHU-2012]**

(a) Keeping the hind fallow

(b) Farming on contour strips

(c) Construction of small reservoirs

(d) Using plastic sheet cover

120. In Rational formula, Q = CiA, i standard for **[BHU-2012]**

(a) Intensity of rainfall

(b) Runoff coefficient

(c) Hydraulic gradient

(d) Mean intensity of rainfall for a duration equal to time of concentration

121. If the saturated hydraulic conductivity of a soil is 1 m/day, the rate of water transmission across a rectangular area 100 m long and 1 m height under a unit hydraulic gradient will be **[BHU-2012]**

(a) 10 m^3/day (b) 1 m^3/day

(c) 100 m^3/ day (d) 1000 m^3/day

Answers	**115. (b)**	**117. (a)**	**119. (b)**	**121. (c)**
	116. (b)	**118. (c)**	**120. (d)**	

122. Hydraulic conductivity is the proportionality constant in **[BHU-2012]**

(a) Bernoulli's equation (b) Rational formula
(c) Darcy's equation (d) Laplace's equation

123. Hydrologic soil Group - A stands for **[BHU-2012]**

(a) Low runoff potential
(b) Moderately low runoff potential
(c) Moderately high runoff potential
(d) High runoff potential

124. Thiessen polygon is used to **[BHU-2012]**

(a) Find area of a polygon
(b) Average depth of rainfall
(c) Perimeter of a polygon
(d) Average depth of runoff

125. Measure of dryness of a region is referred to as **[BHU-2012]**

(a) Aridity index (b) Drying coefficient
(c) Humidity (d) Anti - wetness index

126. Rain drops are spherical in shape because of

(a) Surface tension **[BHU-2014]**
(b) Capillary
(c) Cohesion and adhesion
(d) Acceleration due to gravity

127. A chute spillway is used to convey water for an elevation difference **[BHU-2012]**

(a) Less than 1 m (b) 1 m
(c) 1 m to 2 m (d) More than 3 m

Answers	122. (c)	124. (b)	126. (a)
	123. (a)	125. (a)	127. (d)

128. A 75% dependable rainfall means [BHU-2012]

(a) Magnitude of rainfall equal to 75% of normal

(b) Rainfall will be equal to or more than the given value 75% of the time

(c) Chances of normal rainfall are 75%

(d) Rainfall will be less than the given value 75% of the time

129. The standard recording rain gauge adopted in India [BHU-2010, 2012, ARS-2015]

(a) Weighing bucket type (b) Natural syphon type

(c) Tipping bucket type (d) Telemetry type

130. Land use capability classification is primarily based on [BHU-2012]

(a) Soil texture (b) Rainfall

(c) Ground water (d) Land slope

131. Land having slopes of more than 10 per cent should be cultivated only after making [BHU-2012]

(a) Contour trenches (b) Contour benches

(c) Broad based terraces (d) Bench terraces

132. The arithmetic mean method for computing missing rainfall data is suitable, when normal annual precipitations of various stations are within

(a) 10% of the normal annual precipitation of missing station

(b) 20% of the mean annual precipitation at the missing station

(c) 10% of the mean annual precipitation at the missing station

(d) 15% of the normal rainfall at missing station

Answers	**128. (b)**	**130. (d)**	**132. (a)**
	129. (b)	**131. (d)**	

133. The average rainfall in India is about

(a) 1194 mm (b) 1384 mm
(c) 1391 mm (d) 1491 mm

134. Diameter of rainfall collector in Non-recording type rain gauge is

(a) 8 cm (b) 13.5 cm
(c) 12.7 cm (d) 30 cm

135. The mass rainfall curve is drawn as a plot of

(a) Rainfall intensity vs. time
(b) Accumulated rainfall depth vs. time in a chronological order
(c) Cumulative rainfall intensity vs. time
(d) Rainfall volume vs. time

136. Thiessen polygons are drawn by

(a) Joining rain gauge stations
(b) Drawing lines of equal elevation
(c) Drawing perpendiculars of lines joining rain gauge stations
(d) Drawing lines of equal rainfall

137. While calculating optimal number of stations in a watershed, the allowable error for estimation of rainfall is generally taken as

(a) 2% (b) 8%
(c) 10% (d) 25%

138. Which of the following is the most accurate instrument for measuring stream velocity ?

(a) Coshocton wheel (b) Surface float
(c) H flume (d) Current meter

139. Base flow is separated from a **[IARI PhD-2013]**

(a) Surface hydrograph (b) Unit hydro graph
(c) Flood hydrograph (d) Hyetograph

Answers	**133. (a)**	**135. (b)**	**137. (c)**	**139. (c)**
	134. (c)	**136. (c)**	**138. (d)**	

140. A Unit hydrograph consist of one unit of

(a) Effective rainfall duration (b) Peak discharge
(c) Hydrograph time base (d) Direct runoff

141. In a watershed the number of non-recording rain gauge is installed as

(a) 10
(b) 20
(c) 90% of the total estimated rain gauge station
(d) 5

142. In Rational formula i.e. Q_p = CIA/360. The value of rainfall intensity (I) is expressed as

(a) cm/hr (b) mm/hr
(c) m/hr (d) None of the above

143. Unit of run - off coefficient in the Rational formula is

(a) Dimensionless (b) mm
(c) cm (d) m

144. A stream in which flow is continued throughout the year is called

(a) Ephemeral stream (b) Perennial stream
(c) Intermittent stream (d) Spring

145. The most economical section of grass water way is

(a) Parabolic (b) Towards outlet
(c) Triangular (d) Rectangular

146. Maximum movement of soil particle takes place, when flow depth is

(a) About or equal to particle diameter
(b) Less than 5 cm
(c) Equal to 10 cm
(d) None of the above

Answers				
	140. (d)	142. (b)	144. (b)	146. (a)
	141. (c)	143. (a)	145. (a)	

147. Detachment and transportation of soil particle is greater in

(a) Splash erosion (b) Rill erosion

(c) Sheet erosion (d) Both (b) & (c)

148. Erosion intensity of severe erosion is

(a) Less than 5 tons/ha/y

(b) 5 to 10 tons/ha/y

(c) 40 to 80 tons/ha/y

(d) Greater than 80 tons/ha/y

149. Stage - 3 gully development refers to

(a) Healing stage (b) Stabilizes stage

(c) Initiation stage (d) Development stage

150. For design of grassed way permissible flow velocity for sparse grass cover condition is taken as

(a) 0.9 to 1.2 m/s (b) 1.5 to 2.0 m/s

(c) 3.0 to 4.5 m/s (d) 1.0 to 2.0 m/s

151. Use of diversion drains is essential when

(a) Specified part of catchment is to keep under protection

(b) Protection of barren land is essential

(c) Diversion of water into gully is required

(d) All the above

152. Mulch tillage is practiced to minimize

(a) Moisture loss from soil

(b) Sediment yield from the field

(c) Splash effect

(d) Sheet erosion

153. When drop height exceeds 4 m and there is possibility of silt accumulation in farm pond, then most suitable mechanical spillway to use is

(a) Drop inlet spillway (b) Chute spillway

(c) Straight drop spillway (d) Grassed waterway

Answers				
	147. (a)	149. (a)	151. (d)	153. (b)
	148. (d)	150. (b)	152. (a)	

154. **Soil loss phenomena is**

(a) a dynamic event (b) a cyclic event

(c) a static event (d) None of the above

155. **Factor - C of USLE is affected by**

(a) Land slope

(b) Slope length

(c) Soil properties

(d) Cropping pattern and management practices

156. **The retaining walls are constructed for the purpose of**

(a) Maintaining unequal ground level

(b) Controlling soil erosion loss

(c) Supporting a soil mass

(d) Both (a) & (b)

157. **Greater soil erosion is observed in case of**

(a) Soil surface covered by plant canopy

(b) Soil surface under grass cover

(c) Soil under forest cover

(d) Soil under cultivated crop

158. **The sequence of water erosion is**

(a) Splash, sheet, rill and gully

(b) Sheet, rill, raindrop and gully erosion

(c) Rill, sheet, splash and gully erosion

(d) Gully, splash, rill and sheet erosion

159. **The purpose of cut-off walls in drop structure is to** **[BHU - 2010]**

(a) Provide structural strength against sliding

(b) Spill the flow safely

(c) Dissipate Kinetic Energy of flow

(d) Support gully walls

Answers	154. (a)	156. (c)	158. (a)
	155. (d)	157. (a)	159. (a)

160. Design of inlet section of drop structures is done by using [BHU-2010]

(a) Weir formula (b) Flume formula
(c) Orifice formula (d) Darcy's formula

161. Gully formation is mainly due to [BHU-2010]

(a) Land surface without vegetative cover and over grazing
(b) Adoption of faulty tillage work
(c) Not checking of developed rills
(d) Improper construction of channels

162. The basic assumption of the unit hydrograph theory is

(a) Non - linear response and time invariance
(b) Linear response and non-linear time variance
(c) Linear response and time invariance
(d) Linear response and time variance

163. Rating curve expresses the relationship between [BHU-2010]

(a) Stage versus discharge
(b) Stage versus velocity
(c) State versus time
(d) Stage versus sediment load

164. Conservation bench terrace is designed for [BHU-2010]

(a) Semi - arid region (b) Humid region
(c) Arid region (d) None of the above

165. The line above which there is no hydrostatic pressure and below which there is hydrostatic pressure is referred as [BHU-2010]

(a) Flow line (b) Seepage line
(c) Streamline (d) Piezometric surface

Answers			
	160. (a)	162. (c)	164. (b)
	161. (a)	163. (a)	165. (b)

166. For the storm runoff analysis, the base flow separation is performed on [BHU-2010]

(a) a unit hydrograph

(b) a flood hydrograph

(c) a hyetograph

(d) a hydrograph of effluent stream only

167. Terraces constructed on contour lines are called [BHU-2010]

(a) Graded terraces (b) Leveller terraces

(c) Bench terraces (d) Drainage type terraces

168. Bench terraces are constructed to change [BHU-2010]

(a) The slope of land only

(b) The length of slope only

(c) Both the land slope and the slope length

(d) None of the above

169. Graded terraces are recommended for the areas where [BHU-2010]

(a) Rainfall is high (b) Rainfall is low

(c) Soil depth is more (d) Soil is of shallow depth

170. The Universal Soil Loss Equation, primarily developed for small watersheds, estimates [BHU-2010]

(a) Permissible annual soil loss

(b) Maximum annual soil loss

(c) Average annual soil loss

(d) Minimum permissible annual soil loss

171. The most active portion of a gully is [BHU-2010]

(a) The gully tail (b) The gully banks

(c) The gully head (d) The gully bed

Answers			
	166. (b)	168. (c)	170. (c)
	167. (a)	169. (a)	171. (d)

172. The stilling basin with a chute spillway is provided for [BHU - 2010]

(a) Energy formation (b) Discharge measurement

(c) Energy dissipation (d) Wave formation

173. The suspended sediment in a flowing stream is measured by [BHU-2010]

(a) a stage level recorder

(b) a Parshall flume

(c) a Coshocton wheel sampler

(d) a Cipoletti weir

174. Shelterbelts are most effective, if installed [BHU-2010]

(a) At an angle of 45° from the prevailing wind direction

(b) At an angle more than 90° from the prevailing wind direction

(c) Parallel to the prevailing wind direction

(d) Perpendicular to the prevailing wind direction

175. The lines of equal rainfall are called [BHU-2010]

(a) Isohyetal (b) Isothyetal

(c) Isothermal (d) Contour

176. Effective rainfall means [BHU-2010]

(a) Rainfall which percolates into groundwater

(b) Total amount of rainfall

(c) Amount of rainfall used by the plants

(d) Amount left in the field after runoff

177. Sudden fall of pressure at a place indicates [IARI PhD-2013]

(a) Storm (b) Rain

(c) Fair weather (d) Cold wave

Answers	172. (a)	174. (a)	176. (c)
	173. (c)	175. (a)	177. (a)

178. Percolation tanks are used for [IARI PhD-2013]

(a) Storage of water to be used for irrigation and domestic purpose

(b) To increase the water carrying capacity of stream

(c) To hold the surface water for recharge

(d) Flood control

179. While designing an earth dam, care should be taken so that the resultant of the forces [IARI PhD-2013]

(a) Passes through the middle of the base

(b) Meets the base within $2/3^{rd}$ distance from the toe

(c) Meets the base within $2/3^{rd}$ distance from the heel

(d) Passes the downstream at $1/3^{rd}$ the height from the base

180. The most accurate method of averaging precipitation over an area is [IARI PhD-2013]

(a) Arithmetical averaging (b) Thiessen method

(c) Grid point method (d) Isohyetal method

181. The stilling well for water stage recorder is used basically [IARI PhD-2013]

(a) To protect the float

(b) To protect the counter weight cables

(c) To suppress fluctuations from surface waves in the stream

(d) To keep away the silt content of water of the stream

182. Multi - slot divisors are used for studying [IARI PhD-2013]

(a) Wind effect on rainfall

(b) Space distribution of rainfall

(c) Drop size distribution of rainfall

(d) Soil loss from experimental plots

Answers	178. (c)	180. (d)	182. (d)
	179. (b)	181. (a)	

183. The formula Q_p= CiA is used to estimate the [IARI PhD-2013]

(a) Peak flow rate of runoff
(b) Average flow rate of runoff
(c) Cumulative flow of runoff
(d) Instantaneous rate of runoff

184. The peak of unit hydrograph is the discharge per unit of [IARI PhD-2013]

(a) Total rainfall (b) Watershed area
(c) Rainfall duration (d) Rainfall excess

185. A rainfall of 5.0 mm recorded between 14.00 h and 14 h 15 min has occurred with an intensity of [IARI PhD-2013]

(a) 5 mm/h (b) 10 mm/h
(c) 20 mm/h (d) 50 mm/h

186. Graded bunds are used in [IARI PhD-2013]

(a) Low rainfall areas for soil conservation
(b) Low rainfall areas for water conservation
(c) Low rainfall areas for soil and water conservation
(d) Relatively high rainfall areas for safe removal of excess rainfall

187. A soil is categorised as 'Group C' soil. It has [IARI PhD-2013]

(a) Very low infiltration rate
(b) Low infiltration rate
(c) Moderate infiltration rate
(d) High infiltration rate

188. The main cause of sheet erosion is [IARI PhD-2013]

(a) Raindrop splash (b) Strong winds
(c) Tillage (d) Cultivation of cereal crops

Answers	183. (a)	185. (c)	187. (c)
	184. (d)	186. (c)	188. (a)

189. In the universal soil loss equation (USLE), the soil erodibility factor K is [IARI PhD-2013]

(a) a measure of the susceptibility of soil particles to detachment and transport

(b) Slope length gradient factor

(c) Crop management factor

(d) Rainfall - runoff factor

190. The difference between observed total rainfall hyetograph and the excess rainfall hyetograph is termed as [IARI PhD-2013]

(a) Soil moisture storage (b) Abstractions

(c) Ground water recharge (d) Detention storage

191. Why the dam of water reservoir is thick at bottom? [IARI PhD-2013]

(a) Quantity of water increases with depth

(b) Density of water increases with depth

(c) Pressure of water increases with depth

(d) None of the above

192. The equation $t_c = 0.0192L^{0.77}S^{-0.385}$ is [IARI PhD-2013]

(a) Boussinesque equation

(b) St. Venant equation

(c) Kirpich formula

(d) Darcy's equation

193. Abstractions includes [IARI PhD-2013]

(a) Interception by vegetation above the surface

(b) Interception by vegetation before surface runoff begins

(c) Interception by vegetation above the ground, depression storage and infiltration

(d) Depression storage and infiltration

Answers	189. (a)	191. (c)	193. (c)
	190. (b)	192. (c)	

194. In hydrologic routing **[IARI PhD-2013]**

(a) Flow is calculated as a function of space only

(b) Flow is calculated as a function of time alone at given location

(c) Flow is calculated as a function of time and space

(d) Flow is calculated as a function of depth at given location

195. In case of saturation overland flow theory **[IARI PhD-2013]**

(a) Soil is saturated from above by infiltration

(b) Soil is saturated from below by sub-surface flow

(c) Entire watershed contributes to overland flow

(d) The top of the watershed contributes to overland flow

196. The portion of a chute spillway, which is known as its controls structure, is **[BHU-2012]**

(a) Low ogee weir

(b) Chute channel

(c) Approach channel leading the water from the reservoir to the ogee weir

(d) Stilling basin at its bottom

197. Removal of a thin and fairly uniform layer of the soil from the land surface by runoff water is called **[IARI PhD-2011, BHU-2012]**

(a) Torrent erosion (b) Glacial erosion

(c) Sheet erosion (d) Geologic erosion

198. The universal soil loss equation, primarily developed for small watersheds, estimates **[BHU-2012]**

(a) Permissible annual soil loss

(b) Average annual soil loss

(c) Maximum annual soil loss

(d) Minimum permissible annual soil

Answers	194. (b)	196. (c)	198. (b)
	195. (b)	197. (c)	

199. Amongst the following, the most effective measure for erosion and soil loss control [IARI PhD-2011]

(a) Contour farming

(b) Strip cropping

(c) Terracing and bunding

(d) Fertilizing

200. A study of the iso-pluvial maps revealed that at Calcutta a maximum rainfall depth of 200 mm in 12h has a return period of 50 years. The probability of a 12h rainfall equal to or greater than 200mm occurring at Calcutta at least once in 30years is.....(Given that 0.98^30=0.55)

(a) 0.45 (b) 0.55

(c) 0.56 (d) 1

201. At a station, Storm I of 5 hour duration with intensity 2 cm/h resulted in a runoff of 4 cm and Storm II of 8hour duration resulted in a runoff of 8.4 cm. Assume that the φ - index is the same for both the storms. The φ - index (in cm/h) is :

(a) 1.2 (b) 1.8

(c) 1.6 (d) 1.4

202. The chemical compound which is generally used to reduce the evaporation from water surface is

(a) DDT (b) Alum

(c) Cetyl alcohol (d) Potassium dichromate

203. An isopluvial line is a line joining points having

(a) Equal evapotranspiration value

(b) Equal barometric pressure

(c) Equal height above the MSL

(d) Equal rainfall depths

Answers	199. (c)	201. (b)	203. (d)
	200. (a)	202. (c)	

204. The most suitable hydraulic structure for conveying water from higher elevation to lower elevation across the earthen bund is [GATE-2016]

(a) Drop structure (b) Pipe drop structure

(c) Chute spillway (d) Gabion structure

205. A drought in India is considered as a severe drought, when the production of the country due to drought falls

(a) Between 50% and 75% of the normal

(b) Between 25% and 50% of the normal

(c) Between 15% and 25% of the normal

(d) Below 15% of the normal

206. Which meteorological phenomenon helps in buildup of pollution levels in atmosphere ?

(a) Radiation (b) Thunder storm

(c) Rainfall (d) Thermal inversion

207. During wind erosion, the maximum amount of soil removal is due to

(a) Sheet (b) Saltation

(c) Surface Creep (d) Shifting

208. The percentage of total world's precipitation, which is lost to the atmosphere through evaporation, approximates to

(a) 27% (b) 7%

(c) 57% (d) 23%

209. Which of the following is not a method for water conservation ?

(a) Rainwater harvesting

(b) Groundwater extraction

(c) Improving irrigation efficiency

(d) Avoiding water wastage

Answers	204. (b)	206. (b)	208. (c)
	205. (a)	207. (b)	209. (b)

210. Tabletop bench terraces are applicable in[NET/ARS-2016]

(a) Medium depth of soil (b) Deep depth of soil

(c) Shallow depth of soil (d) All

211. When cut fill ratio is greater than one then centroid of leveling is [NET/ARS-2016]

(a) Centroid is below half part

(b) Centroid is above half part

(c) Centroid is at centre

(d) None of the above

212. If T denote return period, then (1-1/T) refers to [NET/ARS-2016]

(a) Probability of occurrence of rainfall

(b) Probability of non-occurrence of rainfall

(c) Both

(d) None of the above

213. For one cm effective rainfall, ordinate of unit hydrograph is 120 m^3/s. then for 3 cm effective rainfall ordinate is [NET/ARS-2016]

(a) 360m^3/s (b) 120 m^3/s

(c) 40 m^3/s (d) 0 m^3/s

214. For concrete surface the CN value is [NET/ARS-2016]

(a) 0 (b) 50

(c) 100 (d) 15

215. Vados water refers to [NET/ARS-2016]

(a) Capillary (b) Intermediate

(c) Soil and water surface (d) None

216. An aquifer which does not release water is [NET/ARS-2016]

(a) Aquitard (b) Aquifuge

(c) Aquiclude (d) None

Answers				
	210. (a)	**212. (b)**	**214. (c)**	**216. (c)**
	211. (c)	**213. (a)**	**215. (b)**	

217. A catchment has eight raingauge stations. In a year, the annual rainfall recorded by the gauges (in cm) are 93.8, 106.5, 170.6, 138.7, 87.8, 156.2, 180.9 and 110.3. For a 10% error in the estimation of the mean rainfall, the optimum number of stations in the catchment is [GATE-2019]

(a) 4 (b) 6

(c) 8 (d) 10

218. On a 4% land slope in a medium rainfall zone, the horizontal spacing of bunds in meter and the length of bunds per hectare in meter, respectively are[GATE-2019]

(a) 25 and 300 (b) 25 and 400

(c) 30 and 300 (d) 30 and 400

219. The approximate relationship between Sediment Delivery Ratio (SDR) and drainage area (A) shows that SDR varies [GATE-2021]

(a) directly with $A^{0.2}$ (b) inversely with $A^{0.2}$

(c) directly with A (d) inversely with A

220. It is proposed to develop bench terraces in an area having land slope of 10%. If the vertical interval between the bench terraces is 2.5 m and the batter slope is 100%, working width (in m) and the area lost for cultivation (in percent), respectively will be [GATE-2021]

(a) 22.50 and 0.05 (b) 25.00 and 0.50

(c) 22.50 and 10.45 (d) 25.00 and 10.45

221. The shape of the Instantaneous Unit Hydrograph (IUH) of a catchment is an isosceles triangle with a peak of 60 $m^3 s^{-1}$ and time to peak of 3 h. If the constant base flow is 7.5 m^3s^{-1}, the peak of the 3 h Unit Hydrograph (UH) in m^3s^{-1} is [GATE-2021]

(a) 43.33 (b) 50.83

(c) 52.50 (d) 60.00

Answers	217. (c)	219. (b)	221. (a)
	218. (b)	220. (c)	

222. **A plot between rainfall intensity versus time is called as** **[BHU-2018]**

(a) Hydrograph (b) Mass curve
(c) Hyetograph (d) Isohyets

223. **The shape of falling limb of a hydrograph is dependent on ....** **[GATE-2022]**

(a) Basin and storm characteristics
(b) Storm characteristics only
(c) Basin characteristics only
(d) Direction of the rainfall only

224. **A parabolic shaped grass-waterway is to be designed to carry a flow of 2.85 m^3 s^{-1}down the slope of 3%. The permissible velocity of water in the waterway is 1.78 ms^{-1}. If the freeboard depth is excluded, the most appropriate top width in mand depth in m, respectively are (Assume Manning's roughness coefficient = 0.04)** **[GATE-2022]**

(a) 4 and 0.6 (b) 6 and 0.4
(c) 7 and 0.5 (d) 5.5 and 0.6

OOOOO

Answers	222. (c) 224. (b) 223. (c)

5 Groundwater Development, Wells and Pumps

1. **The rate of fluid flow through porous media is proportional to the hydraulic gradient is given by [ARS-2013, 2014]**
   (a) Muskingham (b) Darcy
   (c) Dupuit (d) Theis
2. **Corrosion in tube well water is increased due to presence of [NET-2013, ARS-2014, ARS-2015]**
   (a) Dissolved salts (b) Solids contents
   (c) Dissolve gases in water (d) All of the above
3. **An unsteady flow in confined aquifer was derived by [ARS - 2014]**
   (a) Theis (b) Jacob
   (c) Chow (d) All of the above
4. **Characteristics curve shows the relationship between [ARS - 2014]**
   (a) Head (b) Speed
   (c) Discharge (d) All
5. **The head loss due to friction when water flow through pipe is proportional to [IARI PhD-2011, ARS-2013, ARS-2014]**
   (a) Square of velocity (b) Square root of velocity
   (c) Fifth power of velocity (d) Velocity

Answers	**1. (b)**	**3. (d)**	**5. (a)**
	2. (d)	**4. (d)**	

6. **If hydraulic head and length is 5m and 10m respectively. The hydraulic gradient is** **[ARS-2014]**

(a) 5/10 (b) 0.5

(c) 10/5 (d) Both (a) and (b)

7. **If hydraulic conductivity and kinematic viscosity of materials are 5m/day and 10m²/s respectively. The intrinsic permeability (m²) is** **[ARS-2014]**

(a) 5.899×10^{-6} (b) 58.99×10^{-6}

(c) 589.9×10^{-6} (d) 0.589×10^{-6}

8. **Keeping other factors constant, doubling diameter of tube well will increase the discharge by [ARS-2014, BHU-2015]**

(a) 11% (b) 20%

(c) 50% (d) 100%

9. **Cavity well having** **[ARS-2014]**

(a) No strainer

(b) Strainer

(c) Operated in clay layer of soil

(d) Both (a) and (b)

10. **The dispose ash from thermal power plant is mainly used in** **[ARS-2014]**

(a) Road construction (b) Channel design

(c) Agriculture (d) Cement factory

11. **Total head of pump is indicated by** **[ARS-2014]**

(a) Total suction head (b) Total delivery head

(c) Both (a) and (b) (d) None of the above

12. **Well recovery refers to** **[ARS-2014]**

(a) Well loss (b) Well formation

(c) Well characteristics (d) All of the above

Answers	6. (d)	8. (a)	10. (a)	12. (c)
	7. (b)	9. (a)	11. (c)	

13. The discharge of confined aquifer refers to [ARS-2014]

(a) Drawdown (b) Thickness

(c) Porosity (d) Both (a) and (b)

14. The Water entrance velocity in well strainer is [ARS-2014]

(a) 30 mm/s (b) 300 mm/s

(c) 3 mm/s (d) 0.3 mm/s

15. Pumps used in surface drainage works are of the type [BHU-2012, ARS-2014]

(a) Reciprocating pump (b) Centrifugal pump

(c) Submersible pump (d) Propeller pump

16. Well development is a process of [ARS-2014]

(a) Reversal of flow through casing pipe

(b) Increases the rate of water movement from the aquifer into the well

(c) Stabilizes the aquifer to prevent sand pumping, thereby producing better quality water and increasing the service life of the pump cylinder and well

(d) All of above

17. Confined aquifer is operated for testing is [ARS-2014]

(a) 12 - 20 h (b) 24 - 40 h

(c) 24 - 48 h (d) More than 48 h

18. Foot valve is installed in which side of pump[ARS-2014]

(a) Delivery (b) Centre

(c) Suction (d) All of the above

19. Specific capacity of aquifer refers to the ratio [SRF-2013, NET-2013, ARS-2015]

(a) Discharge vs drawdown

(b) Discharge vs radius of influence

(c) Drawdown vs discharge

(d) Both (a) and (b)

Answers				
	13. (d)	15. (b)	17. (b)	19. (a)
	14. (a)	16. (d)	18. (c)	

20. Specific yield of the aquifer is the properties of [SRF-2013]

(a) Confined aquifer (b) Unconfined aquifer
(c) Semi - confined aquifer (d) Both (b) and (c)

21. When two centrifugal pumps are arranged in parallel, the head is [SRF-2013]

(a) Remain constant (b) Increase
(c) Decrease (d) None of the above

22. Ergun equation is applicable to the flow [SRF-2013]

(a) Turbulent (b) Laminar
(c) Porous media (d) Silt

23. A geological formation which neither porous nor permeable is called as [JRF-2012, ARS-2013]

(a) Aquifer (b) Aquiclude
(c) Aquitard (d) Aquifuge

24. The pump used for high discharge and low head is [JRF-2012, NET-2013]

(a) Propeller (b) Centrifugal
(c) Submersible (d) Air jet

25. Perched aquifer is a special case of [NET-2013]

(a) Confined aquifer (b) Unconfined aquifer
(c) Leaky aquifer (d) False aquifer

26. A completely saturated aquifer that is bounded above by a semi-pervious layer and below by a layer that is either impervious or semi-pervious is [NET-2013]

(a) Confined aquifer (b) Leaky aquifer
(c) Unconfined aquifer (d) False aquifer

27. Groundwater flow occurs when Reynolds number is [ARS-2013, NET-2013]

(a) More than 1 (b) Equal to 1
(c) Less than 1 (d) 2 - 10

Answers	20. (d)	22. (c)	24. (a)	26. (b)
	21. (a)	23. (d)	25. (b)	27. (c)

28. Specific speed of pump expresses relationship between [NET-2013]

(a) Speed, discharge and head (b) Speed and head

(c) Speed and capacity (d) Discharge and head

29. The yield of steady flow confined aquifer due to increase in drawdown [NET-2013]

(a) Increases (b) Same

(c) Decreases (d) None of the above

30. Doubling the diameter of confined aquifer increases its yield by [NET-2013]

(a) Marginally (b) 2 times

(c) 3 times (d) 1.1 times

31. Piezometer is used to measure [NET-2013]

(a) Hydrostatic pressure (b) Hydraulic conductivity

(c) Well depth (d) None of the above

32. The effective diameter D_{10} represents [NET-2013]

(a) 10 % finer (b) 90 % finer

(c) 10 % coarser (d) None of the above

33. If uniformity coefficient of gravel pack material is 1, it represents [NET-2013, ARS-2014, ARS-2015]

(a) Complete assortment (b) Uniform material

(c) Non-uniform material (d) None of the above

34. For a uniform aquifer $\frac{D_{50} \text{ of pack}}{D_{50} \text{ of aquifer}}$ should lies between [NET-2013]

(a) 9 and 12.5 (b) 4 and 5

(c) 11 and 15.5 (d) 15.5 and 31

Answers	28. (a)	30. (a)	32. (a)	34. (a)
	29. (a)	31. (a)	33. (b)	

35. Crooked tube wells caused due to [NET-2013]

(a) Misalignment of the line shaft assemble

(b) Higher power consumption

(c) Wear and tear of shaft bearings

(d) All of the above

36. A centrifugal pump delivers 10 lps against total head of 7.5 m. The water power is [IARI PhD-2011, BHU-2012, NET-2013]

(a) 0.746 kW (b) 7.46 W

(c) 0.746 W (d) 74.6 W

37. Water hammer occurs due to [NET-2013]

(a) Sudden starting and stopping of pump

(b) Power failure and rapid close of valve

(c) Abrupt change in pump speed

(d) All of the above

38. The relation due to increase in diameter of impeller results in total pump head (H) in the proportion of [NET-2013]

(a) $D \propto H$ (b) $D \propto H^2$

(c) $D \propto H^3$ (d) None of the above

39. Jet assembly provided in centrifugal pumps to increase [NET-2013]

(a) Suction lift (b) Discharge

(c) Efficiency (d) Head

40. Which method shows the relationship between GW fluctuation (y-axis) and GW draft (x-axis) ? [NET-2013]

(a) Hills' method

(b) Harding's method

(c) Miller's method

(d) All of the above

Answers			
	35. (d)	37. (d)	39. (a)
	36. (a)	38. (b)	40. (a)

41. **If the speed of a centrifugal pump is doubled, the power required will be increased by**
[JRF-2011, BHU-2012, SRF-2013, BHU-2015]

(a) 2 times (b) 4 times
(c) 8 times (d) 16 times

42. **A chemical method used to measure the polluting potential of material in water** **[SRF-2013]**

(a) BOD (b) COD
(c) OD (d) DO

43. **WHP of centrifugal pump of 10 lps capacity and 38 m total head will be**

(a) 3 (b) 4
(c) 5 (d) 6

44. **Hydraulic ram is pump which works on the principle of**

(a) Water hammer (b) Centrifugal pump
(c) Reciprocating action (d) None of the above

45. **The total head of propeller pump is** **[JRF-2011]**

(a) 1 - 2 m (b) 1.5 - 2.5 m
(c) 1 - 2.5 m (d) > 2.5

46. **Submersible pumps are suitable for the condition where**
[BHU-2010]

(a) Water is to be lifted from shallow depth
(b) Water is to be lifted from deep tube-well
(c) Large quantity of water required
(d) Any where

47. **Minimum thickness of gravel packs in case of tube-well is**
[BHU-2010]

(a) 20 cm (b) 7.5 cm
(c) 20 cm (d) None of the above

Answers	41. (c) 42. (a)	43. (c) 44. (a)	45. (c) 46. (b)	47. (b)

48. Multistage centrifugal pump issued for [BHU-2010]

(a) Low discharge condition
(b) High discharge low head condition
(c) Higher head condition
(d) All of the above

49. A pumping device that combines the advantages of both centrifugal and reciprocating pumps is known as [GATE-2012]

(a) Air lift pump (b) Hydraulic ram
(c) Jet pump (d) Rotary pump

50. An unconfined aquifer covering an area of 50 ha has a hydraulic conductivity of 20 m day^{-1} and specific yield of 12%. After a significant rainfall event, the water table rises from 17 m to 14.5 m below the ground level. Assuming no abstraction and outflow of groundwater during the recharge period, the amount of groundwater recharge contributed by the rainfall in m^3 is [GATE-2015]

(a) 120000 (b) 12000
(c) 150000 (d) 15000

51. The discharge of a single suction centrifugal pump operating against a total head of 12 m is 50 $l\ s^{-1}$. If the pump is directly connected to a motor operating at 1440 rpm, the specific speed of the pump will be

(a) 45 (b) 49 [GATE-2014]
(c) 53 (d) 57

52. A centrifugal pump having an overall efficiency of 75% requires 6 kW power at 1450 rpm to deliver water against a suction head of 5 m and a delivery head of 12 m. If the pump runs at 1650rpm and frictional head losses are negligible, the total head developed by the pump in metres will be [GATE-2013]

(a) 22.01 (b) 25.05
(c) 29.35 (d) 31.72

Answers	48. (c) 49. (c)	50. (c) 51. (b)	52. (a)

53. A 200 mm well fully penetrates a confined aquifer. After a long period of pumping at a rate of 1400 litres per minute, the drawdowns in the observation wells located at 25 m and 40 m from the pumping well are found to be 2.6 m and 1.9 m, respectively. The transmissivity of the aquifer in m^2 day^{-1} is **[GATE-2013]**

(a) 190 (b) 198

(c) 206 (d) 215

54. For construction of a tube well, the following formations were obtained from drilling an unconfined aquifer between 12 m and 16 m and a confined aquifer between 30 m and 40 m below ground level. A horizontal centrifugal pump installed on the ground level can pump water from the constructed tube well. Probable static water level from the ground surface in m is

(a) 5 (b) 12

(c) 16 (d) 30

55. When the water level in a well is at a depth of 7m from the surface, the most suitable pump to lift water for irrigation is **[GATE-2007]**

(a) Submersible pump

(b) Axial flow pump

(c) Horizontal centrifugal pump

(d) Reciprocating pump

56. Ratio of volume of water added or removed directly from the saturated aquifer to the resulting change in volume of aquifer below the water table is called **[BHU-2015]**

(a) Apparent specific yield (b) Specific yield

(c) Storage coefficient (d) Specific storage

57. A centrifugal pump running 1450 rpm discharges 20 lps at 30 m total head. The specific speed of pump will be **[BHU-2015]**

(a) 12 (b) 16

(c) 20 (d) 24

Answers	**53. (d)**	**55. (c)**	**57. (b)**
	54. (b)	**56. (c)**	

58. **The well in which the water level remains at water table level are** **[BHU-2015]**
   - (a) Non artisan wells
   - (b) Flowing artesian well
   - (c) Non flowing artesian wells
   - (d) Confined wells

59. **An aquifer bounded by a partially pervious layer and below by a layer that is either impervious or partially pervious is called** **[BHU-2012]**
   - (a) Confined aquifer (b) Unconfined aquifer
   - (c) Semi-confined aquifer (d) Perched aquifer

60. **A foot valve is used in a centrifugal pumping system so as to** **[BHU-2012]**
   - (a) Measure the flow (b) Give strength at the foot
   - (c) Keep it primed (d) Control water entry

61. **The difference between a shallow tube well and a deep tube well is on the basis of** **[BHU-2012, ARS-2015]**
   - (a) Depth of the tube well
   - (b) Type of aquifer
   - (c) Position of water table and pump
   - (d) Depth of aquifer

62. **In a radial centrifugal pump, the inlet angle will be designed to have** **[BHU-2012]**
   - (a) Relative velocity vector in the radial direction
   - (b) Absolute velocity vector in the radial direction
   - (c) Velocity of flow to be zero
   - (d) Peripheral velocity to be zero

63. **Pressure plate apparatus is used for the measurement of soil moisture tension up to** **[BHU-2012]**
   - (a) 10 bars (b) 15 bars
   - (c) 50 bars (d) 100 bars

Answers	**58. (a)**	**60. (c)**	**62. (a)**
	59. (c)	**61. (a)**	**63. (b)**

64. The normal range in specific speeds (MKS units) encountered in single suction impeller design is [BHU-2012]

(a) 10 - 300 (b) 300 - 500
(c) 500 - 1500 (d) None of the above

65. Binding of tiles refers to [BHU-2012]

(a) Trenching the drain
(b) Laying the tiles
(c) Covering the tiles with loose earth
(d) Joining the tiles

66. Coefficient of storage is a property of [BHU-2012]

(a) Confined aquifer (b) Unconfined aquifer
(c) Semi-confined aquifer (d) None of the above

67. Leakage factor has the dimensions of [BHU-2012]

(a) Length (b) Time
(c) Velocity (d) Resistance

68. Corrosion of tube well pipes may cause [BHU-2012]

(a) Reduced discharge from the tube well
(b) Excessive discharge of sand with water
(c) Discharge of highly alkaline water
(d) None of the above

69. The capillary fringe also called [BHU-2012]

(a) Suspended water (b) Gravity water
(c) Vadose water (d) All of the above

70. Confined aquifer is also known as

(a) Water table aquifer (b) Semi - confined aquifer
(c) Artesian aquifer (d) Perched aquifer

Answers				
	64. (a)	66. (a)	68. (b)	70. (c)
	65. (c)	67. (a)	69. (d)	

71. **Unconfined aquifer is also known as [IARI PhD-2011]**
   (a) Water table aquifer
   (b) Artesian aquifer
   (c) Semi - confined aquifer
   (d) Perched aquifer

72. **Perched aquifer is located**
   (a) Below main water table
   (b) Above the main water table
   (c) Just below the water table
   (d) None of the above

73. **A well installed in confined aquifer always contains**
   (a) Higher water level than static groundwater table
   (b) Lower water level than static water table
   (c) Same water level as static water table
   (d) Very less yield of water

74. **Semi - confined aquifer is also known as**
   (a) Semi - unconfined aquifer
   (b) Leaky aquifer
   (c) Perched - aquifer
   (d) Water table aquifer

75. **Porosity of soil formation is the ratio of**
   (a) Volume of formation to the volume of voids
   (b) Volume of voids to the volume of formation
   (c) Water volume to the soil volume
   (d) Per cent micro pores in the formation

76. **Cavity well is the**
   (a) Shallow well (b) Deep well
   (c) Artesian well (d) Well gallery

Answers	71. (a)	73. (a)	75. (b)
	72. (b)	74. (b)	76. (a)

77. **Well log is prepared during**
    (a) Gravel packing (b) Bore drilling
    (c) Well development (d) Strainer installation

78. **Well development refers to**
    (a) Removal of well incrustation
    (b) Increase in well discharge
    (c) Removal of final particle from the area around the well screen
    (d) Well testing

79. **Mechanical incrustation refers to the**
    (a) Deposition of slims of iron bacteria
    (b) Deposition due to calcium carbonate
    (c) Deposition of clay materials around well strainer
    (d) Blockage of aquifer

80. **Piezometer arc installed for measuring pressure head in [IARI PhD-2011]**
    (a) Perched aquifer (b) Confined aquifer
    (c) Unconfined aquifer (d) Open well

81. **Theis method is used for evaluating the parameters of**
    (a) Root zone (b) Confined aquifer
    (c) Unconfined aquifer (d) Perched aquifer

82. **Leakage factor has the dimension of [BHU-2010]**
    (a) Length (b) Velocity
    (c) Time (d) Resistance

83. **Well yield per unit drawdown in an unconfined aquifer is referred as [BHU-2010]**
    (a) Storage coefficient (b) Well yield
    (c) Specific yield (d) Transmissivity

Answers	**77. (b)**	**79. (c)**	**81. (b)**	**83. (b)**
	78. (c)	**80. (b)**	**82. (a)**	

84. **Advantage of a submersible pump is** **[BHU-2010]**
   (a) It gives more discharge at low head.
   (b) It gives high discharge at high head
   (c) It can be used in very deep tube-wells
   (d) Its energy consumption is low

85. **The volute of centrifugal pump changes** **[BHU-2010]**
   (a) Pressure head into velocity head
   (b) Frictional head into velocity head
   (c) Velocity head into pressure head
   (d) Velocity head into frictional head

86. **The pressure of soil water above the water table is** **[BHU-2010]**
   (a) More than atmospheric (b) Less than atmospheric
   (c) Equal to atmospheric (d) None of the above

87. **For partially penetrating well, the depth of observation well should be** **[BHU-2010]**
   (a) Half of the depth of test well
   (b) 2 times the depth of test well
   (c) Equal to depth of test well
   (d) ¾ times the depth of test well

88. **Bridging action in tube-wells can be broken by** **[BHU-2010]**
   (a) Developing well by over primping
   (b) Developing well by surging
   (c) Constructing well by reverse rotary method
   (d) Controlling pH of groundwater

89. **The sum of well loss and formation loss is known as** **[BHU-2010]**
   (a) Total well loss (b) Drawdown
   (c) Friction loss (d) Head loss

Answers	84. (c)	86. (c)	88. (b)
	85. (a)	87. (c)	89. (b)

90. The volume of water, the confined aquifer releases from or takes into storage per unit surface area of the aquifer per unit change in the component of head normal to the surface, is referred to as [BHU-2010]

(a) Coefficient of storage (b) Transmissibility
(c) Hydraulic conductivity (d) Specific yield

91. A tube well which does not make use of strainer and contracted at a location where high yielding sand stratum is underlain by strong impervious stratum of day is known as [BHU-2010]

(a) Collector well (b) Cavity well
(c) Fully penetrating well (d) None of the above

92. Aquifers which are overlain or underlain by semipermeable strata are referred to as [BHU-2010]

(a) Confined aquifer (b) Perched aquifer
(c) Leaky aquifer (d) Unconfined aquifer

93. Horizontal centrifugal pump has [BHU-2010]

(a) Vertical impeller mounted on a horizontal shaft
(b) Horizontal impeller mounted on a vertical shaft
(c) Impeller mounted on a shaft having 30° tilt from vertical
(d) None of the above

94. Jet pumps arc the combination of centrifugal pump and jet mechanism where [BHU-2010]

(a) Jet is placed at ground surface and centrifugal pump in the well below water surface
(b) Centrifugal pump is placed at ground surface and jet in the well below water surface
(c) Centrifugal pump and jet, both are placed in the well below water surface
(d) Centrifugal pump and jet, both are placed at ground surface

Answers	90. (a) 91. (b)	92. (c) 93. (a)	94. (b)

95. **The efficiency of reciprocating pump compared to that of centrifugal pump to handle small discharge at high head is** [BHU-2010]

(a) Same (b) More

(c) Less (d) None of the above

96. **A steady state water flow condition exists when** [BHU-2010]

(a) The water level responds to change in atmosphere pressure

(b) The water level drops as the pumping is continued

(c) The water level first drops then it starts rising

(d) The water level in the well ceases to decline

97. **The term isotropic means** [BHU-2010]

(a) Hydraulic conductivity varies with direction

(b) Hydraulic conductivity varies with space

(c) Hydraulic conductivity is constant in all directions

(d) Hydraulic head is constant with time

98. **A perched water table** [BHU-2010]

(a) May lie below the groundwater table

(b) Gives a fair amount of sustained yield

(c) May lie above the groundwater table

(d) May be present in artesian aquifer

99. **The foot valve is installed in the suction line while pumping with** [BHU-2010]

(a) Cavity well

(b) Deep tube - wells in confined aquifer

(c) Deep tube - wells in unconfined aquifer

(d) Open well

Answers	95. (b) 97. (c) 99. (c) 96. (d) 98. (c)

100. Cavity wells are usually constructed in [BHU-2010]

(a) Perched aquifer

(b) Deep confined aquifer

(c) Shallow confined aquifer

(d) Unconfined aquifer

101. Keeping the hydraulic properties as constant, doubling the diameter of well screen in a phreatic aquifer, well discharge will increase about [BHU-2010]

(a) 10 m (b) 50%

(c) No effect (d) About 11%

102. The length of screen in cavity well is decided

(a) By using well log **[BHU-2010]**

(b) By sieve analysis of aquifer material

(c) 1/3 of confined aquifer

(d) No screen is provided

103. Hydraulic ram is a [BHU-2010]

(a) Positive displacement pump

(b) Centrifugal pump

(c) Impulse type pump

(d) None of the above

104. Normal discharge of a 10 cm diameter tube-well is about [BHU-2010]

(a) 10 lit/sec (b) 100 lit/sec

(c) 20 lit/sec (d) None of the above

105. For operation of a centrifugal pump without cavitation, the suction lift plus other losses must be [BHU-2010]

(a) Equal to atmospheric pressure

(b) < atmospheric pressure

(c) > atmospheric pressure

(d) None of the above

Answers	100. (d)	102. (d)	104. (a)
	101. (d)	103. (c)	105. (b)

106. Submersible pumps are suitable for the condition where [BHU-2010]

(a) Water is to be lifted from shallow depth

(b) Water is to be lifted from deep tube-well

(c) Large quantity of water required

(d) Any where

107. Minimum thickness of gravel packs in case of tube-well is [BHU-2010]

(a) 20 cm (b) 7.5 cm

(c) 20 m (d) None of the above

108. Multistage centrifugal pump issued for [BHU-2010]

(a) Low discharge condition

(b) High discharge low head condition

(c) Higher head condition

(d) All of the above

109. Jacob's modification of Theis non-equilibrium equation is valid for [BHU-2010]

(a) Smaller value of 'u'

(b) Higher value of well function

(c) Early pumping data

(d) Long duration pumping data

110. Rotary pumps are commonly used [BHU-2010]

(a) For lifting irrigation water

(b) For lifting lubricating oils etc.

(c) For lifting air vapour mixture

(d) None of the above

111. The dimensions of specific coefficient of an aquifer are [IARI PhD-2013]

(a) L/T (b) L^2

(c) L^{-1} (d) Dimensionless

Answers	**106. (b)**	**108. (c)**	**110. (b)**
	107. (b)	**109. (a)**	**111. (d)**

112. In case of submersible pump set, the motor is **[IARI PhD-2013]**

(a) Completely submerged in water

(b) Partially submerged in water

(c) Not submerged in water

(d) Kept on the ground surface

113. The intrusion of salty ground water in any area is caused due to **[IARI PhD-2013]**

(a) Lowering of water table

(b) Raising of the water table

(c) Application of irrigation water

(d) Rain water flooding

114. If the speed of a centrifugal pump is doubled, the power required will be increased by **[IARI PhD-2013]**

(a) 2 times (b) 4 times

(c) 6 times (d) 8 times

115. In a soil if the porosity is 0.2, the void ratio will be **[IARI PhD-2011, 2013]**

(a) 0.2 (b) 0.25

(c) 0.75 (d) 0.8

116. An Archimedean screw is **[IARI PhD-2013]**

(a) A reverse threaded screw

(b) A popular water lift

(c) A device for lifting water from shallow and open water body

(d) The item that helped Archimedes discover the law of buoyancy

117. A submersible pump is required when one of the following is too high **[IARI PhD-2013]**

(a) Suction lift (b) Delivery head

(c) Diesel cost (d) Water demand

Answers			
	112. (a)	114. (d)	116. (b)
	113. (a)	115. (b)	117. (b)

118. **The pump efficiency, motor efficiency and drive efficiency of a centrifugal pump set are 80%, 90% and 75%, respectively. The overall efficiency of the pump set is** **[IARI PhD-2013]**

(a) 50% (b) 54%
(c) 75% (d) 90%

119. **The hydraulic head in salt water is 30.0 m above the reference level that coincides with the bottom of the piezometer. Mass density of the saline ground water is 1025 kg/m^3. The length of the column of fresh water is** **[IARI PhD-2013]**

(a) 30.75 m (b) 3.075 m
(c) 35.20 m (d) 40.00 m

120. **Water level in a well is 6.8 m from the surface. The most suitable pump to lift the water is** **[IARI PhD-2013]**

(a) Axial flow pump
(b) Submersible pump
(c) Reciprocating pump
(d) Horizontal centrifugal pump

121. **Occurrence of groundwater can be detected by** **[IARI PhD-2011]**

(a) Water meter (b) Current meter
(c) Neutron meter (d) Resistivity meter

122. **Louver type screen have opening in the form of** **[ARS-2013]**

(a) Rectangular Slot (b) Round opening
(c) Shutter (d) Continuous slot

123. **Which of the following pumps is preferred for flood control and irrigation applications ?**

(a) Centrifugal pump (b) Mixed flow pump
(c) Axial flow pump (d) Reciprocating Pump

Answers	**118. (b)**	**120. (d)**	**122. (c)**
	119. (a)	**121. (d)**	**123. (c)**

124. In order to avoid cavitation in centrifugal pumps

(a) the suction pressure should be high

(b) the delivery pressure should be high

(c) the suction pressure should be low

(d) the delivery pressure should be low

125. The head loss due to friction in pipe flow for a given discharge can be reduced by

(a) Increasing pipe length

(b) Increasing flow velocity

(c) Increasing the number of bends

(d) Increasing pipe diameter

126. A pump used in high pressure orchard sprayer is **[GATE-2017]**

(a) centrifugal sprayer

(b) rotary sprayer

(c) turbine pump

(d) plunger type positive displacement pump

127. Power requirement of centrifugal pump depends on **[NET/ARS-2016]**

(a) Impeller diameter (b) Pump speed

(c) Both (d) None of the above

128. If KH and KV are horizontal and vertical hydraulic conductivity, then the resultant hydraulic conductivity is **[NET/ARS-2016]**

(a) $(K_H + K_V)^2/2$ (b) $[(K_H)^2 + (K_V)^2]/2$

(c) $(K_H + K_V)/2$ (d) $(K_H \times K_V)^{1/2}$

129. The line joining of equal water table depth is called as **[NET/ARS-2016]**

(a) Isobath (b) Isochrone

(c) Isohyte (d) None of the above

Answers			
	124. (c)	126. (d)	128. (d)
	125. (d)	127. (c)	129. (a)

130. Well hydrostatic pressure is measured by **[NET/ARS-2016]**

(a) Piezometer (b) Relief well

(c) Both (d) None of the above

131. Piezometric surface is found in the aquifer **[NET/ARS-2016]**

(a) Unconfined (b) Confined

(c) Semi confined (d) All

132. Perched aquifer is special case of **[NET/ARS-2016]**

(a) Confined

(b) Semi - confined

(c) Unconfined

(d) All

133. Which one of the following is a wrong statement ? **[GATE-2018]**

(a) The head generated by a centrifugal pump at zero discharge is the 'shutoff head'.

(b) To avoid cavitation in centrifugal pumps, the net positive suction head should be more than the theoretical atmospheric pressure.

(c) According to the affinity laws of centrifugal pumps, the head varies with the square of the impeller speed.

(d) Most of the turbine pumps have operational characteristics closer to those of the centrifugal pumps than the propeller pumps.

134. Determine the water horse power of a pump discharging at a rate of 10 lps against a total heal of 25 m **[BHU-2018]**

(a) 2 (b) 2.3

(c) 3.3 (d) 5

Answers			
	130. (a)	132. (c)	134. (c)
	131. (b)	133. (b)	

135. In construction of gravel packed wells, the pack-aquifer ratio is generally defined as .... [GATE-2022]

(a) $\dfrac{\text{50\% of the size of gravel pack}}{\text{50\% of the size of aquifer}}$

(b) $\dfrac{\text{60\% of the size of gravel pack}}{\text{10\% of the size of aquifer}}$

(c) $\dfrac{\text{50\% of the size of aquifer}}{\text{50\% of the size of gravel pack}}$

(d) $\dfrac{\text{60\% of the size of aquifer}}{\text{10\% of the size of gravel pack}}$

OOOOO

Answers	135. (a)

6 Management of Degraded, Waterlogged and other Problematic Soils and Water

1. **The discharge entering a drain per unit length of the drain is** **[ARS - 2014]**

   (a) $RL^2/2$ (b) RL/2

   (c) L/2 (d) All

2. **The maximum permissible length of mole drain is** **[ARS - 2014]**

   (a) 50 m (b) 100 m

   (c) 200 m (d) 400 m

3. **A saline - sodic soil have** **[ARS-2014]**

   (a) EC > 4ds/m, ESP > 15 and pH > 8.5

   (b) EC > 4ds/m, ESP > 15 and pH < 8.5

   (c) EC < 4ds/m, ESP > 15 and pH > 8.5

   (d) EC > 4ds/m, ESP < 15 and pH > 8.5

4. **A minimum grade for tile drains should be** **[ARS-2014]**

   (a) 0.2% (b) 0.02

   (c) 0.5 (d) 1

5. **If EC of water is 1 dS/m. What is value of salinity in (ppm)** **[ARS-2014]**

   (a) 64 (b) 640

   (c) 6400 (d) 6.4

Answers	1. (b) 3. (a) 5. (b) 2. (c) 4. (a)

6. **The Hooghoudt's equation for spacing drain is applicable in [IARI PhD-2011, ARS-2014]**
   (a) Homogeneous soil with an impermeable layer below it
   (b) Only for sandy soil
   (c) Any type soil
   (d) Non - homogenous soil

7. **The nature of Hooghoudt's equation for drain spacing is [GATE-2010, ARS-2014]**
   (a) Parabolic (b) Elliptic
   (c) Hyperbolic (d) Circular

8. **Which equation is most applicable under fluctuation water table condition ? [ARS-2014]**
   (a) De Zeeuw Hellinga (b) Hooghoudts
   (c) Glover Dumm (d) All of the above

9. **Mole drainage is a type of [ARS-2014]**
   (a) Sub - surface drainage
   (b) Surface drainage
   (c) Underground drainage
   (d) Both (a) and (c)

10. **Envelope is provided to [ARS-2014]**
   (a) Reduce the resistance of flow
   (b) Increase the resistance of flow
   (c) Unaltered
   (d) All of the above

11. **The percentage of total quantity of water in the world that is saline is about**
   (a) 71% (b) 33%
   (c) 67% (d) 97%

Answers	6. (a)	8. (a)	10. (a)
	7. (b)	9. (d)	11. (d)

12. **Subsurface drain removes** **[ARS-2014]**
    (a) Excess runoff water from rainfall
    (b) Hygroscopic water
    (c) Sub - surface gravitational water
    (d) Capillary water

13. **The Haryana collaborations with Netherland for the objective** **[ARS-2014]**
    (a) Drainage (b) Irrigation
    (c) Erosion control (d) All of the above

14. **Drain spacing in unsteady flow condition is calculated by using** **[SRF-2013, NET-2013]**
    (a) Hooghoudts' equation
    (b) De Zeeuw Hellinga equation
    (c) Glover Dum equation
    (d) All of the above

15. **Herringbone refers to** **[SRF-2013]**
    (a) Milk parlor (b) Relief drain
    (c) Both (d) None of the above

16. **The salinity of irrigation water is measured in terms** **[IARI PhD-2011, SRF-2013]**
    (a) EC value (b) pH value
    (c) SAR value (d) ESP value

17. **Ergun equation is applicable to** **[SRF-2013]**
    (a) Turbulent flow (b) Laminar flow
    (c) Porous media flow (d) Slit flow

18. **If porosity and specific retention of aquifer is 60% and 20% respectively. What is its specific yield ?** **[NET-2013]**
    (a) 0.4 (b) 0.8
    (c) 0.6 (d) None of the above

Answers	12. (c)	14. (c)	16. (a)	18. (a)
	13. (a)	15. (c)	17. (c)	

19. If the drainage coefficient is 3 cm, flow rate through drains of watershed of area 1500 ha is [NET-2013, ARS-2014]

(a) 5.2 m^3/s (b) 0.5 m^3/s

(c) 0.2 m^3/s (d) 2.0 m^3/s

20. Dupuit - Forchheimer's assumption used in Hooghoudt's equation [NET-2013]

(a) Hydraulic gradient $\propto$ slope of water table

(b) Soil is homogeneous

(c) Flow is horizontal

(d) Both (a) & (c)

21. Water quality criteria used for irrigation water include [NET-2013, ARS-2015]

(a) C1 - S1 (b) C3 - S3

(c) C2 - S2 (d) C4 - S4

22. If EC > 4 dS/m and ESP < 15, the soil water is said to be [NET-2013]

(a) Saline (b) Saline - alkali

(c) Alkali (d) Acidic

23. The units for expressing anion exchange capacity [NET-2013]

(a) meq / lit (b) mmole

(c) ppm (d) EC

24. If Na, Ca, and Mg added in water with quantity 4, 5 and 7 meq/lit respectively. What will be the salinity of water? [NET-2013]

(a) 1.6 dS/m (b) 0.6 dS/m

(c) 2.6 dS/m (d) 4 dS/m

25. Leaching requirement is the ratio of [NET-2013]

(a) Depth of percolated water to depth of irrigation water

(b) Depth of leaching water to depth of field water

(c) Depth of irrigation water to depth of percolated water

(d) None of the above

Answers	**19. (a)**	**21. (a)**	**23. (a)**	**25. (a)**
	20. (d)	**22. (a)**	**24. (a)**	

26. **Which type of subsurface drainage is used to drain seepage water across hill areas ? [NET-2013]**

(a) Interceptor drain (b) Herringbone

(c) Grid iron (d) Random

27. **Mole drain is the most suitable drainage system for [NET-2013, GATE-2015, ARS-2015]**

(a) Heavy clay soil (b) Loamy soil

(c) Sandy soil (d) Silty soil

28. **Ditch conduit formula is used for estimation of [NET-2013 & 2014, ARS-2015]**

(a) Load of pipes (b) Spacing

(c) Capacity (d) None of the above

29. **If 10 cm of water added to a field area of 1ha which has salinity of 1 dS/m. How much of salt added to the field? [NET-2013]**

(a) 10 Kg (b) 640 Kg

(c) 6400 Kg (d) 64 Kg

30. **Among Sodium (Na), potash (K) and phosphorus (P) which of the element causes more hazard to plant growth ? [NET-2013]**

(a) K (b) Na

(c) P (d) None of the above

31. **Residual Sodium Carbonate (RSC) for good quality irrigation water [NET-2013, ARS-2015]**

(a) Less than 1.25 meq/l (b) 1.25-2.50meq/l

(c) More than 2.50meq/l (d) None of the above

32. **Leaching of saline water causes or results [NET-2013]**

(a) Decrease of EC (b) Decrease of ESP

(c) Both (a) & (b) (d) Increase of EC

Answers	26. (a)	28. (a)	30. (a)	32. (c)
	27. (a)	29. (b)	31. (a)	

33. The movement of ground water is represented by [NET-2013]

(a)	Hooghdoudt's	(b)	Earnst
(c)	Darcy	(d)	Glover - Dumn

34. Isobath are used to measure [NET-2013, ARS-2015]

(a) Waterlogged areas
(b) Water table
(c) Ground water flow direction
(d) None of the above

35. Which sub-surface drainage system consists of laterals that enter the main drain at an angle, generally from both sides ? [SRF-2013]

(a)	Random	(b)	Gridiron
(c)	Interceptor	(d)	Herringbone

36. A soil having EC < 4, pH > 8.5 and ESP > 15 is known as [JRF-2011]

(a)	Saline soil	(b)	Sodic (alkali) soil
(c)	Saline - alkali soil	(d)	None of the above

37. If the discharge of drainage canal is 1000 lps and drainage area is 360 ha, the drainage coefficient (cm) will be equal to [JRF-2011]

(a)	2.4	(b)	0.24
(c)	24	(d)	240

38. The gridiron pipe drainage system is more economical than the herringbone pipe drainage system because [GATE-2013]

(a) It is adopted in the fields which do not require complete drainage
(b) The number of main or sub-main lines is reduced
(c) The number of junctions and the double-drained area are reduced
(d) It has only main or sub - main lines

Answers			
	33. (c)	35. (d)	37. (a)
	34. (a)	36. (b)	38. (c)

39. **The USDA classification of irrigation water with regard to alkali and salinity hazards is based on [GATE-2015]**
   (a) Exchangeable sodium percentage and pH
   (b) Electrical conductivity and Sodium adsorption ratio
   (c) Electrical conductivity and pH
   (d) Sodium percentage and pH

40. **Dupuit - Forchheimer assumptions are used for analyzing groundwater flow in [GATE-2015]**
   (a) Confined aquifers
   (b) Leaky confined aquifers
   (c) Unconfined aquifers
   (d) Both confined and unconfined aquifers

41. **If an irrigation water source has the concentrations of Na^{+}, Ca^{++} and Mg^{++} as 28, 10 and 5 milliequivalents per litre, respectively, then the Sodium adsorption ratio of this water is [GATE-2015]**
   (a) 10.3 (b) 11
   (c) 9 (d) 9.5

42. **If the drainable porosity of a command area is 5% and the design rate of drop of the water table is 0.25 m day^{-1}, the drainage coefficient of the command area in mm day^{-1} will be [GATE - 2013]**
   (a) 250 (b) 12.5
   (c) 1.25 (d) 0.0125

43. **Schoonover's method is used for estimation of**
   (a) Leaching requirement (b) Gypsum requirement
   (c) water requirement (d) None of the above

44. **Wheat supplied with similar quantity of water will cause greater uptake in [BHU-2015]**
   (a) Saline soils (b) Alkali soils
   (c) Sodic soils (d) Normal soils

Answers	39. (b)	41. (a)	43. (b)
	40. (c)	42. (b)	44. (b)

45. **Which term is not related to drainage ?** **[BHU-2015]**

(a) Venturi meter (b) Mole

(c) 20 - 40 rule (d) Water logging

46. **Drainable water is the** **[BHU-2015]**

(a) Hygroscopic water (b) Capillary water

(c) Gravitational water (d) Perched water

47. **Conjunctive use of water in a basin means**
[IARI PhD-2011, BHU-2012]

(a) Combined use of water for irrigation and hydro power generation

(b) Use of water by co-operative farmers

(c) Use of water for irrigating both *rabi* and *kharif* crops

(d) Combined use of surface and ground water for crop production

48. **If the electrical conductivity of irrigation and drainage water is 0.2 mmhos/cm and 0.4 mmhos/cm respectively, the leaching requirement will be equal to** **[BHU-2012]**

(a) 80% (b) 50%

(c) 40% (d) 20%

49. **Mathematical equation used to describe saturated-unsaturated flow of water in drip irrigation**
[IARI PhD-2011, BHU-2012]

(a) Richard equation (b) Bernoulli's theorem

(c) Continuity equation (d) Laplace equation

50. **Water logging is eliminated by** **[BHU-2012]**

(a) Deep ploughing (b) Irrigation

(c) Shallow ploughing (d) Providing the drains

51. **Irrigation water having an SAR value of 20 is called as**
[BHU-2012]

(a) Very high sodium water (b) High sodium water

(c) Medium sodium water (d) Low sodium water

Answers				
	45. (a)	47. (d)	49. (a)	51. (b)
	46. (c)	48. (b)	50. (d)	

52. An agricultural land is said to be waterlogged, when **[BHU-2010]**

(a) The land is completely submerged under standing water
(b) There is flowing water over the land
(c) The pH value of the soil becomes as high as 8.5
(d) The soil pores in the root zone get saturated with water either by the actual water table or by its capillary fringe for a longer period

53. When water from a confined aquifer is pumped, which one of the following is lowered ? **[BHU-2010]**

(a) Water table (b) Drawdown
(c) Piezometric surface (d) None of the above

54. The ratio of the equivalent depth of drainage water to the depth of irrigation water is referred to as **[BHU-2010, ARS-2015]**

(a) Drainage coefficient
(b) Leaching requirement
(c) Fraction of drainage water
(d) None of the above

55. If a soil has pH < 8.5, EC > 4 mmhos/cm at 25°C and ESP < 15, the soil is referred as **[BHU-2010]**

(a) Saline - alkali (b) Saline
(c) Alkali (d) None of the above

56. Almost all natural groundwater motion has Reynold's number equal to **[BHU-2010]**

(a) One (b) > One
(c) < One (d) None of the above

57. The method to analyse pumping test data for unsteady flow to a well in confined aquifer which is applicable for large value of time and small values of distance of observation well from test well was given by

(a) Hantush (b) Theis [BHU-2010]
(c) De - Glee (d) Cooper and Jacob

Answers	52. (d)	54. (b)	56. (c)
	53. (c)	55. (b)	57. (d)

58. If a saturation extract of soil has Electrical Conductivity less than 4 m mhos/m and SAR less than 13, the soil is referred to as [BHU-2010]

(a) Normal (b) Saline - sodic

(c) Sodic (d) Saline

59. The surface drains which are best suited to the drainage of scattered depression or pot holes where the depth of cut is not over 1 m are referred to as [BHU-2010]

(a) Bedding

(b) Parallel field ditch system

(c) Random field ditch system

(d) Parallel lateral ditch system

60. The portion of the precipitation that makes its way towards stream channels, lakes or oceans as surface flow is referred to as [BHU-2010]

(a) Drain flow (b) Runoff

(c) Surface flow (d) Drainage coefficient

61. Drainage coefficient means, depth of water to be removed from a drainage field in [BHU-2010]

(a) Three days (b) One day

(c) Two days (d) Depends on type of crop

62. A sodic soil has [IARI PhD-2013]

(a) ESP > 15, EC > 4 ds/m (b) ESP > 15, EC < 4 ds/m

(c) ESP < 15, EC < 4 ds/m (d) ESP < 15, EC > 4 ds/m

63. The extreme alkali soil can be reclaimed by using [IARI PhD-2013]

(a) Soil amendments like gypsum

(b) Nitrogen fertilizer

(c) Leaching of salts

(d) Green manuring

Answers	**58. (c)**	**60. (b)**	**62. (b)**
	59. (c)	**61. (b)**	**63. (a)**

64. Sum of specific yield and specific retention is equal to the **[IARI PhD-2011, 2013]**

(a) Porosity (b) Void ratio

(c) Degree of saturation (d) Storage coefficient

65. The flow towards a sub-surface drain at mid spacing is **[IARI PhD-2013]**

(a) Vertical (b) Parallel

(c) Radial (d) Horizontal

66. The drainable porosity of soil is important parameter for designing **[IARI PhD-2013]**

(a) Surface drainage system

(b) Surface irrigation system

(c) Drip irrigation system

(d) Sub - surface drainage system

67. Drain spacing in steady flow condition is calculated by using **[ARS-2015]**

(a) Hooghoudts' equation

(b) De Zeeuw Hellinga equation

(c) Glover Dum equation

(d) All of the above

68. Acidic soil is reclaimed by the addition of

(a) Gypsum (b) Lime

(c) Potash (d) All of the above

69. Saline soil is characterized by the physical properties value

(a) pH < 8.5, EC > 4 (b) pH < 8.5, EC < 4

(c) pH > 8.5, EC > 4 (d) pH > 8.5, EC < 4

70. Saline soil has the properties of

(a) Low permeability (b) High permeability

(c) Not varied (d) All of the above

Answers	**64. (a)**	**66. (d)**	**68. (b)**	**70. (b)**
	65. (d)	**67. (a)**	**69. (a)**	

71. Saline soil is reclaimed by

(a) Leaching (b) Drainage

(c) Both (a) and (b) (d) Lime

72. Sodic soil (Alkali soil) is reclaimed by ....

(a) Gypsum (b) Lime

(c) Rock phosphate (d) Both (a) and (c)

73. Soluble salts in ground water originate mainly from

(a) The recharge of contaminated water

(b) The excessive irrigation water percolating through the root zones of cultivated area

(c) The solution of the rock material

(d) The water originally entrapped in sedimentary strata since the time of deposition

74. For water logged condition the water table depth [NET/ARS-2016]

(a) 2 m (b) 2 - 3 m

(c) 4 m (d) 5 m

75. An area is said to be waterlogged on the basis of [NET/ARS-2016]

(a) Isobath (b) Isochrone

(c) Isohyte (d) None of the above

76. Ditch conduit formula is applicable in[NET/ARS-2016]

(a) Load on pipe (b) Pressure on pipe

(c) Discharge of pipe (d) None of the above

77. Drag line method used for estimating [NET/ARS-2016]

(a) Open drain (b) Groundwater

(c) Surface water (d) All

Answers	**71. (c)**	**73. (b)**	**75. (a)**	**77. (a)**
	72. (d)	**74. (a)**	**76. (a)**	

78. **Non clayey soil is reclaimed by using [NET/ARS-2016]**

(a) Gypsum (b) Sulphur

(c) HCL (d) Iron pyrites

79. **Residual sodium carbonate is used for checking [NET/ARS-2016]**

(a) Irrigation water quality

(b) Soil quality

(c) Both

(d) None

80. **The most salt tolerant crop is [NET/ARS-2016]**

(a) Barley

(b) Sugarcane

(c) Wheat

(d) Paddy

81. **One of the key assumptions made by Dupuit-Forchheimer about the flow behavior in the porous medium towards subsurface drains is [GATE-2018]**

(a) homogeneous medium

(b) isotropic medium

(c) horizontal streamlines

(d) uniform recharge

82. **The depths from the soil surface to subsurface tile drains, impermeable soil layer and the highest water table are measured as 2.8 m, 5.0 m and 0.8 m, respectively. The effective hydraulic head for drainage in meter is [GATE-2018]**

(a) 0.8 (b) 2.0

(c) 2.2 (d) 4.2

Answers			
	78. (a)	**80. (a)**	**82. (b)**
	79. (a)	**81. (c)**	

83. In a drainage area of 15 ha, the slope and drainage coefficient are 0.4% and 11 mm/day, respectively. The value of Manning's roughness coefficient is 0.016.The inside diameter (in mm) of the corrugated plastic tubing used for drainage is [GATE-2019]

    (a) 200.51

    (b) 205.52

    (c) 209.51

    (d) 215.23

OOOOO

Answers	83. (c)

7 Soil, Water and Atmosphere Relationship

1. **The available water content is high in the soil texture [ARS-2014, NET-2014]**
   (a) Sandy loam (b) Sandy
   (c) Clay (d) Silty clay loam
2. **The capillary rise of water is maximum in the soil texture [ARS-2014]**
   (a) Silty clay (b) Sandy
   (c) Sandy loam (d) Clay
3. **Available water lies at soil moisture tension [ARS-2014]**
   (a) 1/10 to 1/3 atm (b) 1/3 to 32 atm
   (c) 60 atm (d) 1/3 to 15 atm
4. **If particles size is increased by ½ times then the value of hydraulic conductivity will be increased by [ARS-2014]**
   (a) 1/16 times (b) ½ times
   (c) ¼ times (d) 1/8 times
5. **The consumptive use is highest in areas [ARS-2014]**
   (a) Humid (b) Dry
   (c) Sub - humid (d) All of the above

Answers	
	1. (c) 3. (d) 5. (a)
	2. (d) 4. (c)

6. **Salt addition to irrigation water** **[ARS-2014]**
   (a) Increase the evaporation
   (b) Reduces the evaporation
   (c) Unaltered the evaporation
   (d) All of the above

7. **The Porosity of clay soil** **[ARS-2014]**
   (a) 40 - 60% (b) 30 - 40%
   (c) 60 - 70% (d) 35 - 45%

8. **Hydraulic conductivity of clay soil** **[ARS-2014]**
   (a) More than 0.5 m/day (b) Less than 0.5 m/day
   (c) 0.5 - 2.5 m/day (d) 2.5 - 10 m/day

9. **Capillary water held at pressure** **[JRF-2012, ARS-2014]**
   (a) 1/3 to 31 atm (b) 1/10 to 1/3 atm
   (c) 1/3 to 15 atm (d) 60 atm

10. **Pan coefficient refers to** **[ARS-2013]**
   (a) Coefficient to correlate a high rate of evaporation in a pan to an evaporation rate from larger water bodies
   (b) Ratio of ET observed for the crop studied over that observed for the well calibrated reference crop under the same conditions
   (c) Both (a) and (b)
   (d) None of the above

11. **Which of the following types of soil water is generally used by plant ?** **[SRF-2013]**
   (a) Hygroscopic water (b) Gravitational water
   (c) Capillary water (d) All of the above

12. **The moisture content (%) at field capacity for clay soil is** **[SRF-2013]**
   (a) 3 - 5 (b) 15 - 30
   (c) 25 - 40 (d) None of the above

Answers	**6. (b)**	**8. (b)**	**10. (c)**	**12. (c)**
	7. (a)	**9. (a)**	**11. (c)**	

13. **A part of the precipitation moves laterally through upper crust of the soil and returns to the surface at some location away from the point of entry into the soil is [NET-2013]**
    (a) Interflow (b) Seepage
    (c) Percolation (d) Depression storage

14. **Water held by a force of surface tension and continuous films around soil particles is [BHU-2010, NET-2013]**
    (a) Capillary water (b) Gravity water
    (c) Hygroscopic water (d) Saturated water

15. **The particle size (mm) of fine sand according to USDA [NET-2013]**
    (a) 0.1 - 0.25 (b) 0.02 - 0.2
    (c) 0.05 - 0.1 (d) 0.25 - 0.5

16. **At 50% saturation capacity clay soil has water potential of [NET-2013, 2014; ARS-2015]**
    (a) 4.33 atm (b) 15 atm
    (c) 0 atm (d) 7 atm

17. **The water which moves freely in the plant and does not tightly bind to components of cell is [NET-2013]**
    (a) Gravitation water (b) Hygroscopic water
    (c) Capillary water (d) None of the above

18. **Total flow rate of water in a saturated soil is proportional to [NET-2013]**
    (a) Radius of pores
    (b) Cube of radius of pores
    (c) Square of radius of pores
    (d) Four times of radius of pores

19. **The most sensitive stage in wheat crop is [NET-2013]**
    (a) Crown root initiation (b) Tillering
    (b) Grain formation (c) Milky stage

Answers	13. (a)	15. (a)	17. (a)	19. (a)
	14. (a)	16. (a)	18. (d)	

20. **Clay is chemically active soil material due to [NET-2013]**
   (a) Specific surface (b) Shrinking
   (c) Swelling (d) Hardpan

21. **Accumulated infiltration is $I = 0.5\, t^{0.5}$; Infiltration rate (cm/min) for t = 100 min [IARI PhD-2011, NET-2013]**
   (a) 0.025 (b) 0.25
   (c) 0.5 (d) 2.5

22. **Infiltration using Philip model is given by [NET-2013]**
   (a) $f = \frac{S}{2} r^{-0.5} + C$ (b) $f = \frac{S}{2} r^{0.5} + C$
   (c) $f = \frac{S}{2} r^{-0.5}$ (d) $f = \frac{S}{2} r^{2} + C$

23. **The pF of soil for 1000 cm of soil moisture tension [NET-2013]**
   (a) 3 (b) 1
   (c) 2 (d) 0

24. **Infrared thermometers are used to measure [NET-2013]**
   (a) Crop Canopy temperature
   (b) Soil temperature
   (c) Plant temperature
   (d) Air temperature

25. **Diffusion pressure deficit of water in plant cell or solution is given by [NET-2013]**
   (a) Osmotic pressure (OP) - Turgor pressure (TP)
   (b) TP - OP
   (c) TP + OP
   (d) TP / OP

Answers	20. (a)	22. (a)	24. (a)
	21. (a)	23. (a)	25. (a)

26. Transportation rate in plants when there is no shortage of moisture depends on [NET-2013]

(a) Moisture gradient from plant to atmosphere
(b) Plant canopy
(c) Plant height
(d) None of the above

27. In Penman formula the symbol γ represents [NET-2013]

(a) Psychometric constant
(b) Wind speed
(c) Slope of saturation vapor pressure
(d) Net radiation

28. Penman method measures [JRF-2010, NET-2013]

(a) Evaporation from open water surface
(b) Irrigation requirement
(c) Actual ET
(d) All of the above

29. Lake evaporation measured by [NET-2013]

(a) USWB Class A pan (b) Field plot
(c) Lysimeter (d) All of the above

30. Plant roots extract moisture from soil by a process called [BHU-2012, NET-2013, ARS-2015]

(a) Osmosis (b) Diffusion
(c) Root system (d) Respiration

31. If bulk and particle density of soil are 1.35 and 2.7 respectively. The void ratio is [JRF-2012, NET-2013]

(a) 1.0 (b) 0.4
(c) 0.5 (d) 0.2

32. Lysimeter is used to measure [JRF-2011, IARI PhD-2011]

(a) Evapotranspiration (b) Infiltration
(c) Evaporation (d) Transpiration

Answers	**26. (a)**	**28. (a)**	**30. (a)**	**32. (a)**
	27. (a)	**29. (a)**	**31. (a)**	

33. The concept of Potential Evapotranspiration was suggested by

(a) Blaney - Criddle (b) Thonthwaite

(c) Penman (d) Hargreaves

34. The pressure that does not have any measurable influence on the void ratio or shearing resistance of the soil mass is [GATE-2013]

(a) Pore water pressure (b) Intergranular pressure

(c) Capillary pressure (d) Surcharge pressure

35. Capillary water is held in the soil due to [GATE-2011]

(a) Absorption force (b) Surface tension force

(c) Gravitational force (d) Osmotic force

36. The soil moisture tension at field capacity is [ARS-2013]

(a) 1/10 to 1/3 atm (b) 1/3 to 32 atm

(c) 1/3 to 1/10 atm (d) 1/3 to 15 atm

37. Relative porosity is also called as [ARS-2013]

(a) Porosity (b) Void ratio

(c) Specific gravity (d) Relative density

38. Soil texture refers to [BHU-2015]

(a) Arrangement of soil particles

(b) Size of soil particles

(c) Colour of soil particles

(d) None of the above

39. Cohesion is [BHU-2011 &2015, IARI PhD-2013]

(a) Attraction of similar molecules

(b) Attraction between two different molecules

(c) Both (a) & (b)

(d) None of the above

Answers	**33. (b)**	**35. (b)**	**37. (b)**	**39. (a)**
	34. (a)	**36. (a)**	**38. (b)**	

40. Permeability of clay soil as compared to sandy soil is [BHU-2015]

(a) Equal (b) More
(c) Lesser (d) Difficult to say

41. Modified Penmann method for computing Potential Evapotranspiration includes [BHU-2015]

(a) Energy terms (b) Aerodynamic terms
(c) Both (a) & (b) (d) None of the above

42. Infiltration is measured by [BHU-2011, 2015]

(a) Cylindrical metal rings
(b) USWB class A pan
(c) Lysimeter
(d) Rain gauge

43. Evaporation from water surface is the process by which liquid on free surface is transformed into [BHU-2011, 2015]

(a) A solid state (b) Clouds
(c) A gaseous state (d) Rainfall

44. The latest method of the estimation of PET (potential evapotranspiration) is [BHU-2012, ARS-2013]

(a) Penman's Equation
(b) Blaney criddle formula
(c) Class A pan evaporation
(d) Penman Monteith Equation

45. With increase in supplied irrigation water, the yield of crops [BHU-2012, ARS-2014]

(a) Increases continuously
(b) Increases up to a certain limit and then becomes constant
(c) Decreases continuously
(d) Increases up to a certain limit and then decreases

Answers			
	40. (c)	42. (a)	44. (d)
	41. (c)	43. (c)	45. (d)

46. **Field capacity, wilting point and available soil moisture are referred to as** **[BHU-2012, NET-2013]**
   (a) Soil moisture coefficients
   (b) Soil moisture indices
   (c) Soil moisture constants
   (d) Soil moisture standards

47. **Effective rainfall in irrigation planning is equal to** **[BHU-2012]**
   (a) Total rainfall
   (b) Rain water stored in root zone
   (c) Rainfall – runoff
   (d) Rainfall + runoff

48. **IW / CPE ratio is used for** **[BHU-2012, ARS-2015]**
   (a) Irrigation scheduling
   (b) Fixing fertilizer dose
   (c) Fixing irrigation duration
   (d) Determining soil moisture

49. **Wheat crop requires about 7.5 cm depth of water after every 28 days and base period for wheat is 140 days. What will be the value of delta for wheat ?** **[BHU-2012]**
   (a) 40.2 cm (b) 37.5 cm
   (c) 36 cm (d) 30.2 cm

50. **Which of the following mineral particle size is classified as silt according to ISSS ?** **[BHU-2012]**
   (a) 0.05 to 0.1 mm (b) 0.002 to 0.05 mm
   (c) 0.002 to 0.02 mm (d) None of the above

51. **Flow in an irrigation channel is considered as** **[IARI PhD-2011, BHU-2012]**
   (a) Gradually varied (b) Rapidly varied
   (c) Spatially varied (d) Uniform

Answers			
	46. (b)	48. (a)	50. (c)
	47. (b)	49. (b)	51. (d)

52. Evaporation from a free water surface is measured by **[ARS-2015]**

(a) Lysimeter (b) Infiltrometer
(c) USWB class A Pan (d) Anemometer

53. Infiltration index is the most commonly used method for determination of the

(a) Infiltration rate
(b) Cumulative infiltration
(c) Abstraction from precipitation
(d) Consumptive use

54. Tensiometer can effectively measure soil moisture tension in the range of **[ARS-2014]**

(a) 0.0 to 1 atm (b) < 0.8 atm
(c) 0 to 15 atm (d) 15 to 33

55. Readily available soil moisture to plants in the soil profile (root zone) is approximately equal to **[ARS-2013]**

(a) 100% of available water holding capacity (AWHC)
(b) 50% of AWHC
(c) 10% of AWHC
(d) 50% of field capacity

56. Adhesion is

(a) Attraction of similar molecules
(b) Attraction between two different molecules
(c) Both (a) & (b)
(d) None of the above

57. Weighted creep ratio (WCR) is defined as the ratio of **[BHU-2010]**

(a) Critical head and seepage path
(b) Weighted creep distance and total head loss
(c) Weighted creep distance and seepage path
(d) Critical head and weighted creep distance

Answers	
	52. (c) 54. (b) 56. (b)
	53. (c) 55. (b) 57. (b)

58. Net outgoing long wave radiation is equal to [BHU-2010]

(a) Short ware radiation reflected from ground surface

(b) Difference between radiation from ground surface upward and thedownward long wave radiation

(c) Radiation because of temperature of earth surface

(d) None of the above

59. The consumptive use of water for crop represents [BHU-2010]

(a) Transpiration needs of the crop

(b) Evaporation needs of the cropped area

(c) Evapotranspiration needs of the cropped area plus the minor quantity required in plant metabolism

(d) None of the above

60. The relative proportion of silt, sand and clay determines [BHU-2010]

(a) Soil structure (b) Soil series

(c) Soil texture (d) Soil stratification

61. Volume of water present in total pore volume is referred to as [BHU-2010]

(a) Volume of wetness (b) Degree of saturation

(c) Saturation (d) Moisture content

62. The sum of exchangeable cations absorbed by soil expressed in mill equivalents per 100 gm of soil is referred to as [BHU-2010]

(a) Cation exchange

(b) Cation percent

(c) Exchangeable cation

(d) Cation exchange capacity

Answers	58. (b)	60. (c)	62. (d)
	59. (c)	61. (b)	

63. **Effective root zone depth of sugarcane, lucerne, citrus, and safflower is considered as** **[BHU-2010]**

(a) 60 cm (b) 90 cm
(c) 120 cm (d) 180 cm

64. **The pressure of water above water table will be** **[BHU-2010]**

(a) Positive (b) Negative
(c) Atmospheric (d) None of the above

65. **The number of the days that can be allowed for applying one irrigation to a given design area during the peak period of consumptive use of the crop is referred to as** **[BHU-2010]**

(a) Irrigation interval (b) Irrigation frequency
(c) Irrigation intensity (d) Irrigation period

66. **Recommended safe limit of land slope for efficient irrigation in medium (loamy) soils is** **[BHU-2010]**

(a) 0.4 - 0.6 per cent (b) 0.2 - 0.4 per cent
(c) 1.0 - 2.0per cent (d) 2.0 - 4.0 per cent

67. **The weight of oven dry soil per unit volume of wet soil divided by density of water is referred to** **[BHU-2010]**

(a) Bulk density (b) Density of soil
(c) Apparent specific gravity (d) None of the above

68. **The albedo is the ratio of**

(a) Actual to yearly average rainfall/ day
(b) Actual to monthly average temperature/day
(c) Actual to maximum possible hours of bright sun shine/day
(d) None of the above

Answers			
	63. (d)	65. (d)	67. (c)
	64. (b)	66. (b)	68. (c)

69. Water application efficiency is defined as [BHU-2010]

(a) (Water stored in the root zone during irrigation)/(Water needed in the root zone prior to irrigation)

(b) (Water stored in the root zone)/(Water delivered to the field)

(c) (Water stored in the field) / (Water diverted from the source)

(d) None of the above

70. At ultimate wilting point, if water is added to soil

(a) Plant will regain life

(b) Plant fail to regain life

(c) Plant recovers during night

(d) None of the above

71. Uniformity coefficient is [IARI PhD-2013]

(a) d_{60}/d_{10} (b) d_{60}/d_{50}

(c) d_{60}/d_{30} (d) d_{30}/d_{60}

72. How does ploughing help in retaining subsoil water ? [IARI PhD-2013]

(a) By creating capillaries

(b) By breaking capillaries

(c) By turning the soil upside down

(d) None of the above

73. Hydraulic conductivity of soil depends on [IARI PhD-2013]

(a) Property of porous medium only

(b) Property of fluid only

(c) Property of porous medium and fluid

(d) None of the above

74. The process of removing soluble constituents from the soil layer by action of percolating water is known as [IARI PhD-2013]

(a) Diffusion (b) Percolation

(c) Leaching (d) Infiltration

Answers			
	69. (a)	71. (a)	73. (c)
	70. (b)	72. (b)	74. (c)

75. **The infiltration rate curve after a long time becomes** **[IARI PhD-2013]**

(a) Vertical

(b) Horizontal

(c) Asymptotic to rate axis

(d) Asymptotic to time axis

76. **The understanding of soil-water-plant relationship is important for** **[IARI PhD-2013]**

(a) Tillage operation

(b) Sowing of crops

(c) Harvesting of crops

(d) Design and management of irrigation system

77. **Permeability is measure of** **[IARI PhD-2013]**

(a) Available soil moisture

(b) Porosity

(c) Water holding and transmitting capacity

(d) Ability to transmit water

78. **A soil has available water capacity 200 mm per meter of soil depth. For a crop root zone depth of 1.5 m the depth of applied irrigation water should not exceed** **[IARI PhD-2013]**

(a) 20 cm (b) 30 cm

(c) 40 cm (d) 60 cm

79. **In arid and semi-arid region, the additional irrigation is needed to** **[IARI PhD-2013]**

(a) Control the temperature

(b) Soften the soil for plant roots penetration

(c) Control soil salinity

(d) For ground water recharge

Answers	75. (d) 77. (d) 79. (c) 76. (d) 78. (b)

80. Open channel flow takes place **[IARI PhD-2013]**

(a) Under pressure (b) Under gravity

(c) Both pressure and gravity (d) None of the above

81. Atmometer is used to measure **[IARI PhD-2013]**

(a) Rainfall (b) Wind velocity

(c) Evaporation (d) None of the above

82. Clay is defined as the fraction of soil particles less than 0.05 mm in

(a) ISSS (International Society of Soil Science)

(b) USPRA (United States Public Roads Administration)

(c) USDA (United States Department of Agriculture)

(d) DIN (German Standards)

83. Size of silt and clay particles (mm) of soil are (ISSS)

(a) 0.02-0.002, >.002 (b) 0.02-0.002, <.002

(c) 0.2-0.02 (d) None of the above

84. Which soil particles have maximum porosity ?

(a) Sand (b) Clay

(c) Silt (d) Alluvial

85. Moisture content is measured by

(a) Tensiometer (b) Neutron probe

(c) TDR, FDR (d) All of the above

86. Which soil properties don't change after tillage operations?

(a) Soil structure (b) Soil permeability

(c) Soil texture (d) Infiltration

87. Which of the following type of soil lies between sand and clay ?

(a) Rock (b) Stone

(c) Fine sand (d) Silt

Answers				
	80. (b)	82. (c)	84. (b)	86. (c)
	81. (c)	83. (b)	85. (d)	87. (d)

88. Which water is tightly held by adsorption forces ?

(a) Capillary water

(b) Hygroscopic water

(c) Gravitational water

(d) None of the above

89. Measurement of soil - moisture by TDR is based on

(a) Neutron scattering

(b) Dielectric constant of water

(c) Electrical resistance of soil

(d) Viscosity of water

90. The ratio of actual evapo-transpiration to potential evapo-transpiration is in the range

(a) 0 - 0.4 (b) 0.6 - 0.9

(c) 0.4 - 1.2 (d) 1 - 2

91. The dividing line is the groundwater table (also known as phreatic surface) where the pressure will be

(a) Positive

(b) Negative

(c) Equal to Atmospheric pressure

(d) None of the above

92. Bulk density of soil normally decreases with increase of

(a) Sand particles (b) Silt particles

(c) Clay particles (d) Stone particles

93. In unsaturated flow condition water movement in soil is in order **[NET/ARS-2016]**

(a) sand > silt > clay (b) sand < silt < clay

(c) sand > silt < clay (d) sand < silt > clay

Answers			
	88. (b)	90. (c)	92. (a)
	89. (b)	91. (c)	93. (b)

94. For sandy soil, the soil texture is **[NET/ARS-2016]**

(a) 25 % of clay (b) 15 % of silt

(c) 15 % of clay + silt (d) None of the above

95. Effective size of soil refers to **[NET/ARS-2016]**

(a) 90 % coarser, 10 % finer

(b) 10 % coarser, 90 % finer

(c) 50 % coarser, 50 % finer

(d) None of the above

96. Capillary water in soil is held by **[NET/ARS-2016]**

(a) Surface tension (b) Adhesion

(c) Cohesion (d) None of the above

97. Electrical resistivity meter measured at tension **[NET/ARS-2016]**

(a) 0 bar (b) 5 bar

(c) 100 bar (d) 15 bar

98. Conjunctive use of water include **[NET/ARS-2016]**

(a) Surface water (b) Ground water

(c) Both (d) None

99. Delta is associated with **[NET/ARS-2016]**

(a) Depth of rainfall

(b) Depth of irrigation water excluding rainfall

(c) Depth of irrigation water with rainfall

(d) None

100. The efficient method for measuring evapotranspiration is **[NET/ARS-2016]**

(a) Field plot method (b) Weighing lysimeters

(c) Non weighing lysimeters

(d) Plot method

Answers	94. (c)	96. (a)	98. (c)	100. (b)
	95. (a)	97. (d)	99. (b)	

101. In dryland area which method of evapotranspiration will be more suitable ? [NET/ARS-2016]

(a) Blaney-criddle (b) Penmann

(c) Thornthwaite (d) Christancian

102. While assessing the intensity of agricultural drought, a negative value of aridity index indicates that the area is classified as [GATE-2021]

(a) Severely arid

(b) Moderately arid

(c) Mildly arid

(d) Non - arid

OOOOO

Answers	**101. (a)** **102. (d)**

8 Miscellaneous Questions

1. **GPS is a device** **[BHU-2012]**
   (a) To indicate position of a point on the globe
   (b) To indicate position of the globe in a room
   (c) To indicate position of earth in respect of the sun
   (d) To determine if a series is GP (geometric progression)

2. **Soil water moves from** **[BHU-2012]**
   (a) High potential to low potential
   (b) Low potential to high potential
   (c) High to low as well as low to high
   (d) Potential and water flow are unrelated

3. **Sky radiation (Diffuse sky radiation) is defined as** **[BHU-2010]**
   (a) Total direct solar radiation on earth surface
   (b) Downward scattered and reflected component of thermal radiation
   (c) Total reflected radiation from earth surface
   (d) Night time radiation coming from extra-terrestrial bodies

Answers	1. (a) 3. (a) 2. (a)

4. Humidity is measured by **[BHU-2010]**

(a) Hygrometer (b) Hydrometer

(c) Hyetometer (d) Pyrheliometer

5. Yearly sequence and spatial arrangements of crops and fallow in given area is referred to as **[BHU-2010]**

(a) Cropping intensity (b) Cropping pattern

(c) Cropping system (d) Cropping arrangements

6. Ethanol can be easily obtained from substances rich in **[BHU-2010]**

(a) Lipids (b) Carbohydrates

(c) Proteins (d) Secondary metabolites

7. Which of the following is concerned with phasing out of CFCs ? **[BHU-2010]**

(a) Montreal Protocol (b) Outer space treaty

(c) Ramsar convention (d) SAARC summit

8. Photochemical smog formation starts with **[BHU-2010]**

(a) NOx

(b) Hydrocarbons

(c) SOx

(d) Volatile Organic Compounds (VOCs)

9. PAN is the **[BHU-2010]**

(a) Initiation material of Photochemical smog

(b) Intermediate product of Photochemical smog

(c) Termination product of Photochemical smog

(d) Harmless product of Photochemical smog

10. Methane in biogas accounts for **[BHU-2010]**

(a) 50 - 65% (b) 80 - 85%

(c) 90 - 95% (d) 100%

Answers	4. (a)	6. (b)	8. (a)	10. (a)
	5. (b)	7. (a)	9. (c)	

11. Water vapours are present in the [BHU-2010]

(a) Troposphere (b) Mesosphere

(c) Stratosphere (d) Thermosphere

12. URL stands for [BHU-2010]

(a) Uniform Resource Locator

(b) Universal Resource Locator

(c) Unlimited Resource Locator

(d) Upgraded Resource Locator

13. The geographically distributed information can best be stored analysed and printed by using the following software [IARI PhD-2013]

(a) MS Office (b) PRO Engineer

(c) ILWIS (d) AUTOCAD

14. The topographical details of any area can be derived using the remote sensing data of the following type [IARI PhD-2013]

(a) PAN data

(b) Multi - spectral band data

(c) Stereoscopic high resolution remote sensing data

(d) Multi - spectral multi-date data

15. The term 'VES', with reference to geohydrology, stands for [IARI PhD-2013]

(a) Visibly Efficient Systems

(b) Visibly Equitable Systems

(c) Variable Echo Sounding

(d) Vertical Electrical Sounding

16. The term "conservation agriculture" represents [BHU-2012]

(a) Agriculture profession is conservative

(b) Conserving the agricultural produce

(c) Protecting crops

(d) Optimize use of available natural resources

Answers			
	11. (a)	**13. (c)**	**15. (d)**
	12. (a)	**14. (b)**	**16. (d)**

17. Pradhan Mantri Krishi Sinchayi Yojana (PMKSY) was launched in the year

(a) 2011 - 12 (b) 2012 - 13

(c) 2013 - 14 (d) 2014 - 15

18. How much fund (crore) was allocated to the proposed Pradhan Mantri Krishi Sinchayi Yojana (PMKSY) for irrigation, which was announced in the Union Budget 2014-15 ?

(a) 500 (b) 1000

(c) 700 (d) 2000

19. World forest day and world water day is celebrated on

(a) 21 March, 22 March

(b) 23 March, 22 March

(c) 23 April and 21 March

(d) None of the above

20. World soil day is celebrated on

(a) 5 Oct. (b) 5 Dec.

(c) 23 April (d) 23 Nov.

21. "National Bureau of Soil Survey and Land Use Planning (NBSS & LUP)" is situated at

(a) Pune (b) Nashik

(c) Nagpur (d) Dehradun

22. A meter suitable for flow totalisation is

(a) Turbine flow meter (b) Venturimeter

(c) Rotameter (d) Orifice Plate

23. A flow meter that is independent of fluid density is

(a) Rotameter (b) Electromagnetic flow meter

(c) Venturimeter (d) Orifice meter

Answers	**17. (d)**	**19. (a)**	**21. (c)**	**23. (b)**
	18. (b)	**20. (b)**	**22. (a)**	

24. The tube of the rotameter

(a) Tapers upwards
(b) is of uniform cross-section
(c) Tapers downwards
(d) Tapers in the horizontal direction

25. A rotameter can be used

(a) only in vertical direction
(b) only in horizontal orientation
(c) in any orientation
(d) only for air

26. The UN Framework Convention on Climate Change (UNFCCC) COP-21, 2015 was held in

(a) Paris (b) Ankara
(c) Beijing (d) New Delhi

27. N - s / m^2 is used in S.I. system for

(a) Kinematic viscosity (b) Dynamic viscosity
(c) Mass density (d) Weight density

28. In S.I. system, symbol for the specific weight is

(a) kg/m^3 (b) N/m^3
(c) N/m^2 (d) None of the above

29. Stress in SI units is expressed in

(a) kg per sq cm (b) kg per sq mm
(c) Newton per sq mm (d) Newton per sq m

30. One Newton is equivalent to

(a) 0.10197 kgf (b) 0.20197 kgf
(c) 9.80665 kgf (d) 0.980665 kgf

31. m^2/s is used in S.I. system for

(a) Surface tension (b) Kinematic viscosity
(c) Pressure (d) Power

Answers				
	24. (c)	26. (a)	28. (b)	30. (a)
	25. (a)	27. (b)	29. (d)	31. (b)

32. The intensity of pressure at a certain place is 1 kg (f)/m², the intensity of pressure in SI units will be

(a) 47.88 N/m^2 (b) 9.81 N/m^2

(c) 4.882 N/m^2 (d) 0.07013 N/m^2

33. 10^{-12} is called

(a) Terra (b) Pica

(c) Giga (d) Mega

34. 100 kN/m^2 pressure is equal to

(a) 1 atm (b) 1 bar

(c) 1 m bar (d) 1 mm Hg

35. The fundamental units in S.I. system, are the same as that of

(a) C.G.S. units (b) F.P.S. units

(c) M.K.S. units (d) None of the above

36. The thickness of a micron is

(a) 10^{-3} m (b) 10^{-6} m

(c) 10^{-6} mm (d) 10^{-9} m

37. Pick up the correct statement from the following:

(a) 1 N force = 0.10197 kgf

(b) 1 kgf = 9.80665 N

(c) 1 kgf/cm^2 = 98.0665 kN/m^2

(d) All of the above

38. 1 kg wt in gravitational unit equals............. N in SI system

(a) 8.9 (b) 9.8

(c) 4.5 (d) 0.98

39. The relationship between Arithmetic mean (A), Harmonic mean (H) and Geometric mean (G) is [IARI PhD 2013]

Answers				
	32. (b)	34. (b)	36. (b)	38. (b)
	33. (b)	35. (c)	37. (d)	39. (a)

(a) $G^2 = AH$ (b) $G = \sqrt{AH}$

(c) $H^2 = GA$ (d) $A^2 = GH$

40. For the data 1, -2, 4, geometric mean is [IARI PhD 2013]

(a) 2 (b) 4

(c) -7/3 (d) -2

41. Puddling is used to [IARI PhD 2013]

(a) Reduce percolation of water

(b) Pulverize soil

(c) Level the field

(d) Compact the soil

42. The dimension of surface tension is [IARI PhD 2013]

(a) [MLT] (b) $[ML^{-1}T^{-2}]$

(c) $[ML^{-1}]$ (d) $[MT^{-2}]$

43. The first derivation of e^{x^2} wrt x is. [IARI PhD 2013]

(a) e^{x^2} (b) $2xe^{x^2}$

(c) $x^2e^{x^2}$ (d) $\frac{e^{x^2}}{x^2}$

44. Two forces of magnitude 30 N and 40 N acts at right angle to each other. The resultant force is [IARI PhD 2013]

(a) 40N (b) 50N

(c) 60N (d) 70N

45. The speed of CPU of computer is given by [IARI PhD 2013]

(a) GB (b) GHz

(c) m/s (d) GJ

Answers	40. (d)	42. (d)	44. (b)
	41. (a)	43. (b)	45. (b)

46. The value of $\lim_{x\to 2}\left(\frac{x^2-3x+2}{x^2+x-6}\right)^1$ will be [IARI PhD 2013]

(a) 0 (b) 1
(c) 1/5 (d) 1/6

47. **If the inverse of matrix P is P, then P is called**

(a) Symmetric Matrix (b) Skew symmetric
(c) Diagonal (d) Involutory

48. **The instrument used to measure area of map is** [IARI PhD 2013]

(a) Dumpy level (b) Theodolite
(c) Planimeter (d) Dynamometer

49. **Ozone layer in atmosphere is contained in** [IARI PhD 2013]

(a) Troposphere (b) Stratosphere
(c) Ionosphere (d) Mesosphere

50. **The product of two orthogonal matrices is** [IARI PhD 2013, 2016]

(a) Unitary matrix (b) Orthogonal matrix
(c) Unit matrix (d) Null matrix

51. **The ratio of the volume of the voids to the total soil volume is called** [IARI PhD 2013]

(a) Void ratio (b) Porosity
(c) Dry bulk density (d) Wet bulk density

52. **In which flow meter, the pressure drop remains nearly constant but the area changes ?** [IARI PhD 2013]

(a) Pitot tube (b) Venturimeter
(c) Rotameter (d) Orifice meter

Answers				
	46. (c)	48. (c)	50. (b)	52. (c)
	47. (d)	49. (b)	51. (b)	

53. If f(x) is a perfect normal distribution with mean and standard deviation of 5 and 1, respectively, then the value of f(x) for $x = 6$ is

(a) 0.124 (b) 0.242

(c) 0.482 (d) 0.524

54. The system of linear equations has [IARI PhD 2013]

$$a + 3b + 4c = 11$$

$$2a + 6b + 8c = 22$$

(a) Unique solution (b) Many solution

(c) No solution (d) Imaginary solution

55. The conjugate of a complex number a+bi is denoted by

(a) b+ai (b) b-ai

(c) $\sqrt{a^2 - b^2}$ (d) a-bi

56. Archimedes' principle is used in determining the

(a) Shape of a solid

(b) Surface area of an irregular solid

(c) Centre of gravity of a floating body

(d) Volume of an irregular solid

57. The rate of change of volume of a ball with respect to its radius (r) is

(a) $4/3\ \pi r^3$ (b) $4/3\ \pi r^2$

(c) $4\ \pi r^2$ (d) $¾\ \pi r^2$

58. Indicate the value of (2+3i) (1-i)

(a) 1+i (b) 1-i

(c) 5-i (d) 5+i

59. Closeness of the instrument output to the true value of measured quantity is known as [IARI PhD 2013]

(a) Precision (b) Resolution

(c) Accuracy (d) Threshold

Answers	53. (a)	55. (d)	57. (c)	59. (c)
	54. (c)	56. (c)	58. (d)	

60. The angle between the lines $2x - y + 5 = 0$ and $3x + y + 4 = 0$ is

(a) 30° (b) 45°

(c) 60° (d) 90°

61. The lines $2x - 3y = 5$ and $3x - 4y = 7$ are diameter of a circle of area 154 sq. units. Then the equation of the circle is

(a) $x^2+y^2+2x-2y=62$ (b) $x^2+y^2+2x-2y=47$

(c) $x^2+y^2-2x+2y=47$ (d) $x^2+y^2-2x+2y=62$

62. Coordinates of point which divides the line segments joining point A (0,0) and B(9,12) in the ratio 1 : 2 are

(a) (-3,4) (b) (3,4)

(c) (3,-4) (d) (4,-3)

63. If $y = \log \sqrt{\tan x}$ then the value of dy/dx at $x = \pi/4$ is

[IARI PhD 2013]

(a) ∞ (b) 0

(c) 1 (d) 1/2

64. If $x^y = e^{x-y}$ then dy/dx is equal to

(a) $\dfrac{\log x}{(1 + \log x)^2}$ (b) $\dfrac{x - y}{(1 + \log x)}$

(c) $\dfrac{x - y}{(1 + \log x)^2}$ (d) $\dfrac{1}{(1 + \log x)}$

65. The radius of sphere is changing at the rate of 0.1 cm/sec. The rate of change of its surface area when the radius is 200 cm is

(a) $8\ \pi cm^2/sec$ (b) $12\ \pi cm^2/sec$

(c) $160\ \pi cm^2/sec$ (d) $200\ \pi cm^2/sec$

Answers	60. (b)	62. (b)	64. (a)
	61. (c)	63. (c)	65. (c)

66. Electron volt is unit of

(a) Charge (b) Potential
(c) Energy (d) Electric power

67. The dimensional formula for change in momentum is same as that for

(a) Force (b) Impulse
(c) Acceleration (d) Velocity

68. If the displacement of a particle is zero, then distance covered

(a) Must be zero (b) Cannot be zero
(c) Is negative (d) May or may not be zero

69. Sudden fall of pressure at a place indicates

(a) Storm (b) Rain
(c) Fair weather (d) Cold wave

70. The conversion factor to change from g/cc to kg/m^3 is

(a) 100 (b) 500
(c) 1000 (d) 1500

71. If $a^x = b$, $b^y = c$, $c^z = a$, then the value of xyz is

(a) 0 (b) 1
(c) 2 (d) 3

72. If $\frac{\log 2}{b - c} = \frac{\log 3}{c - a} = \frac{\log 5}{a - b}$ then $2^a 3^b 5^c =$

(a) 0 (b) 1
(c) -1 (d) None of the above

73. The water from a hand pump is warm in winter because

(a) Inside water comes out and absorbs heat from the environment

Answers	66. (c)	68. (d)	70. (c)	72. (b)
	67. (a)	69. (a)	71. (b)	73. (c)

(b) The pumping process causes friction which warms up the water

(c) The temperature inside the earth is higher than the atmospheric temperature

(d) Our body is cold in winter and the water appears to be warm

74. When hot liquid is poured into a thick glass tumbler, it cracks because glass

(a) is a bad conductor of heat so only inner surface expands

(b) has high temperature coefficient of expansion

(c) has low temperature coefficient of expansion

(d) has a very low specific heat

75. Which of the following instruments is used to measure humidity ?

(a) Kata Thermometer (b) Anemometer

(c) Clinical Thermometer (d) Sling Psychrometer

76. The series $a + ar + ar^2 + ... ar^{n-1}$ is a [IARI PhD 2011]

(a) Geometric series (b) Harmonic series

(c) Logarithmic series (d) Taylor's series

77. For the condition when θ tends to zero, the value of sinθ tends to [IARI PhD 2011]

(a) $\cos\theta$ (b) $\tan\theta$

(c) $\cot\theta$ (d) $\sec\theta$

78. The sum of a complex number (a+bi) and that of its conjugate complex number is equal to [IARI PhD 2011]

(a) a (b) 2a

(c) 2a+2b (d) 2a-2b

Answers	74. (a) 76. (a) 78. (b) 75. (d) 77. (b)

79. A point moves in a straight line so that its displacement 'x' meters at time 't' seconds is given by $x^2 = 1 + t^2$. Its acceleration at a time 't' is [IARI PhD 2011]

(a) $1/x^3$ (b) $-t/x^2$

(c) $1/x - t^2/x^3$ (d) $1/x - 1/x^2$

80. A 5 hp motor with mechanical efficiency of 60 per cent works for 2 hours. The energy consumed by motor will be [IARI PhD 2011]

(a) 16.67 kWh (b) 12.5 kWh

(c) 4.4 kWh (d) None of the above

81. In hyperbolic function, tanhx is equal to [IARI PhD 2011]

(a) $\frac{e^x - e^{-x}}{e^x + e^{-x}}$ (b) $\frac{e^x + e^{-x}}{e^x - e^{-x}}$

(c) $\frac{e^x + e^{-x}}{2}$ (d) $\frac{e^x - e^{-x}}{2}$

82. In F - test, the test criterion F is the ratio of

(a) Means (b) CV's

(c) Variances (d) None of the above

83. Initial velocity of an object is 2m/s. How much will it travel in 10 seconds if acceleration is $4 m/s^2$?

(a) 20 m (b) 80 m

(c) 180 m (d) 220 m

84. The equation $x^2 + ix + 1 = 0$, where $i = \sqrt{-1}$ has

(a) Two real roots

(b) Two imaginary roots

(c) One real and one imaginary root

(d) Infinite number of roots.

Answers	79. (c)	81. (a)	83. (d)
	80. (c)	82. (c)	84. (b)

85. The slope of the curve $Y=(5/3)X^2$ at X=2 is given by

(a) 5/3 (b) 10/3

(c) 20/3 (d) 10

86. If $\sin \lambda = 1/2$, the value of $\cot \lambda$ will be [IARI PhD 2011]

(a) $\sqrt{3}$ (b) $1/\sqrt{3}$

(c) $\frac{\sqrt{3}}{2}$ (d) $\frac{1}{\sqrt{2}}$

87. $Y^2 = 4ax$ is the form of equation [IARI PhD 2011]

(a) Hyperbola (b) Circle

(c) Parabola (d) Ellipse

88. Consider two vectors $\vec{F_1} = 2i + 5\hat{k}$ and $\vec{F_2} = 3j + 4\hat{k}$. The magnitude of the scalar product of these vectors is [IARI PhD 2011]

(a) 20 (b) 23

(c) $33^{1/2}$ (d) 26

89. The mean of first 'n' natural numbers is

(a) n(n+1) (b) n(n+1) / 2

(c) (n+1) / 2 (d) (n+1) / 4

90. $x - \frac{x^3}{3!} + \frac{x^5}{5!} - \frac{x^7}{7!} + \frac{x^9}{9!} - \ldots\ldots$ is expansion of [IARI PhD 2016]

(a) cos x (b) sin x

(c) tan x (d) None of the above

91. Product of two orthogonal matrices is [IARI PhD 2016]

(a) Orthogonal (b) Singular

(c) Null (d) None of the above

Answers	85. (c)	87. (c)	89. (c)	91. (a)
	86. (a)	88. (a)	90. (b)	

92. $\int \ln x\, dx$ is **[IARI PhD 2016]**

(a) $x \ln x - x + C$ (b) $x^2 \ln x + C$

(c) $x \ln x + x + C$ (d) $1/x + C$

93. Linear variable differential transformer (LVDT) measures

(a) Linear Force (b) Linear displacement

(c) Resistance (d) None of the above

94. Which of the following is a desirable characteristic of an instrument ?

(a) High drift (b) Poor reproducibility

(c) High fidelity (d) High measuring lag

95. 1 degree Celsius is equal to

(a) 273.15 K (b) 274.15 K

(c) 272.15 K (d) None of the above

96. Which of the following is not the triple point of water ?

(a) 492 R (b) 273 K

(c) 32 R (d) 32°F

97. Load cells are used for the measurement of

(a) Weight (b) Stress

(c) Strain (d) Pressure

98. Which of the following is not a differential pressure flow meter ?

(a) Rotameter (b) Orificemeter

(c) Venturimeter (d) Flow nozzle

99. The function of a transducer is to

(a) Modify the input signal.

(b) Amplify the input signal.

(c) Codify / decodify the input signal.

(d) Convert the primary signal into a more useful quantity, usually an electric impulse.

Answers	**92. (a)**	**94. (c)**	**96. (c)**	**98. (a)**
	93. (b)	**95. (b)**	**97. (a)**	**99. (d)**

100. A mercury barometer measures the ________ pressure.
(a) Gauge (b) Absolute
(c) Atmospheric (d) Vacuum

101. Which of the following is not a mechanical pressure sensing element ?
(a) Diaphram (b) Bellows
(c) Bourdon tube (d) U - tube

102. The rank of the identity matrix of order n is :
(a) n-1 (b) n
(c) n-2 (d) None of the above

103. Determinant value of Non-singular matrix is
(a) Zero (b) Non zero
(c) Cannot be defined (d) None of the above

104. If A is a non-singular matrix of order n, then the rank of A is :
(a) n (b) 0
(c) n - 1 (d) None of the above

105. The rank of the matrix $A = \begin{bmatrix} 1 & 1 & 1 \\ 1 & 1 & 1 \\ 1 & 1 & 1 \end{bmatrix}$
(a) 1 (b) 2
(c) 3 (d) 0

106. Rank of null matrix is
(a) 0 (b) 1
(c) Not defined (d) None of the above

107. If y is expressed in terms of a variable x as Y = f(x), then y is called
(a) Explicit function (b) Implicit function
(c) Linear function (d) Identity function

Answers				
	100. (c)	102. (b)	104. (a)	106. (a)
	101. (d)	103. (b)	105. (a)	107. (a)

108. $\mathbf{Cos(-435°) =}$

(a) cos15° (b) -cos15°

(c) -sin15° (d) sin15°

109. If circumference of a circle is divided into 360 congruent parts, angle subtended by one part at center of circle is called

(a) Angle (b) Radian

(c) Degree (d) Minute

110. If A, G, H are arithmetic, geometric and harmonic means between a and b respectively, then A, G, H are

(a) in G.P (b) in A.P

(c) in H.P (d) Real Numbers

111. $\mathbf{X = at^2}$ **and** $\mathbf{y = 2at}$ **are parametric equations of**

(a) Circle $x^2 + y^2 = a^2$ (b) Parabola $y^2 = 4ax$

(c) Ellipse $x^2/a^2 + y^2/b^2$ (d) Ellipse $x^2/a^2 - y^2/b^2$

112. Transpose of a column matrix is

(a) Zero Matrix (b) Row Matrix

(c) Diagonal Matrix (d) None of the above

113. $\mathbf{3x^2 + 2x + 1}$ **is a**

(a) Polynomial of degree 2

(b) Polynomial of degree 0

(c) Polynomial of degree 3

(d) Polynomial of degree n

114. If $\mathbf{{}^nC_{12} = {}^nC_6}$ **value of n is**

(a) 12 (b) 14

(c) 18 (d) 16

115. If $\mathbf{|A| = 0}$**, then A is**

(a) Zero matrix (b) Singular matrix

(c) Non-singular matrix (d) 0

Answers	108. (d)	110. (a)	112. (b)	114. (c)
	109. (c)	111. (b)	113. (a)	115. (b)

116. **If A is a symmetric matrix, then A^t =**

(a) A (b) |A|

(c) 0 (d) Diagonal matrix

117. **1 radian =**

(a) 57°17′45″ (b) 1°

(c) 180° (d) 180′

118. **In a matrix multiplication for A and B, $(AB)^t$**

(a) $A^t B^t$ (b) $B^t A^t$

(c) 1/AB (d) AB

119. **In 30 minutes, hours hand of a clock turns through**

(a) π/6 radians (b) π/12 radians

(c) π/24 radians (d) π radians

120. $\int_a^b f(x)$ =

(a) $\int_b^a f(x)$ (b) $-\int_b^a f(x)$

(c) $\int_a^b f(-x)$ (d) None of the above

121. **1 are =**

(a) 10 m^2 (b) 100 m^2

(c) 1,000 m^2 (d) 10,000 m^2

122. **The maximum frictional force, which comes into play, when a body just begins to slide over the surface of the other body, is known as**

(a) Static friction

(b) Dynamic friction

(c) Limiting friction

(d) Coefficient of friction

Answers				
	116. (a)	118. (b)	120. (b)	122. (c)
	117. (a)	119. (b)	121. (b)	

123. Two balls of equal mass and of perfectly elastic material are lying on the floor. One of the balls with velocity v is made to struck the second ball. Both the balls after impact will move with a velocity

(a) v (b) v/2
(c) v/4 (d) v/8

124. If the resultant of two equal forces has the same magnitude as either of the forces, then the angle between the two forces is

(a) 30° (b) 60°
(c) 90° (d) 120°

125. The point, through which the whole weight of the body acts, irrespective of its position, is known as

(a) Moment of inertia (b) Centre of gravity
(c) Centre of percussion (d) Centre of mass

126. Which of the following is a scalar quantity ?

(a) Acceleration (b) Force
(c) Speed (d) Velocity

127. The rate of change of momentum is directly proportional to the impressed force, and takes place in the same direction in which the force acts. This statement is known as

(a) Newton's first law of motion
(b) Newton's second law of motion
(c) Newton's third law of motion
(d) None of the above

128. The angular velocity (in rad / s) of a body rotating at N revolutions per minute is

(a) $\pi N / 60$ (b) $\pi N / 180$
(c) $2\pi N / 60$ (d) $2\pi N / 180$

Answers	**123. (b)**	**125. (b)**	**127. (b)**
	124. (d)	**126. (c)**	**128. (c)**

129. Dimensions of impulse is

(a) $[MLT^{-1}]$ (b) $[ML^2T^{-1}]$

(c) $[MLT^{-2}]$ (d) $[M^2LT^{-1}]$

130. "Pascal second" has the dimensions of

(a) Force (b) Energy

(c) Coefficient of Viscosity (d) Pressure

131. "Parsec" is the unit of

(a) Time (b) Distance

(c) Velocity (d) Frequency

132. The most common gas used in gas chromatography is

(a) Feron (b) Helium

(c) Methane (d) Chlorine

133. Which of the error in measurement is a chance error and caused due to unknown reason ?

(a) Instrument error (b) Observational error

(c) Random error (d) None of the above

134. The constant 'a' and 'b' for exponential function ($y = ae^{bx}$) can be easily determined y plotting the data on

(a) Semi-log paper (b) Log - Log paper

(c) Simple graph paper (d) None of the above

135. Unit less measurement of dispersion is

(a) Coefficient of Variation (b) Range

(c) Standard Deviation (d) Mean deviation

136. Which measure of central tendency requires data arrangement in ascending or descending order for its estimation ?

(a) Arithmetic Mean (b) Mode

(c) Median (d) Harmonic Mean

Answers	129. (a)	131. (b)	133. (c)	135. (a)
	130. (c)	132. (b)	134. (a)	136. (c)

137. Mean deviation is least when calculated about

(a) Median (b) Mode

(c) Arithmetic Mean (d) Geometric mean

138. Hypothesis of committing Type I error in statistics is known as

(a) Level of significance (b) Test of significance

(c) Composite hypothesis (d) None of the Above

139. Which is correct for the symmetric distribution of data ?

(a) Mean = Mode = Median (b) Mean > Mode > Median

(c) Mean < Mode < Median (d) Mean = Mode > Median

140. To calculate the average speed, which item of the central tendency is most suited

(a) Mean (b) Weighted Harmonic Mean

(c) Weighted Mean (d) Geometric Mean

141. Arithmetic mean and variance is always equal in

(a) Binomial distribution (b) Normal distribution

(c) Poisson distribution (d) None of the above

142. Which of these is not based on all observations ?

(a) Arithmetic Mean (b) Mode

(c) Median (d) Harmonic mean

143. Data in population census report is

(a) Grouped data (b) Secondary data

(c) Primary data (d) None of the above

144. Which one is not measure of dispersion ?

(a) Range (b) Variance

(c) 50th percentile (d) Inter - quartile range

145. Algebraic sum of deviation from mean is

(a) Zero (b) Undefined

(c) Maximum (d) None of the above

Answers					
	137. (a)	139. (a)	141. (c)	143. (c)	145. (a)
	138. (a)	140. (b)	142. (b)	144. (d)	

146. **Statistic is a numerical quantity, which is calculated from**

(a) Population (b) Sample

(c) Data (d) None of the above

147. **The strength (degree) of correlation between a set of independent variable X and dependent variable Y is measured by**

(a) Coefficient of determination

(b) Coefficient of correlation

(c) Standard error

(d) All of the above

148. **The percent of total variation of the dependent variable Y explained by the set of independent variable X is measured by**

(a) Correlation coefficient

(b) Coefficient of determination

(c) Coefficient of Skewness

(d) Standard error

149. **Correlation coefficient between X and X is**

(a) 0 (b) 1

(c) -1 (d) ∞

150. **The sum of the first *n* cubes is the .... of the sum of the first *n* natural numbers.**

(a) Cube (b) Square

(c) Double (d) Triple

151. **Altimeter is used for measuring**

(a) Height of a place from msl

(b) Air temperature

(c) Longitude of a place

(d) Ground water level

Answers	146. (b)	148. (b)	150. (b)
	147. (d)	149. (b)	151. (a)

152. NDVI refers to **[BHU-2018]**

(a) National Digital Verification Index

(b) Normalized Difference Vegetation Index

(c) Normalized Digitization Value Index

(d) Normalized Difference Value Index

OOOOO

Answers	**152. (b)**

9 Matching

1.

(i)	Rainfall intensity vs time	(A)	Hydrograph
(ii)	Cumulative discharge vs time in chronological order	(B)	Hyetograph
(iii)	Accumulated precipitation vs time in chronological order	(C)	Flow duration curve
(iv)	Stream flow vs time in chronological order	(D)	Mass curve of rainfall
(v)	Stream discharge vs percent time the flow in equalled or exceeded	(E)	Flow mass curve

2.

(i)	Erosivity	(A)	Tubewell
(ii)	Erodibility	(B)	Tubewell spacing
(iii)	Application efficiency	(C)	Rainfall
(iv)	Radial flow	(D)	Soil
(v)	Cone of depression	(E)	Irrigation

Answers	
	1. i-B, ii-E, iii-D, iv-A, v-C
	2. i-C, ii-D, iii-E, iv-A, v-B

3.

(i)	World foresty Day	(A)	23 December
(ii)	World environment day	(B)	16 October
(iii)	Kisan day	(C)	5 June
(iv)	World food day	(D)	8 march
(v)	World Water day	(E)	21 march
(vi)	World earth day	(F)	22 April

4.

(i)	NDRI	(A)	Dehradun
(ii)	CIPHET	(B)	Karnal
(iii)	CIAE	(C)	Hyderabad
(iv)	CRIDA	(D)	Bhopal
(v)	IISWC	(E)	Ludhiana

5.

(i)	Direct runoff	(A)	T-year rainfall depth
(ii)	Peak runoff	(B)	Curve number
(iii)	Tensiometer	(C)	aquifer
(iv)	Isoerodant map	(D)	Rational number
(v)	Isopluvial map	(E)	30-minute rainfall intensity
(vi)	Zone of saturation	(F)	Field capacity

6.

(i)	Unconfined aquifer	(A)	Hard rock area
(ii)	Confined aquifer	(B)	Screen well
(iii)	Pearched aquifer	(C)	Piezometric surface
(iv)	Open well	(D)	Phreatic surface
(v)	Bore well	(E)	False aquifer

Answers		
	3. i-E, ii-C, iii-A, iv-B, v-D, vi-F	**5. i-B, ii-D, iii-F, iv-E, v-A, vi-C**
	4. i-B, ii-E, iii-D, iv-C, v-A	**6. i-D, ii-C, iii-E, iv-B, v-A**

7.

(i)	Hyethograph	(A)	Infiltration
(ii)	Capilliary zone	(B)	Remote sensing
(iii)	Field capacity	(C)	Rainfall
(iv)	Land use/ land cover	(D)	Irrigation
(v)	Duty	(E)	Above water table

8.

(i)	IUH	(A)	Watts
(ii)	Manning's equation	(B)	Newton
(iii)	Work	(C)	Hydrograph
(iv)	Force	(D)	Erg
(v)	Power	(E)	Velocity

9.

(i)	Irrigation	(A)	Terrace
(ii)	Drainage	(B)	Surge
(iii)	Water Pumping	(C)	Foot valve
(iv)	Soil conservation	(D)	Land reclamation
(v)	Water resources	(E)	Dam

10.

(i)	Kennedy's equation	(A)	freeboard
(ii)	Philip's equation	(B)	Synthetic hydrograph
(iii)	Hooghoudt's equation	(C)	Drain spacing
(iv)	Snyder's equation	(D)	Canal design
(v)	Haksley's formula	(E)	infiltration

Answers		
	7. i-C, ii-A, iii-E, iv-B, v-D	**9 i-B, ii-D, iii-C, iv-A, v-E**
	8. i-C, ii-E, iii-D, iv-B, v-A	**10. i-D, ii-E, iii-C, iv-B, v-A**

11.

(i)	Thermocouple	(A)	Stress/ strain
(ii)	Strain gauge	(B)	Velocity of fluids
(iii)	Piezoelectric	(C)	Composition of gases
(iv)	Chromatograph	(D)	Temperature
(v)	Pitot tube	(E)	Pressure

12.

(i)	Venturimeter	(A)	Wilting point
(ii)	Current meter	(B)	Pressure at a point
(iii)	Anemometers	(C)	Wind velocity
(iv)	Pitot tube	(D)	Flow velocity
(v)	Pressure plate apparatus	(E)	Flow measurement

13.

(i)	Campbell stokes's	(A)	Rain fall
(ii)	Wind vane	(B)	Sunshine radiation
(iii)	Seismograph	(C)	Wind direction
(iv)	Rain gauge	(D)	earthquake
(v)	Multi-slot divisnor	(E)	Soil erosion

14.

(i)	Ernst	(A)	Confined aquifer
(ii)	Theis	(B)	Fresh water – Saline water interface
(iii)	Ghyben - Herzberg	(C)	Infiltration
(iv)	Ficks	(D)	Drainage
(v)	Kostikov	(E)	Concentration gradient

Answers	**11. i-D, ii-A, iii-E, iv-C, v-B**	**13. i-B, ii-C, iii-D, iv-A, v-E**
	12. i-E, ii-D, iii-C, iv-B, v-A	**14. i-D, ii-A, iii-B, iv-E, v-C**

15.

(i)	Transmissivity	(A)	T
(ii)	Leakage factor	(B)	L^2T^{-1}
(iii)	Hydraulic resistance	(C)	$M^0L^0T^0$
(iv)	Hydraulic conductivity	(D)	LT^{-1}
(v)	Specific yield	(E)	L

16.

(i)	Rational formula	(A)	Ranking
(ii)	Darcy's law	(B)	Runoff
(iii)	Curve number	(C)	Peak flow rate
(iv)	Weibull's method	(D)	Filter design
(v)	Granulometry	(E)	Hydraulic gradient

17.

(i)	Salinity	(A)	Machinery
(ii)	Compaction	(B)	Water harvesting
(iii)	Levelling	(C)	Groundwater recharge
(iv)	Pond	(D)	Leaching
(v)	Percolation tank	(E)	Earth work

18.

(i)	pH	(A)	Measure of replaceable Na
(ii)	EC	(B)	Measure of Na with respect to Ca and Mg
(iii)	CEC	(C)	Measure of salinity
(iv)	SAR	(D)	Measure of soil reaction
(v)	ESP	(E)	Measure of replaceable cations

Answers		
	15. i-B, ii-E, iii-A, iv-D, v-C	17. i-D, ii-E, iii-A, iv-B, v-C
	16. i-C, ii-E, iii-B, iv-A, v-D	18. i-D, ii-C, iii-E, iv-B, v-A

19

(i)	Work	(A)	Kilo-Watt-hr (kWh)
(ii)	Power	(B)	Newton
(iii)	Momentum	(C)	kg.m/s
(iv)	Force	(D)	Watt
(v)	Energy	(E)	Erg

20

(i)	Auger hole method	(A)	Anisotropy
(ii)	Hanging column	(B)	Non-homogeneous
(iii)	Inflow-outflow method	(C)	Drainable porosity
(iv)	Directional difference	(D)	Seepage loss
(v)	Spatial difference	(E)	Saturated hydraulic conductivity

21.

(i)	Water	(A)	Lines
(ii)	Land	(B)	Curved surface
(iii)	Cone	(C)	Variation
(iv)	Spatial	(D)	Volume
(v)	Equipotential	(E)	Area

22.

(i)	Strahler's law	(A)	Fluid viscosity
(ii)	Stokes' law	(B)	Stream order
(iii)	Darcy's law	(C)	Ground water flow
(iv)	Fick's law of diffusion	(D)	Momentum
(v)	Newton's law	(E)	Salt concentration

Answers		
	19. i-E, ii-D, iii-C, iv-B, v-A	**21. i-D, ii-E, iii-B, iv-C, v-A**
	20. i-E, ii-C, iii-D, iv-A, v-B	**22. i-B, ii-A, iii-C, iv-E, v-D**

23.

(i)	Entrance resistance	(A)	Sprinkler irrigation
(ii)	Coefficient of uniformity	(B)	Subsurface tile drainage
(iii)	Saltation	(C)	Critical flow
(iv)	Hydraulic jump	(D)	Wind erosion
(v)	Seepage	(E)	Phreatic line

24.

(i)	Streamflow velocity	(A)	Anemometer
(ii)	Evapo-transpiration rate	(B)	Penman's method
(iii)	Infiltration rate	(C)	Horton's method
(iv)	Wind velocity	(D)	Current meter

25. [GATE-2016]

(i)	Waste valve	(A)	Jet pump
(ii)	Plunger	(B)	Centrifugal pump
(iii)	Foot valve	(C)	Reciprocating pump
(iv)	Nozzle and venturi	(D)	Hydraulic ram

26. [GATE-2018]

(i)	Flownet	(A)	Soil erosion
(ii)	EI_{30} Index	(B)	Curve number
(iii)	Groynes	(C)	Equipotential line
(iv)	Isobath	(D)	Groundwater
(v)	Runoff	(E)	River bank

Answers		
	23. i-B, ii-A, iii-D, iv-C, v-E	24. i-D, ii-B, iii-C, iv-A
	25. i-D, ii-C, iii-B, iv-A	26. i-C, ii-A, iii-E, iv-D, v-B

27. [GATE-2019]

(i)	Uniformly spaced contour lines	(A)	Flat ground
(ii)	Widely spaced contour lines	(B)	Steep ground
(iii)	Closely spaced contour lines	(C)	Hill
(iv)	A series of close contours with high value inside	(D)	Uniform slope

28. [GATE-2020]

(i)	Properties of confined and semi-confined aquifers	(A)	Perched aquifer
(ii)	Property of unconfined aquifer	(B)	Coefficient of storage
(iii)	Property of semi-confined aquifer	(C)	Specific yield
(iv)	A special case of an unconfined aquifer	(D)	Leakage factor

OOOOO

Answers	27. i-D, ii-A, iii-B, iv-C 28. i-B, ii-C, iii-D, iv-A

Model Set - 1

1. **Sprinkler irrigation system performance is considered satisfactory when the minimum value of the uniformity coefficient (%) is**

   (a) 65 (b) 75
   (c) 85 (d) 95

2. **WHP of centrifugal pump of 10 lps capacity and 38 m total head will be**

   (a) 3 (b) 4
   (c) 5 (d) 6

3. **Total depth of irrigation to a crop is known as**

   (a) Delta (b) Base
   (c) Duty (d) Irrigation intensity

4. **Subsurface drains remove**

   (a) Excess runoff water from rainfall
   (b) Hygroscopicwater
   (c) Sub - surface gravitational water
   (d) Capillary water

5. **If the discharge of drainage canal is 1000 lps and drainage area is 360 ha, the drainage coefficient (cm) will be equal to**

   (a) 2.4 (b) 0.24
   (c) 24 (d) 240

Answers	1. (c) 3. (a) 5. (a) 2. (c) 4. (c)

6. **If the speed of a centrifugal pump is doubled, the power required will be increased by**

(a)	2 times	(b)	4 times
(c)	8 times	(d)	16 times

7. **Hydrograph is a plot of**
   - (a) Rainfall intensity vs time
   - (b) Discharge vs time
   - (c) Cumulative Runoff vs time
   - (d) Cumulative discharge vs time

8. **Lysimeter is used to measure**

(a)	ET	(b)	Infiltration
(c)	Evaporation	(d)	Transpiration

9. **For a given fluid the dynamic viscosity is 0.06 poise, density is 0.9 g/cc, the kinematic viscosity (in stokes) is**

(a)	0.04	(b)	0.054
(c)	0.067	(d)	0.4

10. **The ratio of pressure between two points A and B located respectively at depths 0.5m and 2m below a constant level of water in a tank is**

(a)	1 : 1.414	(b)	1 : 2
(c)	1 : 4	(d)	1 : 16

11. **If the Froude number of flow in an open channel is more than 1, then the flow is said to be**

(a)	Critical	(b)	Sub - critical
(c)	Super - critical	(d)	None of the above

12. **In a static fluid, the pressure or intensity of pressure is same in all directions, the fluid is**

(a)	Real fluid	(b)	Newtonian fluid
(c)	Non-Newtonian fluid	(d)	Ideal fluid

Answers				
	6. (c)	**8. (a)**	**10. (c)**	**12. (d)**
	7. (b)	**9. (c)**	**11. (c)**	

13. The discharge coefficient of an orifice meter is

(a) Greater than the venturimeter

(b) Equal to the venturimeter

(c) Smaller than the venturimeter

(d) Greater than one

14. The dimension of intrinsic permeability is

(a) [MLT] (b) $[M^0LT]$

(c) $[M^0L^2T^0]$ (d) $[M^0L^0T^2]$

15. A soil sample has porosity of 40 %, its void ratio is

(a) 0.06 (b) 0.28

(c) 0.40 (d) 0.66

16. The movement of soil particles having sizes in the range of 0.05 to 0.5 mm through a series of benches is known as

(a) Saltation (b) Suspension

(c) Surface creep (d) All of the above

17. Length of surveyor's chain or Guntur's chain (ft) is

(a) 33 (b) 66

(c) 100 (d) 10

18. Location of permanent gully control structure is decided on the basis of

(a) Gully depth (b) Gully width

(c) Gully bed slope (d) All of the above

19. Permanent gully control structures are designed in respect of

(a) Hydrologic (b) Hydraulic

(c) Structural (d) All of the above

20. Gauge pressure = absolute pressure – ....

(a) Vacuum pressure (b) Atmospheric pressure

(c) Hydrostatic pressure (d) None of the above

Answers				
	13. (c)	15. (d)	17. (b)	19. (d)
	14. (c)	16. (a)	18. (c)	20. (b)

21. The cipoletti weir is contracted trapezoidal weir having side slope [ARS-2015]

(a) 1 : 1 (b) 1 : 2

(c) 1 : 3 (d) 1 : 4

22. Find the hydraulic mean depth (m) of lined canal water course rectangular in section with a bottom width of 50cm and depth of flow of 25cm

(a) 0.125 (b) 0.126

(c) 0.127 (d) 0.128

23. Engineering measures to control erosion are more effective, when land slope

(a) Exceeds 10% (b) Exceeds 2%

(c) Exceeds 5% (d) None of the above

24. A structure will not fail against tension, when

(a) Eccentricity not greater than b/6

(b) Eccentricity is greater than b/6

(c) Eccentricity is equal to b/6

(d) None of the above

25. Berms are provided, when

(a) Embankment height exceeds 15 m

(b) Embankment ht. exceeds 10 m

(c) Embankment ht. exceeds 20 m

(d) All of the above

26. In thin layer drying, generally thickness of grain bed (cm) is taken as

(a) Above 20 (b) Upto 20

(c) 20 only (d) None of the above

27. The method of preservation of food by treating with UV or ionized radiation is called

(a) Radiation (b) Irradiation

(c) Sterilization (d) Pasteurization

Answers	**21. (d)**	**23. (b)**	**25. (b)**	**27. (b)**
	22. (a)	**24. (a)**	**26. (b)**	

28. If moisture content (wb.) is 25%, then what would be the moisture content (db.) (%)

(a) 33 (b) 30

(c) 45 (d) 20

29. Extraction of soluble constituents from a solid by using solvent is called as

(a) Distillation (b) Leaching

(c) Evaporation (d) Sublimation

30. Psychometric charts represents .... properties of air

(a) Chemical (b) Aerodynamic

(c) Physio thermal (d) Hygroscopic

31. A scalper is used for

(a) Grading (b) Stone removing

(c) Fine removal (d) Rough separation

32. In a domestic vapour compression refrigerator, the refrigerant commonly used is

(a) CO_2 (b) Ammonia

(c) Freon 12 (d) CFC

33. The maximum power (hp) that can be developed by average man is

(a) 0.01 (b) 0.10

(c) 1 (d) 0.5

34. Thermal efficiency (%) of diesel engine is

(a) 32 - 38 (b) 25 - 32

(c) 36 - 46 (d) 20 - 26

35. Unit Hydrograph theory was enunciated by

(a) W.W. Horner (b) Le - Roy K. Shermen

(c) Robert E. Horten (d) Merril Bernard

Answers	**28. (a)**	**30. (c)**	**32. (c)**	**34. (a)**
	29. (b)	**31. (d)**	**33. (b)**	**35. (b)**

36. **Conversion efficiency (%) of solar energy of solar energy into electrical energy is**
    (a) 4 - 10 (b) 10 - 15
    (c) 15 - 20 (d) 20 - 25

37. **Calorific value (kcal/m^3) of biogas is about**
    (a) 6800 (b) 4500
    (c) 3400 (d) None of the above

38. **The protocol that web client and servers use to communicate with each other is called**
    (a) HTML (b) HTTP
    (c) URL (d) None of the above

39. **The correct equation from the following is**
    (a) Run off = Surface run off + Ground water flow
    (b) Run off = Surface run off – Ground water flow
    (c) Run off = Surface run off / Ground water flow
    (d) Run off = Surface run off × Ground water flow

40. **According to Robert E. Horton, the equation of infiltration capacity curve, is (where letters carry their usual meanings)**
    (a) $f = f_c (f_o - f_c) e^{kt}$ (b) $f = f_t - (f_o - f_c) e^{-kt}$
    (c) $f = f_t + (f_o - f_c) e^{-kt}$ (d) $f = f + (f_o - f_c) e_{kt}$

41. **Disinfection of drinking water involves removal of**
    (a) Bacteria (b) Turbidity
    (c) Odour (d) Colour

42. **ASPEE is famous for manufacturing**
    (a) Tractor (b) Power tiller
    (c) Ploughs (d) Sprayers

43. **Absolute humidity in air**
    (a) Decreases at higher altitudes
    (b) Increases at higher altitudes

Answers	36. (b)	38. (b)	40. (c)	42. (d)
	37. (b)	39. (a)	41. (a)	43. (a)

(c) Remains constant at all altitudes
(d) None of the above

44. Most important factor affecting threshing efficiency

(a) Peripheral speed of drum
(b) Cylinder concave clearance
(c) Moisture content of crop
(d) Feed rate

45. Horizontal component of pull perpendicular to the line of motion is called

(a) Draft (b) Side draft
(c) Pull (d) None of the above

46. Hollow cone nozzles employed on boom type of sprayers have spray angle between

(a) 30 - 60 (b) 40 - 60
(c) 60 - 95 (d) 100 - 150

47. Power sprayers are operated at a pressure (kg/cm^2)

(a) 5 - 10 (b) 10 - 20
(c) 20 - 55 (d) > 55

48. The standard height of a standard rain gauge, is

(a) 10 cm (b) 20 cm
(c) 30 cm (d) 40 cm

49. In India, rain fall is generally recorded at

(a) 8.30 AM (b) 10.30 AM
(c) 8.30 PM (d) 10.30 PM

50. In electrostatic spraying the total volume of liquid to be sprayed over one hectare is (in litre)

(a) < 1 (b) 50
(c) 100 (d) > 100

Answers	44. (a) 45. (b)	46. (c) 47. (c)	48. (c) 49. (a)	50. (a)

51. Separation of liquids from solids by the application of pressure is known as

(a) Extraction (b) Expression

(c) Filtration (d) Leaching

52. Stokes law is used to find out

(a) Terminal velocity (b) Drag coefficient

(c) Surface tension (d) Viscosity

53. The percentage of bran received from paddy

(a) 5 (b) 10

(c) 15 (d) 20

54. For determination of average annual precipitation in a catchment basin, the best method is

(a) Arithmetical method

(b) Thiessen's mean method

(c) Isohyetal method

(d) None of the above

55. 100 kg of soil is dried from 18 % to 13% (wb). The amount of water removed (kg) is

(a) 4.8 (b) 5.0

(c) 5.7 (d) 6.2

56. Fluid flow in circular pipe is said to be laminar if Reynolds number is

(a) < 1 (b) $= 1$

(c) < 2000 (d) > 4000

57. In heat transfer problem involving buoyancy effects, the relevant dimensionless number is

(a) Reynolds number (b) Nusselt's number

(c) Fourier number (d) Grashof number

Answers				
	51. (b)	53. (a)	55. (b)	57. (d)
	52. (a)	54. (c)	56. (c)	

58. **One unit of electricity is equal to**

(a) 1 KW (b) 1 hp

(c) 1 KW-h (d) 1 hp-h

59. **Among the following materials, the specific heat is the highest for**

(a) Glass (b) Silver

(c) Iron (d) Water

60. **A dimensionless ratio of inertia to viscous forces in case of fluid flow is better known as**

(a) Reynolds number (b) Froude's number

(c) Prandtl number (d) Stanton number

OOOOO

Answers	58. (c) 60. (a) 59. (d)

Model Set - 2

1. **The area irrigated through any source once in a year for a particular crop is known as**
   (a) Gross irrigated area
   (b) Net irrigated area
   (c) Gross net un - irrigated area
   (d) None of the above

2. **Bernoulli's theorem deals with the law of conservation of**
   (a) Mass (b) Momentum
   (c) Energy (d) Force

3. **Pitot tube is used for measurement of**
   (a) Pressure (b) Flow
   (c) Discharge (d) Velocity at a point

4. **Froude's number is defined as the ratio of**
   (a) Inertia force to viscous force
   (b) Inertia force to gravity force
   (c) Inertia force to pressure force
   (d) Inertia force to surface tension force

5. **A Current meter is a device used for measuring**
   (a) Discharge (b) Viscosity
   (c) Velocity (d) Pressure

Answers	1. (b) 3. (d) 5. (c) 2. (c) 4. (b)

6. **Hydraulic ram is pump which works on the principle of**
   (a) Water hammer (b) Centrifugal pump
   (c) Reciprocating action (d) None of the above

7. **If the speed of a centrifugal pump is doubled, the power required will be increased by**
   (a) Four times (b) Two times
   (c) Sixteen times (d) Eight times

8. **A plot between rainfall intensity versus time is called a**
   (a) Hydrograph (b) Isohyets
   (c) Hyetograph (d) Mass curve

9. **The wetted perimeter of a rectangular open channel of bottom width = 1.2 m, depth = 0.8 m is**
   (a) 0.68 (b) 1.74
   (c) 1.36 (d) 2.80

10. **Free board is provided to accommodate the embankment height against**
    (a) Overtopping (b) Overturning
    (c) Sliding (d) All of the above

11. **Hygrometer is used to measure**
    (a) Specific gravity (b) Humidity
    (c) Viscosity (d) Wind speed

12. **The line of equal depths of precipitation is known as**
    (a) Isobar (b) Isochrones
    (c) Isosines (d) Isohyets

13. **Rational formula is used to calculate**
    (a) Total discharge (b) Peak discharge
    (c) Runoff volume (d) None of the above

Answers	6. (a)	8. (c)	10. (a)	12. (d)
	7. (d)	9. (d)	11. (a)	13. (b)

14. TDR and Tensiometer is used to measure

(a) Moisture content (b) Pressure
(c) Frequency (d) Power

15. In wind erosion, movement of particle is carried out by

(a) Saltation (b) Surface creep
(c) Suspension (d) All of the above

16. Chute spillway is suitable in

(a) Low slope (b) Steep slope
(c) Moderate slope (d) None of the above

17. Indian Institute of Soil and Water Conservation (IISWC) is located at

(a) Dehradun (b) Jhansi
(c) Karnal (d) Jhodhpur

18. The drop head of drop spillway is

(a) More than 3 m (b) Less than 3 m
(c) Equal to 3 (d) None of the above

19. The emitter discharge of drip irrigation is

(a) 2 - 10 lit/ h (b) 2 - 10 lit/s
(c) 2 - 10 lit/ days (d) 2 - 10 lit/min

20. Terracing is constructed in the area of

(a) High rainfall
(b) Low rainfall
(c) Moderate to high rainfall
(d) None of the above

21. Drainage density is defined as the ratio of

(a) Length of individual stream to area
(b) Total length of stream to total area
(c) Area of stream to length of stream
(d) None of the above

Answers				
	14. (a)	16. (b)	18. (b)	20. (c)
	15. (d)	17. (a)	19. (a)	21. (b)

22. **Darcy's law is applicable for**

(a) Turbulent flow (b) Steady flow

(c) Unsteady flow (d) Laminar flow

23. **Water hp of a centrifugal pump at 10 lit/s and 38 m total head will be equal to**

(a) 5 (b) 4

(c) 6 (d) 3

24. **Propeller pump is suitable for**

(a) High discharge and high head

(b) High discharge and low head

(c) Low discharge and low head

(d) Low discharge and high head

25. **The total head of propeller pump is**

(a) 1 - 2 m (b) 1.5 - 2.5 m

(c) 1 - 2.5 m (d) > 2.5

26. **Void ratio is defined as the ratio of**

(a) Volume of void to total volume

(b) Volume of void to volume of solid

(c) Volume of void to volume of water

(d) None

27. **What is porosity (%), if particle density is 2.67 g/cc and bulk density is 1.45 g/cc ?**

(a) 42 (b) 47

(c) 44 (d) 46

28. **Hydrometer is used to measure**

(a) Soil structure (b) Specific gravity

(c) Soil texture (d) Bulk density

Answers	22. (d)	24. (b)	26. (b)	28. (c)
	23. (a)	25. (c)	27. (d)	

29. A soil sample has porosity of 40%, its void ratio is

(a) 0.06 (b) 0.28

(c) 0.40 (d) 0.66

30. Hydrological flood routing methods use

(a) Equation of continuity only

(b) Both momentum and continuity equation

(c) Energy equation only

(d) Equation of motion only

31. Central Ground Water Board was established by renaming

(a) Exploratory Tube wells Organization

(b) Extrapolatory Tube wells Organization

(c) Exploratory tundra well organization

(d) None of the above

32. Which of the following formation does not contain any ground water ?

(a) Aquifer (b) Aquifuge

(c) Aquitard (d) Aquiclude

33. The science which deals with surface stream is

(a) Limnology (b) Cryology

(b) Geomorphology (d) Potamology

34. The science that deals with occurrence, distribution & circulation of water is

(a) Hydrology (b) Hydrography

(c) Hydrometry (d) Hydraulics

35. The science which deals with lakes is known as

(a) Cryology (b) Limnology

(b) Geomorphology (d) Potamology

Answers				
	29. (d)	31. (a)	33. (d)	35. (b)
	30. (a)	32. (b)	34. (a)	

36. **The concept of hydrologic cycle was correctly postulated for the first time by**
   (a) Aristotle (b) Vitruvius
   (c) Plato (d) Leonardo da Vinci

37. **The percentage of earth covered by ocean is**
   (a) 32% (b) 50%
   (c) 71% (d) 96%

38. **The long term average runoff for India is**
   (a) 23% (b) 46%
   (c) 76% (d) 90%

39. **The self – recording rain gauge gives a continuous**
   (a) Intensity & duration of rainfall
   (b) hourly rainfall
   (c) one day rainfall
   (d) underground freshwaters

40. **Shrouding is provided in**
   (a) cavity type tube wells
   (b) slotted type tube wells
   (c) strainer type tube wells
   (d) perforated type tube wells

OOOOO

Answers			
	36. (b)	38. (b)	40. (b)
	37. (c)	39. (a)	

Model Set - 3

1. **The pump efficiency, motor efficiency and drive efficiency of a centrifugal pump set are 80%, 90% and 75%, respectively. The overall efficiency (%) of the pump set is**

   (a) 50 (b) 54

   (c) 60 (d) 75

2. **The hydraulic head in salt water is 30.0 m above the reference level that coincides with the bottom of the piezometer. Mass density of the saline ground water is 1025 kg/m^3. The length of the column of fresh water is**

   (a) 30.75 m (b) 3.075 m

   (c) 35.20 (d) 40.00 m

3. **Interception loss includes to**

   (a) Abstraction from plant leaves only

   (b) Stem flow only

   (c) Through flow only

   (d) All of the above

4. **NRCS Curve Number method is used for determination of** **[ARS - 2015]**

   (a) Direct runoff (b) Depth of rainfall excess

   (c) Both (d) Peak runoff rate

Answers	1. (b) 3. (a) 2. (a) 4. (a)

5. **In - Situ hydraulic conductivity is measured by** **[IARI PhD-2011]**

   (a) Pipe cavity method (b) Pond infiltration method
   (c) Auger hole method (d) Pumping test

6. **The crop coefficient (Kc) value is highest at the stage**

   (a) Intiation stage (b) Development stage
   (c) Mid stage (d) Harvesting stage

7. **The dimension of intrinsic permeability is**

   (a) m/s^2 (b) m/s
   (c) m^2 (d) None of the above

8. **A 12 hr unit hydrograph of a catchment is triangular in shape with a base width of 144 hr and a peak discharge value of 23 m^3 /s. this unit hydrograph refers to a catchment of area (m^2)**

   (a) 756 (b) 596
   (c) 1000 (d) None of the above

9. **Which of the following is correct ?**

   (a) 1 cusec = 0.0283 cumec
   (b) 1 cusec = 0.00283 cumec
   (c) 1 cusec = 0.283 cumec
   (d) None of the above

10. **An irrigation project is called major irrigation project when CCA (ha) is**

    (a) > 2000 (b) 2000 - 10000
    (c) < 10000 (d) > 10000

11. **Cosochcton wheel is used for measuring**

    (a) Runoff (b) Rainfall
    (c) Sedimentation (d) All of the above

Answers	5. (c)	7. (c)	9. (a)	11. (c)
	6. (c)	8. (b)	10. (d)	

12. The amount of water delivered to the field is 240 mm and water lost from field as runoff is 30mm and as evaporation is 10 mm, then what will be water application efficiency (%) ?

(a) 50 (b) 83.33

(c) 75.65 (d) 93.33

13. Planimeter is used for measurement of

(a) Area of irregular shape (b) Length of stream

(c) Diameter of basin (d) None of the above

14. Hydrograph is applicable for the basin / catchment areas (km^2)

(a) < 5000 (b) 50

(c) > 5000 (d) > 100000

15. Hooghoudt's equation is applicable for

(a) Dry areas (b) Irrigated areas

(c) Both (d) None of the above

16. Persian wheel is a device which is used for
[IARI PhD-2011]

(a) Water lifting (b) Soil moisture measurement

(c) ET (d) Erosion control

17. Rating curve is also called as

(a) Discharge - Area curve

(b) Discharge - Depth curve

(c) Elevation - Head curve

(d) None of the above

18. The safe entrance velocity (mm/s) of through a well screen is

(a) 0.3 (b) 3

(c) 30 (d) 300

Answers	12. (b)	14. (a)	16. (a)	18. (c)
	13. (a)	15. (b)	17. (b)	

19. **In designing regime canal by using Lacey's theory, the velocity depends on several factor except**

(a) Depth of water (b) Hydraulic mean depth
(c) Slope of channel (d) Silt factor

20. **The formula for estimation of ET using only temp. and day length is [ARS - 2015]**

(a) Thornthwaite formula (b) Penman formula
(c) Blaney criddle formula (d) All of the above

21. **A centrifugal pump has cavitation coefficient of 0.3. for a total head of 50 m, the NPSH (m) at the critical point will be**

(a) 12 (b) 15
(c) 10 (d) 166.7

22. **The term 'VES', with reference to geohydrology, stands for**

(a) Visibly Efficient Systems
(b) Variable Echo Sounding
(c) Visibly Equitable Systems
(d) Vertical Electrical Sounding

23. **Atmometer is used to measure**

(a) Rainfall (b) Wind velocity
(c) Evaporation (d) None of the above

24. **The specific yield of soil is 40%, porosity of soil is 80%, what will be specific retention (%)**

(a) 40 (b) 80
(c) 100 (d) 20

25. **The speed of pump is increased by four times, what will be effect on power ?**

(a) 16 (b) Same
(c) 64 (d) None of the above

Answers	19. (d)	21. (b)	23. (c)	25. (c)
	20. (c)	22. (d)	24. (a)	

26. The value of Froude number is lies between 4.5 - 9, the flow will be

(a) Undular (b) Oscillating

(c) Strong (d) Steady

27. If the Froude number is greater than one, then flow will be

(a) Laminar (b) Critical

(c) Supercritical (d) Subcritical

28. The uniformity coefficient is less than two, the material will be

(a) Uniform (b) Non - uniform

(c) Transition (d) None of the above

29. The water requirement (mm) of wheat crop is [ARS-2015]

(a) 1000 (b) 500

(c) 750 (d) 200

30. Strip cropping is suitable when the land slope (%) is

(a) > 10 (b) < 2

(c) < 6 (d) > 20

31. Rice field is irrigated by

(a) Furrow (b) Border

(c) Basin (d) Drip

32. If pH < 8.5, EC > 4dS/m, ESP < 15, the soil will be

(a) Acidic (b) Alkali

(c) Saline (d) Sodic

33. Confined aquifer is also called as

(a) Pressure aquifer (b) Non - artesian aquifer

(c) Both (d) None of the above

Answers				
	26. (d)	**28. (a)**	**30. (b)**	**32. (c)**
	27. (c)	**29. (b)**	**31. (c)**	**33. (c)**

34. **The NIR is 300mm and ET of crop is 60mm/day, the irrigation interval (day) of crop will be**

(a) 5 (b) 10
(c) 6 (d) 3

35. **The EC of irrigation water is 1 dS/m, what will be osmotic pressure (atm)**

(a) 36 (b) 3.6
(c) 0.036 (d) 0.36

36. **Rain shadow region in India is found to the**

(a) West of western ghats (b) East of western ghats
(c) West of eastern ghats (d) South of Himalayas

37. **Higher values of PH indicates ....**

(a) Stronger acids (b) Stronger alkalis
(c) Stronger contamination (d) None of the above

38. **One micron meter is equal to**

(a) 10^{-7} centi meter (b) 10^{-8} centi meter
(c) 10^{-4} centi meter (d) 10^{-10} centi meter

39. **The per capita water demand include**

(a) Domestic water demand only
(b) Domestic as well as commercial water demand
(c) Domestic, commercial, as well as industrial water demand
(d) None of the above

40. **The Symons rain gauge gives**

(a) Total depth
(b) Zones of occurrence and recharge
(c) Optimum sparing of wells
(d) All of the above

OOOOO

Answers				
	34. (a)	36. (b)	38. (c)	40. (a)
	35. (d)	37. (b)	39. (c)	

Model Set - 4

1. **The main constituent of biogas is**
   (a) Methane (b) Carbon dioxide
   (c) Hydrogen Sulphide (d) n-Butane

2. **The concentration of carbon dioxide (%) in atmosphere is**
   (a) 3 (b) 0.03
   (c) 0.3 (d) 30

3. **Full form of "ISO" is**
   (a) International Standardization Organization
   (b) Inter Organization for Standardization
   (c) International Organization for Standardization
   (d) None of the above

4. **The instrument accelerometer is used for measurement of**
   (a) Acceleration (b) Pressure
   (c) Tolerance (d) Vibration

5. **Vibration of sound is measure in**
   (a) Stoke (b) Erg
   (c) Pascal (d) Decibel

6. **What is the maximum length (m) of graded terrace is**
   (a) 40 - 50 (b) 300 - 500
   (c) 1200 - 1400 (d) 120 - 300

Answers			
	1. (a)	3. (c)	5. (d)
	2. (b)	4. (d)	6. (b)

7. **The anemometer instrument is used for measuring**
   (a) Velocity of gases (b) Velocity of flowing water
   (c) Pressure (d) Discharge

8. **ISO 14001, the world's most popular standard for**
   (a) Environmental Management
   (b) Safety management
   (c) Food safety and standard
   (d) Energy management

9. **Thermostat is used for**
   (a) Maintain the pressure
   (b) Maintain the correct temperature
   (c) Maintain the viscosity
   (d) Maintain the heat

10. **Drain spacing in unsteady flow condition is calculated by using .... equation**
   (a) Hooghoudts' (b) De Zeeuw Hellinga
   (c) Glover Dum (d) All of the above

11. **World Food Day is celebrated on**
   (a) 16 Nov. (b) 16 Dec.
   (c) 16 Sept. (d) 16 Oct.

12. **Which class of LUCC is most suitable for forestry ?**
   (a) V (b) VI
   (c) VIII (d) VII

13. **Which is the most common method of land levelling**
   (a) Plan inspection method
   (b) Contour adjustment method
   (c) Plane method
   (d) Profile method

Answers								
	7.	(a)	9.	(b)	11.	(d)	13.	(c)
	8.	(a)	10.	(c)	12.	(d)		

14. National Water Policy was constituted in the year

(a) 2012 (b) 1987

(c) 1989 (d) 2002

15. Conjunctive use refers to the application of water

(a) By augment (b) In time

(c) In space (d) All of the above

16. The Food Safety and Standards Act has been established in the year

(a) 2004 (b) 2009

(c) 2006 (d) 1989

17. Solar cell is connected in

(a) Parallel (b) Series

(c) Both (d) None of the above

18. Rice crop is irrigated by which irrigation method

(a) Border (b) Furrow

(c) Surge (d) Basin

19. If the speed of the pump is increased by 2 times, power is increased by

a. 2 times b. 4 times

c. 8 times d. 16 times

20. W/m.° C is the unit of

(a) Enthalpy (b) Entropy

(c) Thermal diffusivity (d) Thermal conductivity

21. Henderson equation for determination of EMC is based on

(a) Gibbs adsorption equation

(b) Chung - pfost equation

(c) Kelvin equation

(d) Harkins - jura equation

Answers	14. (b)	16. (c)	18. (d)	20. (d)
	15. (d)	17. (c)	19. (c)	21. (a)

22. **The ratio of actual vapour pressurein air water mixture and the saturated water vapour at same temperature is known as**
(a) Percentage humidity (b) Relative humidity
(c) Absolute humidity (d) None of the above

23. **Viscosity of oil is measured in terms of**
(a) Its resistance to flow (b) Its cooling effect
(c) Both (d) None of the above

24. **The moisture contained by a substance in excess of the equilibrium moisture is known as**
(a) Free moisture (b) Bound moisture
(c) Unbound moisture (d) Critical moisture

25. **The optimum moisture content (%) for harvesting of paddy is**
(a) 10 - 12 (b) 14 - 18
(c) 20 - 22 (d) 24 - 26

26. **Dry ice is**
(a) Frozen water (b) Frozen milk
(c) Frozen CO_2 (d) None of the above

27. **Conduction heat transfer is quantified by**
(a) Fourier's law (b) Laplace law
(c) Bukeplummer equation (d) Blake kozeny equation

28. **The amount of heat required to raise the temperature of a given object by unit volume is known as**
(a) Specific heat (b) Thermal conductivity
(c) Thermal capacity (d) Volumetric heat capacity

29. **Nusselt number in convective heat transfer is equivalent to the following in convective mass transfer**
(a) Schmidt number (b) Prandtl number
(c) Sherwood number (d) Archemedes number

Answers	22. (b) 23. (a)	24. (a) 25. (c)	26. (c) 27. (a)	28. (a) 29. (c)

30. The thermocouple is a common device for the measurement of

(a) Air flow (b) Wind velocity

(c) Pressure (d) Temperature

31. Mode of heat transfer in solids is

(a) Conduction (b) Convection

(c) Radiation (d) All of the above

32. The relationship between the equilibrium moisture content and RH for biological materials has been given by

(a) Hicks (b) Pearson

(c) Jenseen (d) Henderson

33. Which of these materials has the least thermal conductivity?

(a) Concrete (b) Water

(c) Glass (d) Air

34. Plank's equation is basically used for calculation of

(a) Drying time (b) Freezing time

(c) Boiling time (d) None of the above

35. At 100% RH, wet bulb temperature is .... Dew point

(a) Same as (b) More than

(c) Less than (d) None of the above

36. A chemical method used to measure the polluting potential of material in water

(a) BOD (b) COD

(c) OD (d) DO

37. The angle of repose is generally .... the angle of internal friction for grain of approximately at the same moisture content

(a) Smaller (b) Higher

(c) No change (d) None of the above

Answers	30. (d)	32. (d)	34. (b)	36. (a)
	31. (a)	33. (d)	35. (a)	37. (b)

38. A devise that qualitatively or quantitatively measures the dose of irradiation received by a food

(a) Dosimeter (b) Tintometer

(c) Jelmeter (d) Salometer

39. Two solutions are separated by a semi-permeable membrane. The one which is of lower osmotic pressure is called

(a) Hypotonic (b) Hypertonic

(c) Isoosmotic (d) Isomorphic

40. The osmosis taking place from solution to pure water by application of pressure greater than osmotic pressure on the solution is called

(a) Equilibrium osmosis (b) Irreversible osmosis

(c) Reversible osmosis (d) Reverse osmosis

41. The size (lakh hectare) of Micro watershed varies

(a) 0.0001 - 0.001 (b) 0.001 - 0.01

(c) 0.10 - 0.50 (d) 2 - 10

42. The salinity of irrigation water is measured in terms of

(a) EC (b) pH

(c) SAR (d) None of the above

43. Which of the following types of soil water is generally used by plant ?

(a) Hygroscopic water (b) Gravitational water

(c) Capillary water (d) All of the above

44. Airy equation is generally used for

(a) Shallow bin (b) Deep bin

(c) Both (d) None of the above

Answers	38. (a)	40. (d)	42. (a)	44. (c)
	39. (a)	41. (a)	43. (c)	

45. "Super passage" in canal irrigation refers to

(a) Irrigation channel passes over drainage channel
(b) Drainage channel passes over irrigation channel
(c) Both
(d) None of the above

46. Tensiometer reading indicates to

(a) Soil moisture content (b) Soil moisture potential
(c) Soil moisture tension (d) None of the above

47. Which sub-surface drainage system consists of laterals that enter the main drain at an angle, generally from both sides ?

(a) Random (b) Gridiron
(c) Interceptor (d) Herringbone

48. Specific capacity of aquifer refers to the ratio of

(a) Discharge vs drawdown
(b) Discharge vs radius of influence
(c) Both
(d) None of the above

49. Hyetograph refers to the ratio of

(a) Rainfall intensity vs time
(b) Discharge vs time
(c) Rainfall depth vs time
(d) Accumulated rainfall vs time

50. Specific yield of the aquifer is the properties of

(a) Confined aquifer (b) Unconfined aquifer
(c) Semi - confined aquifer (d) Both (b) and (c)

51. What is the unit of bulk density ?

(a) g/cc (b) Kg/cc
(c) both (d) None of the above

Answers	45. (b)	47. (d)	49. (a)	51. (c)
	46. (c)	48. (a)	50. (d)	

52. Which state of India having maximum cultivated areas is irrigated by canal ?

(a) Haryana (b) UP

(c) Bihar (d) Punjab

53. The moisture content (%) at field capacity for clay soil is

(a) 3 - 5 (b) 15 - 30

(c) 25 - 40 (d) None of the above

54. For an annual series arranged in decreasing order of magnitude, the return period for a magnitude listed at positon m in a total of N entries is

(a) m/N (b) m/(N+1)

(c) (N+1)/m (d) N/(m+1)

55. When two centrifugal pumps are arranged in parallel, the head is

(a) Remain constant (b) Increase

(c) Decrease (d) None of the above

56. The recommended safe value of longitudinal slope (%) for medium soil is

(a) 0.05 - 0.2 (b) 0.2 - 0.4

(c) 0.25 - 0.6 (d) None of the above

57. The Froude number of steady flow in permanent structure is

(a) 1 - 1.7 (b) 1.7 - 2.5

(c) 2.5 - 4.5 (d) 4.5 - 9

58. Puddling is done to

(a) Reduce percolation of water

(b) Kill weeds

(c) Pulverize soil

(d) Level the field

Answers	**52. (b)**	**54. (c)**	**56. (b)**	**58. (a)**
	53. (c)	**55. (a)**	**57. (d)**	

59. A reciprocating type mower is fitted with

(a) A reciprocating cutter bar

(b) A rotary blade

(c) Fixed knives

(d) Free swinging knives

60. Nozzle spacing on boom is governed by

(a) Type of spray (b) Height of crops

(c) Density of crop (d) All of the above

61. Rotary tillers are characterized by

(a) Low or negative draft requirement

(b) High power requirements

(c) Excessive pulverization

(d) All of the above

62. An adiabatic process taken place at constant

(a) Enthalpy (b) Heat

(c) Pressure (d) Temperature

63. A flowmeter that is independent of fluid density is

(a) Rotameter (b) Orifice meter

(c) Venturimeter (d) Electromagnetic flow meter

64. Gobar gas contains which gas in a larger proportion

(a) Methane (b) Ethane

(c) CO (d) CO_2

65. The temperature to which a vapor gas mixture must be cooled to saturate it is

(a) Dew point

(b) Wet bulb temperature

(c) Ambient temperature

(d) None of the above

Answers	**59. (a)**	**61. (d)**	**63. (a)**	**65. (a)**
	60. (d)	**62. (b)**	**64. (a)**	

66. Ergun equation is applicable to

(a) Turbulent flow (b) Laminar flow

(c) Porous media flow (d) Slit flow

67. If mean and median is 3 and 4 respectively, mode will be

(a) 4 (b) 6

(c) 1 (d) 18

68. In normal distribution

(a) Mean > mode > median

(b) Mean = median = mode

(c) Mode < median < mean

(d) Mode > median > mean

69. Slump test for concrete is carried out determine

(a) Durability (b) Strength

(c) Water content (d) Work ability

70. Reynolds number is the ratio of

(a) Inertia to gravity force

(b) Inertia to elastic force

(c) Inertia to viscous force

(d) Viscous to inertia force

71. The pressure plate apparatus is used for measuring

(a) Wilting point (b) Field capacity

(c) Pressure (d) All of the above

72. The number of first order stream is 16 and second order stream is 4, bifurcation ratio will be

(a) 4 (b) 0.25

(c) 64 (d) None of the above

OOOOO

Answers	66. (c)	68. (b)	70. (c)	72. (a)
	67. (b)	69. (d)	71. (b)	

Model Set - 5

1. **Drainage density refers to the ratio of**
   (a) Catchment area / total stream length
   (b) Total stream length / catchment areas
   (c) Number of streams / catchment areas
   (d) None of the above

2. **Line joining of equal travel time is known as**
   (a) Isohyet (b) Isohaline
   (c) Isotech (d) Isochrone

3. **Design of permanent structures is based on**
   (a) Hydraulic (b) Hydrologic
   (c) Structural (d) All of the above

4. **Campbell - Stokes instruments is used for measuring**
   (a) Sunshine hour (b) Wind speed
   (c) Wind direction (d) All of the above

5. **pH > 8.5, EC < 4, ESP > 15 refers to the properties of**
   (a) Saline soil (b) Alkali soil
   (c) Saline - alkali (d) None of the above

6. **If no. of 1st and 2nd order stream is 10 and 2 resp. what will be bifurcation ratio**
   (a) 3 (b) 4
   (c) 5 (d) 6

Answers	1. (b)	3. (d)	5. (b)
	2. (d)	4. (a)	6. (c)

7. Application efficiency = 50%, GIR = 24mm then NIR=

(a) 40 mm (b) 50 mm
(c) 10 mm (d) 12 mm

8. If discharge = 76 l/s, head = 10 m then WHP=

(a) 5 (b) 4
(c) 1 (d) 10

9. Berm is provided when embankment height

(a) Exceed 10 m (b) Exceed 20 m
(c) Below 10 m (d) None of the above

10. Soil moisture is done by

(a) Tensiometer (b) TDR
(c) FDR (d) All of the above

11. If speed of pump is increased by twice then what will be effects on discharge

(a) 2 (b) 4
(c) 8 (d) 1

12. Which state has highest canal irrigated cultivable command area ?

(a) Haryana (b) Punjab
(c) Uttar Pradesh (d) Bihar

13. Which crops have maximum water requirement ?

(a) Rice (b) Wheat
(c) Cotton (d) Sugarcane

14. What quantity of water needed to wheat and rice crops (mm) ?

(a) 500, 1700 (b) 1700, 500
(c) 500, 500 (d) 1700, 1700

Answers				
	7. (d)	9. (a)	11. (a)	13. (d)
	8. (d)	10. (d)	12. (c)	14. (a)

15. Parched aquifer is localized in .... aquifer

(a) Confined (b) Un - confined

(c) Semi - confined (d) None of the above

16. What is the efficiency of canal command ?

(a) 40% (b) 50%

(c) 20% (d) 60%

17. Single - auger hole method is used for determining the

(a) Hydraulic conductivity (b) Porosity

(c) Intrinsic permeability (d) Void ratio

18. Hooghoudt's formula is used for

(a) Hydraulic conductivity (b) Drain spacing

(c) Water - logging (d) None of the above

19. The pressure at the field capacity is

(a) 1/3 to 1/10 bar (b) 1/10 to 1/3 bar

(c) 1 bar (d) 0 bar

20. Movement of water in plants takes place due to

(a) Diffusion (b) Capillarity

(c) Pore (d) Osmosis

21. UHO is calculated by

(a) DRO/rainfall (b) DRO/effective rainfall

(c) DRO/runoff (d) None of the above

22. Kirpich formula is used for estimation of

(a) Stream length (b) Stream frequency

(c) Time of concentration (d) Relief of the above

23. Mean = Median = Mode characteristics of

(a) Poission distribution (b) Normal distribution

(c) Binomial distribution (d) All of the above

Answers	**15. (b)**	**17. (a)**	**19. (b)**	**21. (b)**	**23. (b)**
	16. (a)	**18. (b)**	**20. (d)**	**22. (c)**	

24. USLE is a function of

(a) RKLSCP (b) RKLSC

(c) RKLCP (d) None of the above

25. USLE doesn't accounts the

(a) Gully erosion (b) Rill erosion

(c) Both (d) None of the above

26. The amount of water drained from an area in one day is called

(a) Irrigation intensity (b) Drainage coefficient

(c) Irrigation coefficient (d) None of the above

27. Which kind of soil-water is used by plants ?

(a) Capillary (b) Gravitational

(c) Hygrosopic (d) All of the above

28. Phillip's equation, Horton's equation is used for estimation of

(a) Evaporation (b) Infiltration

(c) Percolation (d) Runoff

29. Presently, the average annual rainfall of India is (cm)

(a) 119 (b) 105

(c) 90 (d) 200

30. Rainfall simulator is used for measuring

[IARI PhD-2011]

(a) Rainfall (b) Sedimentation

(c) Runoff (d) Erosion

31. Current meter, anemometer and pitot- tube is used for measuring

(a) Current (b) Velocity

(c) Discharge (d) None of the above

Answers	24. (a)	26. (b)	28. (b)	30. (d)
	25. (a)	27. (a)	29. (a)	31. (b)

32. Rational formula is used for the estimation of

(a) Total discharge (b) Peak discharge

(c) Total runoff (d) None of the above

33. National water policy came into effect from

(a) 1989 (b) 1987

(c) 2005 (d) 2012

34. Propeller pump is used for and head is

(a) High discharge and low head, < 1m

(b) High head and low discharge, 1 - 2.5m

(c) High discharge and low head, 1 - 2.5

(d) None of the above

35. Central Soil and Water Conservation Research and Training Institute is renamed as

(a) IISWC (b) IIWSC

(c) ISWC (d) IISWCI

36. Consumptive use of a crop during growth, is the amount of

(a) Interception (b) Evaporation

(c) Transpiration (d) All of the above

37. Rain simulators are used for the determination of

(a) Evaporation (b) Precipitation

(c) Run off (d) Infiltration capacity

38. Discharge curve may be extended by logarithmic method if

(a) Cross section of river is uniform

(b) River is broader and shallower

(c) River is of any type

(d) None of the above

Answers	32. (b)	34. (c)	36. (d)	38. (a)
	33. (b)	35. (a)	37. (d)	

Model Set - 6

1. **One Ton of refrigeration implies to cooling effect equal to**
   (a) 1 ton of ice melted in 1 h
   (b) 200 BTU/min
   (c) 60 kCal/min
   (d) 144 BTU/sec

2. **In a ball mill or pebble mill, most of the size reduction is done by**
   (a) Shearing (b) Cutting
   (c) Impact (d) Crushing

3. **Particle density of an agricultural produce is 1.95 g/cc. The porosity of the bulk is 36%. The bulk density of the produce is**
   (a) 1 (b) 1.25
   (c) 1.50 (d) 1.75

4. **Percentage of fat in butter is**
   (a) 50 (b) 60
   (c) 70 (d) 80

5. **How much space the milk powder takes up as compared to milk ?**
   (a) One fifth (b) One sixth
   (c) One seventh (d) One eighth

Answers	1. (b) 3. (b) 5. (d) 2. (c) 4. (d)

6. A soil having EC < 4, pH > 8.5 and ESP>15 is known as [ARS - 2015]

(a) Saline soil (b) Sodic (alkali) soil

(c) Saline - alkali soil (d) None of the above

7. An imaginary lines connecting points of equal atmospheric pressures is called as

(a) Isobar (b) Isobath

(c) Isochor (d) Isopleth

8. A forms of precipitation having size of fine drops is < 0.5 mm and intensity is < 1mm/h is called as

(a) Rainfall (b) Drizzle

(c) Glaze (d) Snow

9. The evapotranspiration is measured by the instrument

(a) Tensiometer (b) Cryometer

(c) Lysimeter (d) Evaporimeter

10. Free board is provided to accommodate the embankment height against

(a) Overtopping (b) Overturning

(c) Sliding (d) All of the above

11. Hygrometer is used to measure

(a) Specific gravity (b) Humidity

(c) Viscosity (d) Wind speed

12. The line of equal depth of precipitation are known as

(a) Isobar (b) Isochrones

(c) Isosines (d) Isohyets

13. Rational formula is used to calculate

(a) Total discharge (b) Peak discharge

(c) Runoff volume (d) None of the above

Answers								
	6.	(b)	8.	(b)	10.	(a)	12.	(d)
	7.	(a)	9.	(c)	11.	(b)	13.	(b)

14. TDR and Tensiometer is used to measure

(a) Moisture content (b) Pressure

(c) Frequency (d) Power

15. In wind erosion, movement of particle is carried out by

(a) Saltation (b) Suspension

(c) Surface creep (d) All of the above

16. Chute spillway is suitable in

(a) Low slope (b) Steep slope

(c) Moderate slope (d) None

17. Indian Institute of Soil and Water Conservation (IISWC) is located at

(a) Dehradun (b) Jhansi

(c) Karnal (d) Jhodhpur

18. The drop head of drop spillway is

(a) More than 3 m (b) Less than 3 m

(c) Equal to 3 (d) None

19. The emitter discharge of drip irrigation is

(a) 2 - 10 lit/h (b) 2 - 10 lit/s

(c) 2 - 10 lit/days (d) 2 - 10 lit/min

20. Terracing is constructed in the area of

(a) High rainfall (b) Low rainfall

(c) Moderate to high rainfall (d) None of the above

21. 'Drainage density' is defined as the ratio of

(a) Length of individual stream to area

(b) Total length of stream to total area

(c) Area of stream to length of stream

(d) None of the above

Answers				
	14. (a)	16. (b)	18. (b)	20. (c)
	15. (d)	17. (a)	19. (a)	21. (b)

22. **Darcy's law is applicable for**
    (a) Turbulent flow (b) Steady flow
    (c) Unsteady flow (d) Laminar flow

23. **Water hp of a centrifugal pump at 10 lit/s and 38 m total head will be equal to**
    (a) 5 (b) 4
    (c) 6 (d) 3

24. **Propeller pump is suitable for**
    (a) High discharge and high head
    (b) High discharge and low head
    (c) Low discharge and low head
    (d) Low discharge and high head

25. **The total head of propeller pump is**
    (a) 1 - 2 m (b) 1.5 - 2.5 m
    (c) 1 - 2.5 m (d) > 2.5

26. **Void ratio is defined as the ratio of**
    (a) Volume of void to total volume
    (b) Volume of void to volume of solid
    (c) Volume of void to volume of water
    (d) None of the above

27. **What is porosity (%), if particle density is 2.67g/cc and bulk density is 1.45g/cc ?**
    (a) 42 (b) 47
    (c) 44 (d) 46

28. **Hydrometer is used to measure**
    (a) Soil structure (b) Specific gravity
    (c) Soil texture (d) Bulk density

Answers	22. (d) 23. (a)	24. (b) 25. (c)	26. (b) 27. (d)	28. (b)

29. **A soil sample has porosity of 40%, its void ratio is**

(a) 0.06 (b) 0.28

(c) 0.40 (d) 0.66

30. **Hydrological flood routing methods use**

(a) Equation of continuity only

(b) Both momentum and continuity equation

(c) Energy equation only

(d) Equation of motion only

OOOOO

Answers	29. (d) 30. (a)

Model Set - 7

1. **Location of permanent gully control structure is decided on the basis of**
   (a) Gully depth (b) Gully width
   (c) Gully bed slope (d) All of the above
2. **Permanent gully control structures are designed in respect of**
   (a) Hydrologic (b) Hydraulic
   (c) Structure (d) All of the above
3. **Hydraulic jump takes place, when flow enters from**
   (a) Sub - critical to supercritical
   (b) Supercritical to sub - critical
   (c) Uniform to non - uniform
   (d) All of the above
4. **Gully development is accomplished under**
   (a) 4 stage (b) 3 stage
   (c) 2 stage (d) 1 stage
5. **Seepage pressure always acts in the**
   (a) Opposite direction of flow
   (b) Lateral direction of flow
   (c) No specific direction
   (d) Direction of flow

Answers	1. (c)	3. (b)	5. (d)
	2. (d)	4. (a)	

6. **For soil conservation purpose, the land is usually classified in**
   (a) 10 (b) 6
   (c) 4 (d) 8

7. **Jhoom cultivation is normally practiced in**
   (a) Plain gangetic region
   (b) North east hilly region
   (c) Deccan plateau region
   (d) All of the above

8. **LVDT refers to**
   (a) Linear variable differential transducer
   (b) Linear variable differential transformer
   (c) Linear variable differential thermometer
   (d) None of the above

9. **Blinding of tiles refers to**
   (a) Trenching the dam
   (b) Laying the tiles
   (c) Joining the tiles
   (d) Covering the tiles with loose earth

10. **Potential evapotranspiration depends on**
    (a) Soil properties (b) Relative humidity
    (c) Types of crop (d) Elevation of the place

11. **The raindrops may have water particles of diameter**
    (a) Less than 0.5 mm (b) 0.5 - 6 mm
    (c) 2 - 7 mm (d) More than 7 mm

12. **The size of drizzle for uniform precipitation**
    (a) Less than 0.5 mm (b) 7 - 10 mm
    (c) 0.5 - 0.7 mm (d) 0.5 mm

Answers	**6. (d)**	**8. (d)**	**10. (b)**	**12. (a)**
	7. (b)	**9. (d)**	**11. (b)**	

13. **Penman method of estimating the evaporation from a free water surface is based on**
    (a) Energy balance (b) Mass transfer
    (c) Both above (d) Heat balance

14. **Water year refers to**
    (a) 1 June - 31 May (b) 1 Jan - 31 Dec
    (c) 1 April - 31 March (d) None of the above

15. **Turbine is used to convert**
    (a) Electrical to hydraulic
    (b) Hydraulic to electrical
    (c) Mechanical to electrical
    (d) Electrical to mechanical

16. **The particle size of silt**
    (a) > 0.002 mm (b) < 0.002 mm
    (c) > 2 mm (d) 0.02-0.002 mm

17. **The intensity of drizzle is**
    (a) 1 mm/h (b) 5 mm/h
    (c) < 1 mm/h (d) 6 mm/h

18. **Acidic soil is reclaimed by**
    (a) Lime (b) Gypsum
    (c) Drainage (d) None of the above

19. **Most salt tolerate crop is**
    (a) Wheat (b) Rice
    (c) Barley (d) All of the above

20. **Chartometer is used to measure**
    (a) Length of stream (b) Area of basin
    (c) Volume of stream (d) None of the above

Answers				
	13. (c)	15. (b)	17. (c)	19. (c)
	14. (a)	16. (d)	18. (a)	20. (a)

21. **Kinetic energy of raindrops depends on**
(a) Terminal velocity of raindrop
(b) Drop diameter
(c) Rainfall intensity
(d) All of the above

22. **The discharge per unit drawdown**
(a) Specific discharge (b) Specific yield
(c) Specific capacity (d) None of the above

23. **A geologic formation which neither transmits and not absorb water is called** **[ARS-2015]**
(a) Aquifuse (b) Aquitard
(c) Aquiclude (d) Aquifer

24. **Critical diameter of clods takes place the wind erosion is**
(a) 0.50 mm (b) 0.84 mm
(c) 0.10 mm (d) 1 mm

25. **Fine clay particles have low detachability but**
(a) High transportability (b) High transportive
(c) High soil loss (d) None of the above

26. **Rational formula is applicable when catchment size is**
(a) Less than 50 km^2 (b) 500 km^2
(c) 5 km^2 (d) 5000 km^2

27. **Unit hydograph formed when the catchment area is**
(a) 50 km^2 (b) 10000 km^2
(c) 5000 km^2 (d) None of the above

28. **The range of C_d for a venturimeter is**
(a) 0.6 - 0.7 (b) 0.8 - 0.9
(c) 0.7 - 0.8 (d) 0.95 - 0.99

Answers	21. (d)	23. (a)	25. (a)	27. (c)
	22. (c)	24. (b)	26. (a)	28. (d)

29. Rotameter is used for measuring

(a) Density of fluid (b) Velocity of fluid in pipes

(c) Discharge of fluid (d) Viscosity of fluid

30. Hypsometric curve shows the relationship between

(a) Relative height and relative areas

(b) Relief and relative areas

(c) Relative areas and relief

(d) None of the above

31. The permeability of aquifer increases with

(a) Increase in temperature

(b) Decrease in temperature

(c) Independent of temperature

(d) None of the above

32. How much of earth's water is fresh water

(a) 97% (b) 50%

(c) 3% (d) 1.5%

33. The velocity distribution across a pipe flowing in full

(a) Triangular (b) Parabolic

(c) Semi - circular (d) Circular

34. The concept used to evaluate the sprinkler irrigation system is

(a) Uniform intensity (b) Uniformity coefficient

(c) Coefficient of variance (d) Uniformity index

35. Flow in irrigation channel is assumed as

(a) Spatially varied (b) Gradually varied

(c) Uniform (d) Rapidly varied

36. Gabions are used for

(a) Flood control (b) Gully stabilization

(c) Storage of runoff (d) Flow measurement

Answers	29. (c)	31. (a)	33. (b)	35. (c)
	30. (a)	32. (c)	34. (b)	36. (b)

37. A rice field is irrigated by

(a) Border irrigation (b) Furrow irrigation
(c) Basin irrigation (d) Corrugation

38. The runoff from a watershed of 18 ha area having rainfall intensity of 10 cm/h and runoff coefficient 0.3 is

(a) $0.5\ m^3/s$ (b) $1\ m^3/s$
(c) $1.5\ m^3/s$ (d) $3\ m^3/s$

39. A centrifugal pump delivers 10 L/s against a total head of 7.5 m. The water power is

(a) 1 kW (b) 0.746 kW
(c) 10 kW (d) 7.5 kW

40. The cumulative infiltration equation is $I = 2\,t^{0.5}$ (I in cm and t in min). the instantaneous infiltration rate at 4minute from start will be

(a) 0.1cm/h (b) 0.5cm/h
(c) 1cm/h (d) 1.5cm/h

41. In - situ hydraulic conductivity is determined by

(a) Pumping test
(b) Permeameter
(c) Double ring infiltrometer
(d) Augar hole method

42. Combine use of surface and groundwater for crop production is called

(a) Consumptive use (b) Conjunctive use
(c) Joint use (d) Optimal use

43. Persian wheel is a

(a) Water lifting device
(b) Wind mill device
(c) Water distribution device
(d) None of the above

Answers				
	37. (c)	39. (b)	41. (d)	43. (a)
	38. (c)	40. (b)	42. (b)	

44. If the speed of rotor of pump is increase by 2 times, then the power of pump will be increase by

(a) 2 (b) 4

(c) 8 (d) None of the above

45. If bulk density of material is given as 600 kg/m^3 and true density as 1000 kg/m^3, it's porosity will be

(a) 20% (b) 40%

(c) 60% (d) 66.66%

46. Net irrigated area (m.ha) and arrange order of source of irrigation in India

(a) 64; Tubewell > Canal > Dugwell > Tanks

(b) 64; Tubewell < Canal < Dugwell < Tanks

(c) 70; Tubewell > Canal > Dugwell > Tanks

(d) 70; Tubewell < Canal < Dugwell < Tanks

47. Which of the highest infiltration capacity ?

(a) Forest land

(b) Grazed pasture

(c) Concrete pavement in airport

(d) Rockey land

48. If the field capacity of the soil is 30%, moisture before irrigation is 20%, the apparent specific gravity of the soil is 1.6, root zone depth 1m and daily consumptive use is 8m the irrigation interval is

(a) 25 days (b) 20 days

(c) 15 days (d) 10 days

49. Saline lands are mostly found in the region which are

(a) Temperate (b) Arid and semi arid

(c) Unirrigated (d) Humid

Answers	44. (d)	46. (a)	48. (b)
	45. (b)	47. (a)	49. (b)

50. **What size of electric motor is required for pumping 300 L/ min against a head of 50 m, assuming a pump efficiency of 65% ?**

(a) 7.5 hp (b) 5 hp
(c) 3 hp (d) 2 hp

51. **Poundal is unit of**

(a) Force (b) Mass
(c) Momentum (d) None of the above

52. **The viscosity decreases with .... in temperature and therefore permeability increase with .... in temperature.**

(a) increase, decrease (b) increase, decrease
(c) increase, increase (d) decrease, decrease

OOOOO

Answers	50. (b) 52. (c) 51. (a)

Rajasthan Public Service Commission (AE) Exam - 2013

Agricultural Engineering (SWCE)

1. **The angle of intersection of the two plane mirrors of an optical square is**

   (a) 0° (b) 45°

   (c) 60° (d) 90°

2. **For earth work estimation during terrace construction, we need to refer a standard ratio which is generally known as,**

   (a) rise : fall ratio (b) up : down ratio

   (c) cut : fill ratio (d) all of the above

3. **Size of a theodolite is specified by**

   (a) The length of the telescope

   (b) The diameter of the vertical circle

   (c) The diameter of the lower plate

   (d) The diameter of the upper plate

4. **The R.L. at the point A which is on the floor is 100 m and Back Side reading on A is 2.455 m. If the Fore Sight reading on point B, which is on the ceiling is 2.745 m, the R.L. of point B will be,**

   (a) 94.80 (b) 99.71

   (c) 100. 29 (d) 105. 20

Answers	1. (b) 3. (c) 2. (c) 4. (d)

5. **Among below given statements, only one statement is correct. Select the correct statement**
   (a) A contour is not necessarily a closed curve
   (b) A contour represents a ridgeline if the concave side of lower value contour lies towards the his her value contour
   (c) Two contours of different elevations do not cross each other except in case of an overhanging cliff
   (d) All of the above

6. **For analysis of rainfall intensities and durations in a given watershed we need to have at least following instrument installed therein,**
   (a) simple rain gauge
   (b) a water stage level recorder
   (c) a water current meter
   (d) NOA

7. **Which is the correct sequence of hydrologic processes initiated on natural catchment just after first rain storm in a monsoon season ?**
   (a) Rainfall > Surface runoff > Streamflow > Percolation > Evaporation
   (b) Rainfall > Interception > Depressionstorage > Infiltration > Surface runoff
   (c) Ground water recharge > Percolation > Evaporation > Surface runoff
   (d) NOA

8. **Direct runoff in a watershed is generally**
   (a) The sun of surface runoff, interflows, and channel precipitation
   (b) Surface runoff and channel flow
   (c) Surface runoff and groundwater recharge
   (d) NOA

Answers	5. (d) 7. (b) 6. (a) 8. (a)

9. **Watershed planning and management requires**
   (a) land use data (b) socio-economic data
   (c) hydrologic data (d) all of the above

10. **The most famous equation of empirical prediction model for computing peak runoff rate on small watersheds is**
   (a) Cook's Method (b) Rational Method
   (c) Phillip's Model (d) Holton's Model

11. **Hydrograph is the graphical representation of**
   (a) Runoff rate versus time
   (b) Infiltration rates versus time
   (c) Rainfall rates versus time
   (d) NOA

12. **The unit hydrograph of a specified duration can be used to synthesize or evaluate the unit hydrograph of storms of**
   (a) Same duration only
   (b) Same or shorter duration only
   (c) Same and longer durations only
   (d) Any duration

13. **Equation of continuity is based on the principle of conservation of**
   (a) Mass (b) Energy
   (c) Momentum (d) NOA

14. **Whenever there exists a sudden drop (say 1 or 2 m) on a channel bed, what kind of soil conservation structure is usually preferred at his point**
   (a) Graded bund
   (b) Deep trench
   (c) Drop inlet structure
   (d) Drop Structure

Answers			
	9. (d)	11. (c)	13. (a)
	10. (b)	12. (d)	14. (c)

15. The two broad categories of gullies predominantly found in India have cross sections of

(a) Rectangular shopped and parabolic shaped
(b) Straight sections and curved sections
(c) U-shaped and V-shaped cross sections
(d) NOA

16. Usually, the highest volume of soil loss per unit area occurs during

(a) Rill erosion (b) Sheet erosion
(c) Stream Bank erosion (d) Land Slides on hills

17. Two prominent grasses used for conserving soil and water offering effective control of soil erosion under Indian conditions is

(a) Doob grass and buffalo grass
(b) Vetiver (Khus) and Sacrum Munja (kloonj)
(c) Napier Grass and stylo grass
(d) both (a) and (c)

18. In terracing the field is divided into

(a) Large number of small channels
(b) Series of strips leveled independently
(c) Small check basins
(d) all of the above

19. Interception loss is

(a) More towards end of a storm
(b) More at the middle of a storm
(c) More at the beginning of a storm
(d) Uniform throughout the storm

20. In a chute spillway the flow is usually

(a) Uniform (b) Subcritical
(c) Critical (d) Supercritical

Answers	**15. (a)**	**17. (b)**	**19. (c)**
	16. (c)	**18. (b)**	**20. (d)**

21. The highly wind erosion affected state in India is

(a) M.P. (b) Gujarat

(c) A.P. (d) Rajasthan

22. Drip fertigation depicts the process of

(a) Applying fresh irritation water

(b) Applying soluble fertilized through drip pipes while irrigation fields

(c) Applying combination of drip and sprinkler method

(d) All of the above

23. Lines joining the equal depth of water table are known as

(a) Water table lines (b) Isobar lines

(c) Isobath lines (4) NOA

24. The ratio of total cropped land and the actual net cultivated land in a given catchment is known as

(a) Cropped area

(b) Sown area

(c) Cropping intensity

(d) All of the above

25. The capacity of a farm pond is computed by adopting which formula

(a) Trapezoidal rule

(b) Clark's formula

(c) Rational formula

(d) All of the above

26. The term "middle third" rule is generally used while designing the check dams. What does it really deal in stich designing process ?

(a) Crushing (b) Sliding

(c) Breaking (d) None of the above

Answers			
	21. (d)	23. (c)	25. (a)
	22. (b)	24. (c)	26. (b)

27. **Which of the following is not the component of a water harvesting pond ?**
    (a) Emergency outlet
    (b) Inlet conduit/channel/weir
    (c) Earthen embankment
    (d) Drainage well

28. **Soil moisture tension at field capacity varies from**
    (a) 0 to 0.1 atmosphere (b) 0.1 to 0.33 atmosphere
    (c) 0.33 to 5 atmosphere (d) 5 to 30 atmosphere

29. **Water use efficiency is simply defined as**
    (a) Crop yield per unit volume of irrigation water utilized
    (b) % of irrigation water' actually consumed by the plants
    (c) Ratio of water delivered at field and the water remained unutilized at the end
    (d) NOA

30. **A tubewell with an average discharge of 250 litres per minute is used to irrigate one hectare wheat crop in 40 hours. What is the average depth of irrigation ?**
    (a) 40 mm (b) 50 mm
    (c) 25 mm (d) 60 mm

31. **Depth of irrigation water required to brings the soil moisture content of a given soil upto its field capacity is called**
    (a) Hygroscopic water (b) Equivalent moisture
    (c) Soil moisture deficiency (d) Peculiar water

32. **The velocity of flow in an open channel can be measured withthe help of**
    (a) v - notch (b) infiltrometer
    (c) water current meter (d) NOA

Answers	27. (d)	29. (a)	31. (c)
	28. (b)	30. (d)	32. (c)

33. The difference between advance and recession curve in border strip denotes

(a) overlapping time (b) opportunity time

(c) time of concentration (d) depth of ponding

34. Depth of water required for a crop excluding rainfall is called

(a) Base (b) Duty

(c) Delta (d) none of these

35. Which pairs of components are most vital while designing a grassed waterway ?

(a) Permissible flow velocity and type of grass

(b) Type of soil and volume of water

(c) Permissible velocity of flow and most economical channel cross section

(d) All of the above

36. Which equation is most commonly used for designing drainage system in an agricultural catchment, specifically the distance and configurations of drainage tiles etc.

(a) USDA equation (b) USLE

(c) Hooghoudt's equation (d) All of the above

37. Drainage coefficient in a given area can be defined as

(a) Ratio of total channel length to the total drainage area

(b) Ratio of total channel length to number of channels in the area

(c) Both (a) and (b)

(d) NOA

38. When a channel receive supply from ground water it is known as

(a) Ground water recharging (b) Effluent stream

(c) Effective stream (d) NOA

Answers	33. (b)	35. (c)	37. (d)
	34. (c)	36. (c)	38. (b)

39. Catchment area can be described as extent of area, where

(a) Encompassing all net work of small and big natural channels
(b) Total area whose runoff water passes through the single outlet point
(c) Both (a) and (b)
(d) NOA

40. The ratio of the quantity of water delivered to the field and water diverted from the source is known as

(a) Water conveyance efficiency
(b) Water application efficiency
(c) Water rise efficiency
(d) NOA

41. Specific speed of a pump is

(a) Directly proportional to the discharge
(b) Proportional to the square of the discharge
(c) Proportional to cube root of the discharge
(d) Proportional to square root of the discharge

42. The major component used in a centrifugal pump is

(a) Turbine (b) Impeller
(c) Valve inlet (d) All of the above

43. The primps which are installed completely under water, including motor is called

(a) Displacement pump (b) Submersible pump
(c) Solar pump (d) NOA

44. Propeller pump is used for

(a) low head and low discharge
(b) high head and low discharge
(c) low head and high discharge
(d) high head and high discharge

Answers	39. (c)	41. (a)	43. (b)
	40. (a)	42. (b)	44. (c)

45. The conveyance efficiency of canal usually depends upon

(a) Length of canal, soil types and the permeability

(b) Only canal flow rates

(c) Gates of canal

(d) NOA

46. An artesian aquifer is the one where

(a) Water surface under fire ground is at atmospheric pressure

(b) Water is under pressure between two impervious layers

(c) Water table serves as upper surface of zone of saturation

(d) NOA

47. A flow in which the velocity of fluid at a particular fixed point does not change with time is known as

(a) Unsteady flow (b) Laminar flow

(c) Turbulent flow (d) NOA

48. Maximum practical drawdown in a well is the distance between

(a) Static water level and middle of well screen

(b) Static water level and top of well screen

(c) Static water level and pumping water level

(d) Static water level and end of well screen

49. For good uniformity the overlap should be at least .... percent of the wetted diameter.

(a) less than 20 (b) 20 - 50

(c) at least 65 (d) More than 75

OOOOO

Answers	45. (a) 46. (a) 47. (d) 48. (c) 49. (c)

Uttarakhand Public Service Commission (AE) Exam - 2012 Agricultural Engineering (SWCE)

1. **A planimeter is used to**
   (a) measure length of contour lines
   (b) measure area of a closed plan
   (c) draw contour lines
   (d) survey in water

2. **The dimension of calorie are**
   (a) $ML^2 T^{-2}$ (b) $ML T^{-2}$
   (c) $ML^{-2} T^{-1}$ (d) $ML^2 T^{-1}$

3. **The parameter which is least important for selection of a pump for irrigation is**
   (a) Discharge (b) Horsepower
   (c) Head (d) Quality of water

4. **In an open channel water flows due to**
   (a) force of gravity (b) atmosphere pressure
   (c) dynamic pressure (d) static pressure

5. **Hydraulic jump is used to**
   (a) increase flow energy (b) dissipate flow energy
   (c) reduce depth of flow (d) NOA

Answers	1. (b) 3. (d) 5. (b) 2. (a) 4. (a)

6. If the value of Froude number is less than one, the flow will be

(a) Critical flow (b) Super critical flow

(c) Sub-critical flow (d) Laminar flow

7. When both ends of a survey line are not intervisible, then the method of ranging used as

(a) Direct ranging method

(b) Indirect ranging method

(c) Improper ranging method

(d) NOA

8. In an open channel flow, the specific energy at critical flow condition would be

(a) Minimum (b) Maximum

(c) Average (d) Zero

9. One square kilometre (km^2) area is equal to (hectare)

(a) 100 (b) 1000

(c) 10 (d) 40

10. A type of survey in which the curvature of earth is taken into account is called as

(a) Plane table survey

(b) Geodetic survey

(c) Reconnaissance survey

(d) NOA

11. The upper most line of seepage in an earth dam is also called as

(a) Water pressure line

(b) Hydraulic gradient line

(c) Phreatic line

(d) Parabolic seepage line

Answers	**6. (c)**	**8. (a)**	**10. (b)**
	7. (b)	**9. (a)**	**11. (c)**

12. **Contour lines, cross ridge lines and valley lines are on the angle of**

(a) 45° (b) 90°

(c) 180° (d) 60°

13. **Contour line is a line joining the points of**

(a) equal elevation (b) equal slope

(c) equal bearing (d) NOA

14. **Which is the method related to plane table survey ?**

(a) Conduction method

(b) Radiation method

(c) Multiplication method

(d) Subtraction method

15. **The most suitable structure for reducing channel grades is**

(a) drop spillway (b) chute spillway

(c) drop inlet spillway (d) culvert

16. **When water is added to cement ?**

(a) Chemical reaction starts

(b) Heat is absorbed

(c) Heat is generated

(d) NOA

17. **Irregular area may be computed by an instrument known as the**

(a) Pantograph (b) Planimeter

(c) Passometer (d) Speedometer

18. **The sum of interior angle's of a closed traverse is**

(a) (2n – 4) × 90° (b) (2n + 4) × 90°

(c) (n – 4) × 90° (d) (n + 4) × 90°

Answers	12. (b) 13. (a)	14. (b) 15. (b)	16. (c) 17. (b)	18. (a)

19. Pumps based on method of energy imparted to the liquid are

(a) Positive displacement pump

(b) Variable displacement pump

(c) Both (a) and (b)

(d) NOA

20. The depth from which the liquid has to be lifted by the pump is known as

(a) Suction head (b) Delivery head

(c) Velocity head (d) NOA

21. The cross slope of the road is called

(a) Road crown (b) Road gradient

(c) Road camber (d) NOA

22. The quadrantal bearing or reduced bearing in quadrantal system never exceeds

(a) 90° (b) 180°

(c) 270° (d) NOA

23. Where is the submersible pump located ?

(a) over water in the well

(b) submerged in water but above draw down level

(c) submerged in water below draw down level

(d) kept over ground

24. A suitable pump for a situation where flooding is a hazard is

(a) Turbine pump (b) Centrifugal pump

(c) Submersible pump (d) NOA

25. A contour line represents point of

(a) Different elevations (b) Equal elevations

(c) The ridge line (d) The valley line

Answers				
	19. (b)	21. (a)	23. (c)	25. (b)
	20. (a)	22. (b)	24. (b)	

26. **Increasing contours towards centre represents a**

(a) Ridge (b) Valley
(c) Hillock (d) Pond

27. **Batter slope in bench terraces is primarily provided for**

(a) Moisture retention
(b) Controlling sloughing
(c) Both (a) & (b)
(d) Stability to the fill material

28. **Contour lines on a map cut one another only in case of**

(a) overhanging cliff (b) ridge line
(c) valley line (d) flat land

29. **When the chain is found to be too long, the error in measuring distance will be**

(a) Positive (b) Negative
(c) Compensating (d) NOA

30. **The correction to be applied to each 30 m chain for a line measured along 60° slope could be (m)**

(a) 3 (b) 10 (c) 15 (d) 45

31. **A pipe of circular cross section of diameter 'd' is flowing half-full. It's hydraulic radius will be**

(a) d (b) d/2 (c) d/3 (d) d/4

32. **The hydraulic depth for a full-flowing semi-circular channel of radius 'r' will be**

(a) r (b) r/2
(c) r/4 (d) $r^2/2$

33. **If the Froude number for hydraulic jump is 4.0, it is called**

(a) Oscillating jump (b) Weak jump
(c) Steady jump (d) Strong jump

Answers	26. (a)	28. (a)	30. (c)	32. (b)
	27. (d)	29. (b)	31. (d)	33. (a)

34. In a submersible pump, the motor and pump are such that

(a) only pump is submerged
(b) only motor is submerged
(c) both motor and pump are submerged
(d) NOA

35. Which of the following glass is used in doors and windows ?

(a) Soda lime glass (b) Lead glass
(c) Boro silicate glass (d) None of the above

36. If the speed of a pump is doubled then the head developed by it will be

(a) Double (b) Three times
(c) Four times (d) Half

37. The required shaft power for a centrifugal pump will be equal to

(a) Water horsepower / pump efficiency
(b) Water horsepower × pump efficiency
(c) Pump efficiency / water horsepower
(d) two times of water horsepower

38. A pump will not lift water, when

(a) direction of impeller rotation is reverse
(b) pump is not primed
(c) speed of impeller is not high
(d) both (a) and (b)

39. Pump efficiency is higher when

(a) impeller blades are bent backward
(b) impeller are with straight blades
(c) impeller blades are ending radially
(d) all of the above

Answers			
	34. (c)	36. (c)	38. (d)
	35. (b)	37. (a)	39. (a)

40. **In a multistage centrifugal pump**
   (a) two or more impellers are keyed to a single shaft
   (b) impellers are surrounded by guide vanes
   (c) pressure is built in steps
   (d) all of the above

41. **Dynamic similarity between model and prototype means**
   (a) the similarity of forces (b) the similarity of motion
   (c) the similarity of shape (d) NOA

42. **Strip cropping for erosion control is more effective when it is practiced under**
   (a) Terracing (b) Crop rotation
   (c) Bunding (d) Mono-cropping

43. **In vertical turbine pump the shaft used made of stainless steel in the length of only**
   (a) 1 m (b) 2 m
   (c) 2.5 m (d) 3 m

44. **Method of surveying in which the field work and plotting are done simultaneously is called**
   (a) Plane tabling (b) Mapping
   (c) Compass surveying (d) Drawing

45. **The elevation of a point can be determined by using the instrument named**
   (a) Cross staff (b) Optical square
   (c) Dumpy level (d) Prismatic compass

46. **In a pumping system, a float valve is placed at the**
   (a) end of delivery pipe
   (b) end of suction pipe
   (c) between suction pipe
   (d) inside impeller of the pump

Answers	40. (a)	42. (b)	44. (a)	46. (b)
	41. (a)	43. (a)	45. (c)	

47. **Filling water before its operation in a centrifugal pump is called**

(a) testing of pump (b) energizing of pump

(c) priming of pump (d) none of the above

48. **The specific energy diagram is a plot between specific energy and flow depth for aconstant**

(a) Turbulence (b) Discharge

(c) Specific force (d) Specific yield

49. **For high degree of precision measurement which type of tape is more suitable**

(a) Cloth tape (b) Metallic tape

(c) Steel tape (d) Invar tape

50. **Mechanical efficiency of a centrifugal pump is about**

(a) 40% (b) 60%

(c) 90% (d) NOA

51. **Propeller pump are used for**

(a) low head and low discharge

(b) high head and low discharge

(c) high head and high discharge

(d) low head and high discharge

52. **Gauge pressure at a point is equal to**

(a) absolute pressure plus atmospheric pressure

(b) absolute pressure minus atmospheric pressure

(c) vacuum pressure plus absolute pressure

(d) NOA

53. **The operation of levelling to determine the elevation between two points is known as**

(a) Simple levelling (b) Fly levelling

(c) Differential levelling (d) NOA

Answers				
	47. (c)	49. (d)	51. (d)	53. (c)
	48. (b)	50. (b)	52. (b)	

54. The velocity with which water approaches a weir is called

(a) Velocity of flow (b) Velocity of approach

(c) Velocity of Nappe (d) NOA

55. The discharge capacity and efficiency of multistage pump is almost

(a) same as for a single stage of the pump

(b) less than as single stage pump

(c) more than single stage pump

(d) NOA

56. In gear pump number of gears fitted in a housing are

(a) one (b) two

(c) three (d) four

57. In an optical square, the mirrors are fixed at an angle of

(a) 30° (b) 60°

(c) 45° (d) 90°

58. The impeller used for pumping sewerage is

(a) Open (b) Semi-open

(c) Non-clog (d) Closed

59. Only linear measurements are made by

(a) Chain survey

(b) Plane table survey

(c) Compass survey

(d) Theodolite survey

60. Gear pump is a

(a) Non-positive displacement pump

(b) Positive displacement pump

(c) Centrifugal type pump

(d) NOA

Answers	54. (b)	56. (b)	58. (a,b)	60. (b)
	55. (a)	57. (c)	59. (a)	

61. **Contour lines will always be**
    (a) Parallel to general slope of the field
    (b) Across the general slope of the field
    (c) They can be in any direction
    (d) NOA

62. **A mechanical device used to increase the pressure energy of a liquid is called as**
    (a) Machine (b) Engine
    (c) Pump (d) All above

63. **The object of a survey is to prepare plan or map so that it may represent the area on a**
    (a) Vertical plane (b) Horizontal plane
    (c) Circular plane (d) NOA

64. **In Metric chain the length of each link of the chain is (mm)**
    (a) 100 (b) 150
    (c) 200 (d) 250

65. **A one cubic meter per second discharge is equal to (litre/second)**
    (a) 100 (b) 10
    (c) 1000 (d) 50

66. **The length of Engineer's chain is (ft)**
    (a) 50 (b) 100
    (c) 200 (d) 400

67. **The method of plane table surveying which is performed by having a single station only**
    (a) Radiation method (b) Intersection method
    (c) Traversing method (d) NOA

Answers	**61. (a)**	**63. (b)**	**65. (c)**	**67. (a)**
	62. (c)	**64. (c)**	**66. (b)**	

68. **The method used to balance the traverse is based on**
   (a) Rise and fall method (b) Bowditch's rule
   (c) Collimation method (d) NOA

69. **Which of these pumps are also called the axial flow pump ?**
   (a) Centrifugal pump (b) Gear pump
   (c) Propeller pump (d) NOA

70. **If Reynold's number for a flow is 1500, the flow would be**
   (a) Laminar flow (b) Turbulent flow
   (c) Transient flow (d) NOA

71. **The impeller of a centrifugal pump is generally made of**
   (a) Steel (b) Aluminium
   (c) Cast Iron (d) Copper

72. **In pipe flows, the frictional head loss is inversely proportional to**
   (a) Length of pipe
   (b) Square of length of pipe
   (c) Diameter of pipe
   (d) Square of diameter of pipe

73. **If the slopes of channel bottom, hydraulic line and energy line are equal the flow would be**
   (a) Uniform (b) Non-uniform
   (c) Steady (d) NOA

74. **In a rectangular open channel, the critical flow across at 2 m depth of flow, the specificenergy at this depth will be (m)**
   (a) 1 (b) 2
   (c) 3 (d) 4

Answers	68. (b)	70. (a)	72. (c)	74. (c)
	69. (c)	71. (a)	73. (a)	

75. **In an open channel flow, the specific force for critical flow condition will be**

(a) Zero (b) Average

(c) Maximum (d) Minimum

76. **When Mach number is more than 1, the speed of object will be**

(a) Sonic (b) Super-sonic

(c) Sub-sonic (d) none of the above

77. **Dip of magnetic needle at equator is (degree)**

(a) zero (b) 45

(c) 90 (d) 180

78. **Which pump operates using the compressed air injected into water ?**

(a) Vertical turbine pump (b) Air lift pump

(c) Submersible pump (d) Gear pump

79. **The speed of a centrifugal pump N, and its discharge Q are related as**

(a) $Q \propto N$ (b) $Q \propto N^2$

(c) $Q \propto N^3$ (d) $Q \propto N^{1/2}$

80. **Power requirement of a centrifugal pump will become maximum, when increasing**

(a) Diameter only (b) Speed of pump only

(c) Diameter and speed both (d) NOA

81. **Head developed by a centrifugal pump is proportional to**

(a) Square of speed of pump

(b) Speed of pump

(c) Cube of speed of pump

(d) Square root of speed of pump

Answers	**75. (d)**	**77. (a)**	**79. (a)**	**81. (a)**
	76. (b)	**78. (b)**	**80. (c)**	

82. **A theodolite can measure**
(a) Difference in level (b) Bearing of line
(c) Zenith angle (d) All of the above

83. **In brick wall construction when alternative courses have header and stretcher, the bond is called**
(a) English bond (b) Flemish bond
(c) Alternate bond (d) NOA

84. **Nozzle and venturi are main components of**
(a) Centrifugal pump (b) Jet pump
(c) Reciprocating pump (d) Submersible pump

85. **Open impeller is used in pumps to draw**
(a) Clear water
(b) Water mixed with sand and clay
(c) Viscous liquid
(d) NOA

86. **The channels of first kind have a unique depth in uniform flow for a given discharge. This unique depth is called as**
(a) Special depth (b) Critical depth
(c) Uniform depth (d) Alternate depth

87. **A hand pump is an example of which type of pump**
(a) Turbine pump (b) Centrifugal pump
(c) Submersible pump (d) Reciprocating pump

88. **A rectangular cross section is the most efficient when the flow depth is equal to**
(a) Bottom width
(b) Half of bottom width
(c) Two times of bottom width
(d) Four times of bottom width

Answers	**82. (d)**	**84. (b)**	**86. (c)**	**88. (b)**
	83. (b)	**85. (b)**	**87. (d)**	

89. **If pump is not lifting required amount of water then the pump is suffering with the problem of**
    (a) speed may be very high
    (b) suction head may be very low
    (c) suction pipe may be chocked
    (d) NOA

90. **Water can be lifted from depth beyond 45 meters by**
    (a) Centrifugal pump (b) Submersible pump
    (c) Propeller pump (d) Jet pump

91. **The sum of pressure head and elevation head is known as**
    (a) Kinetic head (b) Critical head
    (c) Piezometric head (d) Acceleration head

93. **Delta represents**
    (a) a crop total depth of water required
    (b) seasonal water requirement
    (c) daily water requirement
    (d) monthly water requirement

94. **Minor irrigation project have cultural command area**
    (a) less than 2000 hectares
    (b) 10,000 hectares
    (c) 2000 to 10,000 hectares
    (d) 1500 hectares

95. **At permanent wilting point soil moisture tension is**
    (a) 5 to 50 bars (b) 50 bars
    (c) 5 to 10 bars (d) 7 to 32 atm

96. **A tile drainage system consists of**
    (a) Tile drain (b) Sub-main
    (c) Drainage outlet (d) All of the above

Answers				
	89. (c)	91. (c)	94. (a)	96. (d)
	90. (b)	93. (a)	95. (d)	

97. A drainage canal discharges 0.2 m^3/sec of water from 250 hectares area, the drainage coefficient of the land will be

(a) 2 mm (b) 7 mm
(c) 10 mm (d) 7 cm

98. If the net amount of irrigation is 8 cm and field efficiency is 75%, the gross amount of water to be applied to the field will be

(a) 10.66 cm (b) 8.75 cm
(c) 10.66 mm (d) 8.75 mm

99. The velocity of water through pipes and open channels may be estimated by

(a) Chezy's formula (b) Manning's formula
(c) both (a) and (b) (d) None of the above

100. A centrifugal pump has a discharge of 5400 litres per minute with total head of 20 m. If the overall efficiency of the pumpset is 64%, the size of the required electric motor will be

(a) 24 HP (b) 37.5 HP
(c) 28 HP (d) 20 HP

101. If gross irrigation is 15 cm and irrigation efficiency is 80%, then net irrigation will be

(a) 10 cm (b) 12 cm
(c) 15 cm (d) 19 cm

102. Evapotranspiration is directly measured by

(a) Penman – Monteith method
(b) Blaney – Criddle method
(c) Penman Method
(d) Lysimeter method

Answers			
	97. (b)	99. (c)	101. (b)
	98. (a)	100. (b)	1C2. (d)

103. The gauge used to measure the depth of flow over a weir is located upstream of a weir at a distance of about

(a) twice the approximate head

(b) thrice the approximate head

(c) four times the approximate head

(d) equal to approximate head

104. For medium loam soils, the length of the border should be

(a) 60 – 120 m (b) 100 – 180 m

(c) 150 – 300 m (d) 300 – 500 m

105. For better uniformity of water application in sprinkler irrigation percent overlap should

(a) decrease with the increase in wind velocity

(b) increase with the increase in wind velocity

(c) be 50%

(d) be 70%

106. If 'q' be the curvature angle of an open ditch the radius of curvature (R) of the open ditch in metres can be calculated using the formula

(a) R = 15/sin(q/4) (b) R = 15/sin(q/2)

(c) R = 15/cos(q/4) (d) R = 15/cos(q/2)

107. 20 – 40 rule is used to compute the

(a) head loss in a drainage pipe

(b) slope of drainage ditch

(c) design discharge below the function point of the ditch

(d) hydraulic radius of drainage ditch

108. The spacing of mole drain varies from

(a) 1.5 – 2.5 m (b) 10 – 15 m

(c) 12 – 13 m (d) 5 – 10 m

Answers			
	103. (c)	105. (d)	107. (c)
	104. (b)	106. (b)	108. (d)

109. The drainable porosity of clay soil varies from

(a) 10 – 15% by volume (b) 18 – 35% by volume
(c) 3 – 11% by volume (d) 15 – 20% by volume

110. The relationship between porosity (n) and void ratio (e) is given by

(a) $n = e/(1 + e)$ (b) $e = n/(1 - n)$
(c) $n = (1 + e)/e$ (d) Both (a) and (b)

111. In sprinkler irrigation normally water application is considered to be satisfactory when

(a) Uniformity coefficient (Cu) is 100 percent
(b) Uniformity coefficient is 80% or above
(c) Water is uniformly distributed
(d) All the above

112. The depth of flow over a sharp crested rectangular weir should not be more than

(a) width of weir
(b) half of the crest width
(c) two-third of the crest width
(d) three-fourth of the crest width

113. A soil sample has a porosity of 40 percent, its void ratio is

(a) 0.06 (b) 0.28
(c) 0.40 (d) 0.66

114. Minimum slope of an earthen channel for polyethylene lining is

(a) 1.5 : 1 (b) 2 : 1
(c) 2.5 : 1 (d) 3 : 1

115. The principle of working of a meter gate is

(a) Free flow circular orifice
(b) Free flow rectangular orifice

Answers	109. (c)	111. (b)	113. (d)	115. (c)
	110. (d)	112. (c)	114. (c)	

(c) Submerged flow circular orifice

(d) Submerged flow rectangular orifice

116. The capacity of major distributary in India usually varies from

(a) 0.75 to 5.5 cusec (b) 4.0 to 8.5 cumec

(c) 4.0 to 8.5 cusec (d) 0.75 to 5.5 cumec

117. Laminar flow condition in open channel exists if the Reynold's number is less than

(a) 500 (b) 2000

(c) 1500 (d) 1000

118. How the emitter flow varies with kinematic viscosity in non - orifice type emitters ?

(a) Directly proportional

(b) Inversely proportional

(c) Square root of kinematic viscosity

(d) NOA

119. A parshall flume can be used conveniently on

(a) flatter grades (b) mild slopes

(c) both (a) and (b) (d) NOA

120. A cut throat flume is a modified form of

(a) Cipolletti weir (b) Parshall flume

(c) H-flume (d) NOA

121. Coarse textured soils erode mainly through

(a) surface creep (b) saltation

(c) suspension (d) NOA

122. Sides of an earthen channel will be stable if its slope

(a) does not exceed the angle of repose

(b) exceeds the angle of repose

Answers	**116. (d)**	**118. (a)**	**120. (b)**	**122. (a)**
	117. (a)	**119. (c)**	**121. (b)**	

(c) is kept same as angle of repose

(d) NOA

123. The best hydraulic cross-section of a trapezoidal channel under favourable structural condition is

(a) b = 2d (b) b = d/2

(c) b = 2d tan θ/2 (d) b = 4d

124. The average power coefficient of the standard USWB class A pan evaporimeter used for evaporation is

(a) 0.85 (b) 0.70

(c) 0.90 (d) 1.00

125. In check basin design the useful thumb rule is that the ratio of water spread time required to cover the entire basin to the time required to infiltrate the net depth of irrigation is

(a) 0.25 (b) 0.75

(c) 2.00 (d) NOA

126. In drainage projects the design return period usually ranges from

(a) 5 – 25 years (b) 25 – 50 years

(c) 50 – 75 years (d) 75 – 100 years

127. Steady state drainage design equation assumes that the drain discharge

(a) exceeds the recharge to the ground water

(b) equals the recharge to the ground water

(c) Both (a) & (b)

(d) NOA

128. Saline soil has a pH value

(a) > 8.5 (b) Equal to 8.5

(c) 8.5 to 10.5 (d) less than 8.5

Answers			
	123. (c)	125. (b)	127. (b)
	124. (b)	126. (a)	128. (d)

129. The thickness of a spillway apron depends on

(a) Hydraulic jump (b) Water velocity
(c) Uplift pressure (d) All of the above

130. Darcy's law is valid for

(a) Turbulent flow (b) Laminar flow
(c) Both (a) and (b) (d) NOA

131. If the speed of a centrifugal pump is doubled, the power required will be increased by

(a) 2 times (b) 4 times
(c) 6 times (d) 8 times

132. The maximum non-erosive velocity of a water stream which is used for designing furrows laid at 0.2 percent longitudinal slope should be

(a) 1 litre/sec (b) 3 litres/sec
(c) 4 litres/sec (d) 5 litres/sec

133. Blinding of tiles refers to

(a) trenching of the drains
(b) laying the tiles
(c) joining the tiles
(d) covering the tiles with loose earth

134. From the hydraulic efficiency point of view, the most efficient cross - section of an openchannel is

(a) semi-circular (b) trapezoidal
(c) parabolic (d) rectangular

135. The depth of flow over a sharp crested rectangular weir should not be more than about

(a) half the crest width
(b) two-third of the crest width
(c) three-fourth of the crest width
(d) the width of the weir

Answers				
	129. (c)	131. (d)	133. (d)	135. (b)
	130. (b)	132. (b)	134. (a)	

136. Boulton's well function is associated with semi-confined aquifer having

(a) Excessive yield (b) Normal yield
(c) Delayed yield (d) NOA

137. The ratio of D_{60} and D_{10} sieve sizes in sieve analysis of granular material is called

(a) Well coefficient (b) Uniformity coefficient
(c) Recharge coefficient (d) NOA

138. The well development technique through pumping that can also be used for cleaning a clogged strainer

(a) Backwashing (b) Air washing
(c) Both (a) and (b) (d) NOA

139. Leakage factor and hydraulic resistance are important properties of the

(a) unconfined aquifer (b) semi-confined aquifer
(c) confined aquifer (d) All of the above

140. Which of the following is a method of tubewell drilling ?

(a) Percussion drilling (b) Rotary drilling
(c) Core drilling (d) All of the above

141. In alluvial formations the economical method of drilling is

(a) direct rotary (b) reverse rotary
(c) cable tool (d) DTH

142. Which of the following aquifer is related to the term specific yield ?

(a) unconfined aquifer
(b) confined and unconfined aquifers
(c) confined aquifer
(d) NOA

Answers	136. (c)	138. (c)	140. (d)	142. (a)
	137. (b)	139. (b)	141. (a)	

143. By doubling the seven diameter of a well in an unconfined aquifer the discharge is increased only about

(a) 10% (b) 2%
(c) 20% (d) 100%

144. Which of the following cases is associated with surging ?

(a) Gravel packing (b) Well drilling
(c) Well development (d) Sealing of saline water

145. The lines joining points of equal depth of ground water level are known as

(a) Isohytes (b) Isochrones
(c) Isobars (d) Isobaths

146. Specific yield of clay formation varies from

(a) 1 – 10 % (b) 5 – 15 %
(c) 10 – 15 % (d) 15 – 20 %

147. Formations that contain water but transmits water at a slow rate is called as

(a) Hard pan (b) Aquifer
(c) Aquiclude (d) Aquifuge

148. For a water bearing strata, the sum of specific yield and specific retension is equal to

(a) void ratio (b) porosity
(c) bulk density (d) specific gravity

149. Theis method is applicable for well hydraulics under the conditions

(a) unsteady state flow in a confined aquifer
(b) unsteady state flow in an unconfined aquifer
(c) steady state flow in a confined aquifer
(d) steady state flow in an unconfined aquifer

Answers	**143. (a)**	**145. (d)**	**147. (c)**	**149. (a)**
	144. (c)	**146. (a)**	**148. (b)**	

150. **Based on the sieve analysis of the aquifer material, the uniformity coefficient of a uniform material is**

(a) more than 2 (b) less than 2

(c) more than 4 (d) more than 8

151. **Diameter of a dug well varies from**

(a) 2 to 10 m (b) 5 to 10 m

(c) 10 to 20 m (d) 10 to 15 m

152. **The Manning's coefficient of roughness for grassed channels is specifically known as**

(a) Retardance coefficient

(b) Coefficient of discharge

(c) Manning's constant

(d) Flow coefficient

153. **For a watershed having streams of order 1, 2, 3 and 4 the basin order will be**

(a) 1 (b) 2

(c) 3 (d) 4

154. **Rill erosion is the advanced stage of**

(a) Rain drop erosion (b) Gully erosion

(c) Sheet erosion (d) NOA

155. **The Stanford model is used to**

(a) estimate the soil loss

(b) estimate the runoff

(c) estimate the rainfall depth

(d) estimation of soil formation

156. **The value of 'c' in rational equation is generally**

(a) less than 1 (b) more than 1

(c) equal to 5 (d) All of the above

Answers	150. (b)	152. (c)	154. (c)	156. (d)
	151. (a)	153. (d)	155. (a)	

157. The basic assumptions of unit hydrograph theory are

(a) Nonlinear response and time invariance

(b) Time invariance and linear response

(c) Linear response and linear time variance

(d) Non - linear time variance and linear response

158. The time of concentration of a watershed is proportional to

(a) $L^{1.77}$ (b) $S^{-0.385}$

(c) $S^{0.385}$ (d) $L^{1.77}S^{0.385}$

159. Rational formula is used to compute

(a) Design discharge for flat land

(b) Design discharge for sloppy land

(c) Design peak rainfall

(d) Design peak runoff rate

160. Contour bunds are adopted in

(a) High rainfall regions (b) Low rainfall regions

(c) Highly pervious soils (d) NOA

161. Class IV type lands are

(a) suitable for cultivation

(b) not suitable for cultivation

(c) partly suitable for cultivation

(d) NOA

162. Froude number is the ratio of

(a) Inertia force to the shear force

(b) Inertia force to viscous force

(c) Viscous force to the gravitational force

(d) Inertia force to the gravitational force

Answers			
	157. (b)	159. (d)	161. (a)
	158. (b)	160. (b)	162. (d)

163. For design of grassed waterway the average grade used is

(a) 1% (b) 5%

(c) 10% (d) 15%

164. The sheet of water which overflows a weir is called as

(a) Head (b) Static Head

(c) Nappe (d) All of the above

165. Which of the following may be used for measurement of water discharge ?

(a) Rectangular weir (b) V notch

(c) Orifice (d) All of the above

166. Isohyets are the lines of equal

(a) Temperatures (b) pressure

(c) Precipitation (d) NOA

167. Erosion index is based on rainfall intensity

(a) I_{15} (b) I_{30}

(c) I_{45} (d) I_{60}

168. A 4 - hour unit hydrograph means

(a) 1 cm depth of rainfall over the entire watershed

(b) 1 cm of rainfall excess over the entire watershed

(c) a hydrograph resulting from an instantaneous application of 1 cm rainfall excess over the entire watershed

(d) The stream flow for four hours

169. A 4 hour rainfall in a catchment of 250 sq. km, produces rainfall depths of 6.2 cm and 5.0cm in successive 2-hour unit period. Assuming the ϕ index of the soil to be 1.2 cm per hour, the runoff volume in ha.m will be

(a) 16 (b) 22

(c) 1600 (d) 2200

Answers				
	163. (b)	165. (d)	167. (b)	169. (c)
	164. (c)	166. (c)	168. (b)	

170. 'Cox' formula is used to determine

(a) Rainfall velocity
(b) Rainfall intensity
(c) Vertical interval between contour bunds
(d) Earth work in pond design

171. Contour bunds are suitable in areas having rainfall

(a) more than 1500 mm (b) less than 600 mm
(c) 600 – 900 mm (d) NOA

172. The critical flow condition in a channel occurs when specific energy is

(a) maximum (b) minimum
(c) zero (d) negative

173. The phenomenon of removal of material from the foundation of structure through seepage water is called as

(a) piping (b) sliding
(c) overturning (d) NOA

174. For rectangular channels the minimum specific energy is

(a) 2/3 times critical depth
(b) 3/2 times critical depth
(c) 5/4 times critical depth
(d) NOA

175. In a drop structure safety against tension can be achieved by assuming that the resultant of the forces on the head wall pass through

(a) the middle one-third of the base
(b) the left one-third of the base
(c) the right one-third of the base
(d) any point on the base

Answers	170. (c)	172. (b)	174. (b)
	171. (b)	173. (a)	175. (a)

176. On flat lands which of the following types of gullies are formed ?

(a) L-shaped (b) V-shaped

(c) U-shaped (d) Rectangular shaped

177. The difference in elevation between top of the dam and normal reservoir level is called as

(a) minimum free board (b) maximum free board

(c) critical free board (d) normal free board

178. Check dams are provided with the main objective of

(a) ponding of water

(b) causing upstream sedimentation

(c) to reduce channel slope

(d) All of the above

179. Flood routing techniques are generally used for

(a) flood forecasting

(b) design of spillways and reservoir

(c) flood protection works

(d) NOA

180. Graded bund is used for safe disposal of excess runoff in the area with

(a) High rainfall

(b) Relatively impervious soil

(c) Low rainfall

(d) All of the above

181. Rill erosion usually begins in the

(a) lower part of land slope

(b) upper part of land slope

(c) middle part of land slope

(d) entire length of the land slope

Answers	**176. (c)**	**178. (d)**	**180. (d)**
	177. (d)	**179. (a)**	**181. (b)**

182. Those gullies whose dimension does not change with time are called as

(a)	Active gullies	(b)	U-shaped gullies
(c)	Inactive gullies	(d)	V-shaped gullies

183. Drop inlet spillways are located at the place of

(a)	medium gully slope	(b)	high depression
(c)	gully face	(d)	upstream area of gully

OOOOO

Answers	182. (c) 183. (c)

Uttarakhand Public Service Commission (AE) Exam - 2013 Agricultural Engineering (SWCE)

1. **One hectare is equal to**
   (a) 1000 square-m (b) 100 square-m
   (c) 100000 square-m (d) 10000 square-m

2. **Fore sight is also known as**
   (a) Positive sight (b) Minus sight
   (c) Intermediate sight (d) Vertical sight

3. **Reduced level of a point is its height or depth above or below**
   (a) The ground surface
   (b) The assumed datum
   (c) The line of collimation
   (d) Both (a) and (b)

4. **Hygrophilic soils are those**
   (a) attract water (b) do not attract water
   (c) transmit water (d) produce water

5. **Froude number for a triangular channel is given as**
   (a) $F = V\sqrt{2}/\sqrt{gY}$ (b) $F = V/\sqrt{gY}$
   (c) $F = V/\sqrt{gA/Y}$ (d) $F = V2/\sqrt{gY}$

Answers	1. (d) 3. (b) 5. (c) 2. (a) 4. (b)

6. **A laminar flow is associated to**
   (a) Low flow velocity
   (b) Moving of fluid without lateral mixing
   (c) Absence of eddies
   (d) All of the above

7. **A uniform flow generally occurs in**
   (a) An inclined channel of constant bed slope
   (b) A level channel
   (c) A channel with negative slope
   (d) All of the above

8. **The Manning's roughness (n) decreases with**
   (a) Decrease in flow depth
   (b) Increase in flow depth
   (c) Decrease in turbulence
   (d) Both (b) and (c)

9. **At the critical flow condition the velocity head is equal to**
   (a) Half of the flow depth
   (b) Half of the hydraulic depth
   (c) Two times of hydraulic radius
   (d) NOA

10. **Dimension of dynamic viscosity are**
   (a) $ML^{-1}T^{-1}$ (b) MLT^{-1}
   (c) $ML^{-1}T$ (d) $M^{-1}LT$

11. **Bernoulli's equation is applicable for**
   (a) Frictionless steady flow
   (b) Incompressible flow
   (c) Ideal flow
   (d) Both (a) and (b)

Answers	6. (d)	8. (b)	10. (a)
	7. (a)	9. (b)	11. (d)

12. **The value of circulatory ratio of watershed varies from**
    (a) 0.2 to 0.8 (b) 0.4 to 1.0
    (c) 1.5 to 2.0 (d) 4 to 4.5

13. **Frictional head loss in a pipe is directly proportional to**
    (a) Length of pipe (b) Diameter of pipe
    (c) Both of the above (d) NOA

14. **Current meters are used to determine**
    (a) Flow type (b) Flow turbulence
    (c) Flow direction (d) Flow velocity

15. **Seepage force always acts in**
    (a) Upward direction
    (b) Downward direction
    (c) In the direction of flow
    (d) In the opposite direction of flow

16. **The weight of the fluid per unit volume is also called**
    (a) Specific volume (b) Specific weight
    (c) Density (d) NOA

17. **The dynamic viscosity of a fluid expressed as 'poise' equals to**
    (a) 10 Newton second per m^2
    (b) 1 Newton second per m^2
    (c) 1 Newton - meter per second
    (d) 0.1 Newton - second per m^2

18. **The flow is said to be turbulent if the Reynold number in a pipe is**
    (a) 5000 (b) 1800
    (c) 1500 (d) 1000

Answers	12. (a)	14. (d)	16. (b)	18. (a)
	13. (a)	15. (c)	17. (d)	

19. Bernoulli's equation is related to

(a) Mass conservation (b) Energy balance

(c) Heat conservation (d) Water conservation

20. Ratio of buoyant forces to the viscous forces of the fluid flow is known as

(a) Prandlt number (b) Grashof number

(c) Reynolds number (d) NOA

21. Friction factor is important parameter particularly in

(a) Laminar flow (b) Turbulent flow

(c) Viscous flow (d) Vertical flow

22. Venturimeter is used to measure flow of fluids in pipes when pipe is

(a) Horizontal (b) Vertical downward

(c) Vertical upward (d) In any position

23. When flow parameters change with time but remain constant with space the flow is called as

(a) Unsteady uniform flow

(b) Steady uniform flow

(c) Steady non-uniform flow

(d) Unsteady non-uniform flow

24. A submersible pump may be

(a) Single stage pump (b) Multi stage pump

(c) Centrifugal pump (d) Both (a) and (b)

25. Density of water is

(a) 1000 kg/m^3 (b) 500 kg/m^3

(c) 1500 kg/m^3 (d) 2000 kg/m^3

26. Specific energy diagram is plotted between specific energy and depth of flow for

Answers				
	19. (b)	21. (b)	23. (a)	25. (a)
	20. (b)	22. (d)	24. (d)	26. (b)

(a) Variable discharge
(b) Constant discharge
(c) Constant Froude number
(d) NOA

27. Which of the following is not a type of fluid flow ?

(a) Steady (b) Direct
(c) Laminar (d) Compressible

28. Under open flow conditions, the hydraulic jump is formed when the Froude number is

(a) Equal to one (b) More than one
(c) Less than one (d) NOA

29. At critical depth of flow

(a) Specific energy is minimum
(b) Specific energy is maximum
(c) Both (a) and (b)
(d) NOA

30. If a fluid which possess some viscosity is known as

(a) Real fluid (b) Imaginary fluid
(c) Specific fluid (d) NOA

31. A large Reynold's number is indication of

(a) Highly turbulent flow
(b) Laminar flow
(c) Steady flow
(d) Smooth and stream line flow

32. The flow in the open channel may be characterized as laminar flow when Reynold's number is

(a) $Re < 500$ (b) $Re > 2000$
(c) $Re > 1000$ (d) $Re > 800$

Answers	**27. (b)**	**29. (a)**	**31. (a)**
	28. (b)	**30. (a)**	**32. (a)**

33. One stoke is equal to

(a) 1 m^2/s (b) 0.1 m^2/s

(c) 1×10^{-2} m^2/s (d) 1×10^{-4} m^2/s

34. The velocity of water through a circular channel will be maximum when the depth of water is

(a) 0.95 times the diameter of channel

(b) 0.81 times the diameter of channel

(c) 0.67 times the diameter of channel

(d) 0.50 times the diameter of channel

35. Absolute pressure is equal to

(a) Gauge pressure – Atmospheric pressure

(b) Gauge pressure + Vacuum Pressure

(c) Atmospheric pressure + Gauge pressure

(d) Atmospheric pressure - Gauge pressure

36. The dimension of specific gravity are

(a) MLT (b) ML^2T

(c) ML^{-1} (d) NOA

37. The hydraulic radius for a fully flowing pipe of 1 meter diameter will be

(a) 1 meter (b) 0.5 meter

(c) 0.25 meter (d) 2.0 meter

38. The Force per unit area in fluids is exerted

(a) In all directions (b) Lower depths

(c) Horizontal ways (d) Upward

39. The length of Gunter's chain is

(a) 100 feet (b) 50 feet

(c) 66 feet (d) 75 feet

Answers	**33. (d)**	**35. (c)**	**37. (c)**	**39. (c)**
	34. (b)	**36. (d)**	**38. (a)**	

40. **Length of a metric chain is**

(a) 1 m (b) 20 m

(c) 50 m (d) 100 m

41. **The bench mark fixed at the end of a day's of survey work is called**

(a) Permanent bench mark

(b) Arbitrary bench mark

(c) Temporary bench mark

(d) NOA

42. **The imaginary line joining the geographical North and South is known as**

(a) Geographical meridian (b) Magnetic meridian

(c) Arbitrary meridian (d) All of the above

43. **The bearing of line AB is 40° 26' 10" and bearing of AC is 140° 30' 40". What will be angle between lines AB and AC ?**

(a) 180° 56' 50" (b) 130° 26' 10"

(c) 100° 4' (d) 230° 4'

44. **Alidade is an important instrument used in which survey ?**

(a) Plane table survey (b) Chain survey

(c) Theodolite survey (d) Compass survey

45. **Instrument used for measurement of areas of figure having irregular boundaries are**

(a) Anemometer (b) Planimeter

(c) Rolling meter (d) All of the above

46. **Manning's formula is used to determine flow velocity in which type of flow**

(a) Rapidly varied flow (b) Non-uniform flow

(c) Uniform flow (d) Critical flow

Answers	40. (b)	42. (b)	44. (a)	46. (c)
	41. (c)	43. (a)	45. (b)	

47. At critical state of flow the kinetic energy of flow is equal to

(a) One fourth of its potential energy
(b) One half of its potential energy
(c) One third of its potential energy
(d) One fifth of its potential energy

48. In general, the curing of concrete should be continued for the duration of

(a) 1 to 2 days (b) 3 to 5 days
(c) 15 to 20 days (d) 7 to 10 days

49. The hydraulic radius (R) of a channel in terms of its wetted perimeter (P) and cross sectional area (A) is given on

(a) $R = A \times P$ (b) $R = P / A$
(c) $R = A / P$ (d) $R = A^2 / P$

50. Hydraulic jump formula is based on

(a) Froude number of flow
(b) Reynold number of flow
(c) Critical number of flow
(d) Specific number of flow

51. In the centrifugal pump, the liquid enters through

(a) Eye of the impeller (b) Delivery pipe
(c) By-pass line (d) NOA

52. Axial flow pump delivers large quantity of water at

(a) High heads (b) Medium heads
(c) Low heads (d) Zero heads

53. Which of the following type of impeller is used for centrifugal pump dealing with mud

(a) One side shrouded (b) Two side shrouded
(c) Double action (d) Open from both side

Answers	47. (b)	49. (c)	51. (a)	53. (d)
	48. (d)	50. (a)	52. (c)	

54. Quick sand is a state of

(a) Flow (b) Landslide

(c) Land Levelling (d) NOA

55. Filling water before its operation in a centrifugal pump is called

(a) Testing of pump (b) Energizing of pump

(c) Priming of pump (d) All of the above

56. Propeller pumps are used for

(a) Low head and low discharge

(b) Low head and high discharge

(c) High head and low discharge

(d) High head and high discharge

57. If a pump vibrates, the possible reasons may be

(a) Misalignment (b) Poor suction conditions

(c) Bearing failure (d) All of the above

58. In centrifugal pumps, the number of vanes made in impeller varies from

(a) 3 to 12 (b) 5 to 10

(c) 10 to 12 (d) 7 to 12

59. The vertical height to which the liquid can be raised by the pump above center line of pump is called

(a) Suction head (b) Total head

(c) Discharge head (d) Total differential head

60. Semi open impeller is used for

(a) Clean water (b) Hot water

(c) Sewage water (d) NOA

61. For which type of pump verticality of tube well is critical

(a) Jet pump

(b) Submersible pump

Answers				
	54. (b)	56. (b)	58. (a)	60. (c)
	55. (c)	57. (d)	59. (c)	61. (b)

(c) Directly connected centrifugal pump

(d) Reciprocating pump

62. The parameter which is least important for a selection of pump is

(a) Discharge (b) Horse power

(c) Head (d) Quality of water

63. The relationship to determine break horse power in a centrifugal pump is

(a) Water horse power × pump efficiency

(b) Water horse power / pump efficiency

(c) Water horse power + pump efficiency

(d) Pump efficiency / water horse power

64. Water can be lifted from a depth beyond 45 meter by

(a) Centrifugal pump (b) Jet pump

(c) Submersible pump (d) NOA

65. The hand pump used in houses is a type of pump

(a) Submersible pump (b) Reciprocating pump

(c) Centrifugal pump (d) Jet pump

66. Practically, the suction head of a centrifugal pump should not exceed

(a) 8 meters (b) 12.5 meters

(c) 32.5 meters (d) 13.20 meters

67. Nozzle and venturi are main components of

(a) Centrifugal pump (b) Jet pump

(c) Reciprocating pump (d) Submersible pump

68. If a chain is too long, the measured distance will be less than actual, then the correction will be

(a) Can be negative or positive

Answers	62. (d)	64. (c)	66. (a)	68. (c)
	63. (b)	65. (b)	67. (b)	

(b) Zero

(c) Negative only

(d) Positive only

69. Reciprocating pumps are found to be best suited for

(a) Low discharge and high heads

(b) Low discharge and low heads

(c) High discharge and high heads

(d) High discharge and low heads

70. High lift centrifugal pump are generally

(a) Multi stage pumps

(b) Used in deep wells

(c) Both (a) and (b)

(d) Single stage pumps

71. Which of the following is not a type of impeller of a centrifugal pump

(a) Semi-open (b) Closed

(c) Open (d) High speed

72. Discharge of reciprocating pump is constant regardless of

(a) Temperature (b) Speed

(c) Delivery head (d) Suction head

73. Most efficient channel section is

(a) Triangular (b) Trapezoidal

(c) Rectangular (d) Semi circular

74. The type of survey in which the shape of earth is taken into account is called

(a) Geodetic survey (b) Curvature surface

(c) Precise survey (d) All of the above

Answers	69. (a)	71. (d)	73. (d)
	70. (a)	72. (b)	74. (a)

75. What will be the equivalent pressure head of kerosene if its specific gravity of 0.81, if water pressure head is 100m

(a) 123.46m (b) 184.36m

(c) 81.0m (d) 162.0m

76. Which is not the method for drawing flow nets

(a) Analytical method

(b) Graphical method

(c) Electrical analogy method

(d) Curve fitting method

77. Pitot tube is a simple device used to measure

(a) Density of flow (b) Velocity of flow

(c) Type of flow (d) NOA

78. For maximum discharge in a circular channel the depth of flow should be equal to

(a) 0.70 times diameter (b) 0.95 times diameter

(c) 0.82 times diameter (d) 1.15 times diameter

79. Hydraulic jump is based on the principle of

(a) Energy conservation

(b) Velocity conservation

(c) Momentum conservation

(d) Turbulence conservation

80. Pressure drop in fluid flow through granular material is best estimated by

(a) Black - Kozney equation

(b) Burke - Plummer equation

(c) Ergun equation

(d) Fourier equation

Answers	75. (c)	77. (b)	79. (a)
	76. (d)	78. (b)	80. (c)

81. Froude number is the ratio between

(a) Inertia force to viscous forces
(b) Inertia force to gravity force
(c) Inertia force to shear force
(d) Gravity force to inertia force

82. Height of instrument method is used for determination of

(a) Reduced level (b) Discharge
(c) Flow velocity (d) Back bearing

83. A pump may fail to prime due to

(a) Air leakage in suction line or pump
(b) Foot value may be leaking
(c) Leakage in rotary shaft seals
(d) All of the above

84. Direct ranging in survey is done

(a) When one line overlap into other
(b) When two ends of survey line are inter visible
(c) When two ends are not visible
(d) None of the above

85. Seepage force has the direction

(a) Upward side
(b) Downward side
(c) In direction of flow
(d) Opposite direction of flow

86. The shape of rotary and gyratory screen are generally

(a) Triangular
(b) Circular or rectangular
(c) Trapezoidal
(d) NOA

Answers			
	81. (b)	83. (d)	85. (c)
	82. (d)	84. (b)	86. (b)

87. **An "Archimedean screw", is device used for**
    (a) To tight a screw
    (b) To measure electric current
    (c) To lift water
    (d) To lift earth material

88. **For a given cross sectional area the hydraulic radius will increase with**
    (a) Increase in wetted perimeter
    (b) Decrease in wetted perimeter
    (c) Increase in turbulence of flow
    (d) Decrease in turbulence of flow

89. **Elbow joints are generally used to**
    (a) Increase the pressure (b) Reduce flow
    (c) Increase flow (d) Reduce pressure

90. **Curvature of the earth is taken into account in surveying when the extent of the area is more than**
    (a) 50 km^2 (b) 100 km^2
    (c) 250 km^2 (d) NOA

91. **Which of the following is not the characteristic of centrifugal pump**
    (a) Capacity is inversely proportional to speed
    (b) Horse power is the function of capacity, head and efficiency of pump
    (c) Smooth and even flow
    (d) Adaptive to high speed operation

92. **Pump is operating but not delivering water, possible causes are**
    (a) Pump head is too high
    (b) Rotation of driver is incorrect

Answers	**87. (c)**	**89. (d)**	**91. (a)**
	88. (b)	**90. (c)**	**92. (d)**

(c) Pump speed is too low
(d) All of the above

93. **About 90% of full strength of concrete is achieved after curing of**
(a) 7 days (b) 14 days
(c) 21 days (d) 28 days

94. **The chain with 100 links and 100 feet length is known as**
(a) Gunter's chain (b) Engineer's chain
(c) Metric chain (d) NOA

95. **The survey in which curvature of the earth is considered is known as**
(a) Chain survey (b) Aerial survey
(c) Compass survey (d) NOA

96. **The longest chain line in chain surveying is called**
(a) Check line (b) Tie line
(c) Base line (d) All of the above

97. **Errors in surveying are**
(a) Instrumental error (b) Personal error
(c) Measurement error (d) All of the above

98. **The bearing of line taken in the direction of opposite to the progress of work is known as**
(a) Fore bearing (b) Back bearing
(c) Whole circle bearing (d) NOA

99. **Amongst various land levelling methods, the most common method is**
(a) Plane method
(b) Darcy method
(c) Contour adjustment method
(d) Plane inspection method

Answers				
	93. (c)	**95. (d)**	**97. (d)**	**99. (a)**
	94. (b)	**96. (c)**	**98. (b)**	

100. The volume of earthwork in land levelling can be computed by

(a) Trapezoidal rules (b) Prismoidal method

(c) End – area method (d) Both (a) and (b)

101. The permissible depth of earthwork under land levelling work is about

(a) ± 3 cm (b) 4.5 cm

(c) 5.0 cm (d) 10.0 cm

102. Orifice meter is used to measure

(a) Roughness in pipes

(b) Roughness in open channels

(c) Flow in open channels

(d) Flow in pipes

103. The depth from which the liquid has to be lifted by pumps is known as

(a) Suction head (b) Delivery head

(c) Velocity head (d) Static head

104. Which of the following is a correct match ?

(a) Mole drain = pump drainage

(b) Vertical drainage = well drainage

(c) Pipe drain = well drainage

(d) Horizontal drain = bio-drainage

105. Which of the following is the most correct match ?

(a) Manning's formula = Estimation of seepage loss in a scanal

(b) Kennedy theory = open channel flow

(c) Darcy-Weisbach formula = Friction factor

(d) Seepage meter = Design of open channel

Answers	**100. (d)**	**102. (d)**	**104. (b)**
	101. (a)	**103. (a)**	**105. (c)**

106. If the hydraulic radius is more than 5.0m, then for designing an open ditch, the value of Manning's 'n' should be taken as

(a) 0.002 – 0.030 (b) 0.04 – 0.045
(c) 0.035 – 0.040 (d) 0.040 – 0.045

107. The development of a tube well should be started from

(a) Middle of screen (b) Top of screen
(c) Bottom of screen (d) Bottom of casing pipe

108. Which type of gully is formed on flat land ?

(a) U-shaped (b) V-shaped
(c) L-shaped (d) T-shaped

109. Check dams are provided with the main objective of

(a) Ponding of water
(b) Causing upstream sedimentation
(c) Reducing channel (gully) slope
(d) All of the above

110. Dimension of leakage factor is equivalent to

(a) Time (b) Velocity
(c) Resistance (d) Length

111. Contour farming is recommended for lands having slope

(a) Less than 1% (b) 2 – 7%
(c) 7 – 12% (d) More than 12%

112. If rainfall occurs on a perfectly impermeable surface (such as glass), then the Curve Number (CN) for computing runoff will be assumed to be

(a) 50 (b) 75
(c) 100 (d) 25

Answers	106. (a)	108. (a)	110. (d)	112. (c)
	107. (b)	109. (d)	111. (b)	

113. The average soil loss in India from agricultural lands is about

(a) 6-8 t/ha/year (b) 10-12 t/ha/year
(c) 20-30 t/ha/year (d) 80-100 t/ha/year

114. In light sandy soil, with slope 1 to 5%, the maximum water application rate of a sprinkler irrigation system is

(a) 2.0 cm/hr (b) 2.5 cm/hr
(c) 3.0 cm/hr (d) 3.5 cm/hr

115. The water present in the soil between field capacity and permanent wilting point is known as

(a) Ground water (b) Gravitational water
(c) Hygroscopic water (d) Available water

116. The unit draft in silt loam (moist) soil varies from

(a) 0.21 to 0.24 Kg/cm^2 (b) 0.71 to 0.89 Kg/cm^2
(c) 0.64 to 0.71 Kg/cm^2 (d) 0.36 to 0.43 Kg/cm^2

117. Water loss through seepage in earthen channels amounts to about

(a) 15% (b) 20% (c) 25% (d) 30%

118. Contour bunds are adopted

(a) In low rainfall regions
(b) In highly pervious soils
(c) In high rainfall regions
(d) Where conservation of moisture is needed

119. If a soil sample has porosity of 40%, its void ratio will be

(a) 0.06 (b) 0.60 (c) 0.40 (d) 0.30

120. The upper limit of a tensiometer for soil moisture tension measurement is

(a) 0.85 centibar (b) 8.5 centibar
(c) 85 centibar (d) 100 centibar

Answers	**113. (b)**	**115. (d)**	**117. (a)**	**119. (b)**
	114. (b)	**116. (d)**	**118. (a)**	**120. (a)**

121. **Hydraulic ram is**
   (a) A centrifugal pump (b) An impulse pump
   (c) A volute pump (d) A rotary pump

122. **Subsurface drains removes**
   (a) Gravitational water (b) Capillary water
   (c) Hygroscopic water (d) All of the above

123. **As compared to an electrical motor driven pump, the cost of lifting water by an engine driven pump is higher by**
   (a) 5 to 10% (b) 10 to 15%
   (c) 15 to 25% (d) 25 to 40%

124. **If the velocity of overland flow is doubled, the erosive capacity is increased as**
   (a) 2 times (b) 4 times
   (c) 6 times (d) 32 times

125. **The energy of a raindrop causing erosion is expressed in**
   (a) m-mg / ha.mm (b) m.mg / ha
   (c) m.t / ha (d) t / ha-m

126. **Evaporation pan coefficient of class 'A' pan is generally taken as**
   (a) 7.0 (b) 0.7
   (c) 0.007 (d) 5.5

127. **The kinetic energy of raindrops compared to that of runoff is**
   (a) 100 times more (b) 100 times less
   (c) 250 times more (d) 30 times more

128. **Dicken's formula is used to determine**
   (a) Peak discharge (b) Monthly runoff
   (c) Periodic runoff (d) Fortnightly runoff

Answers				
	121. (b)	123. (c)	125. (a)	127. (c)
	122. (a)	124. (d)	126. (b)	128. (a)

129. Tension on a hydraulic structure develops because of

(a) Load of water (b) Action of uneven forces

(c) Structural weight (d) None of these

130. Erodibility is basically associated to

(a) Soil properties (b) Rainfall properties

(c) Crops (d) Cultural practices

131. One hectare is equal to

(a) 10,000 sq.m. (b) 100,000 sq.m.

(c) 1000 sq.m. (d) 100 sq.m.

132. The ratio of total volume of water delivered to a crop, to area on which it has been spread is called

(a) duty (b) delta

(c) critical path (d) specific volume

133. The unit of delta is

(a) cm (b) $cm^{-1/2}$ (c) cm^{-2} (d) cm^2

134. Spacing of drains in flat land under parallel field drain system varies from

(a) 150 - 300 m (b) 100 - 500 m

(c) 100 - 200 m (d) 300 - 450 m

135. Spacing of mole drains varies from

(a) 2 to 5 m (b) 5 to 7.5 m

(c) 7 to 15 m (d) 2 to 10 m

136. Dimension of leakage factor is

(a) L (b) L/T (c) T^{-2} (d) LT^{-2}

137. Velocity Measurement of stream flow is carried out by the device called

(a) Current meter (b) Planimeter

(c) Tachometer (d) Hydrometer

Answers	129. (a)	131. (a)	133. (a)	135. (a)	137. (a)
	130. (a)	132. (a)	134. (a)	136. (a)	

138. **Unconfined aquifer is also called as**
(a) Semi-confined aquifer (b) Water table aquifer
(c) Aquifuge (d) All of the above

139. **Inward slope of a bench terrace is in the range of**
(a) 1 - 5 Percent (b) 5 - 10 Percent
(c) 2 - 10 Percent (d) 8 - 20 Percent

140. **If a soil sample has porosity of 40 percent, its void ratio will be**
(a) 0.06 (b) 0.28
(c) 0.40 (d) 0.66

141. **The uppermost line of seepage in an earth embankment is called**
(a) Phreatic line (b) Lower most flow line
(c) Runoff line (d) Water pressure line

142. **Soil erosion will be more in**
(a) Clay soil (b) Loam soil
(c) Sandy soil (d) Silty clay soil

143. **As per BIS recommendation, the shape of lined channels should be**
(a) Semi-circular (b) Trapezoidal
(c) Parabolic (d) Rectangular

144. **The maximum rate of emission by drippers under normal working condition is**
(a) 15 lit /hr (b) 10 lit /hr
(c) 5 lit /hr (d) 20 lit /hr

145. **If drainage canal discharge is 0.2 m^3/sec and the drainage area is 250 hectares, then the drainage coefficient will be**
(a) 70 cm (b) 70 mm
(c) 0.5 cm (d) 7 mm

Answers	138. (b)	140. (d)	142. (a)	144. (b)
	139. (c)	141. (a)	143. (a)	145. (a)

146. The effect of gravity force upon the state of flow is represented by

(a) Reynold's number (b) Darcy's number

(c) Kennedy's number (d) Froude's number

147. Sub irrigation is useful in a situation where

(a) Saline water is used for irrigation

(b) Soil is heavy clay to permit capillary rise

(c) Capillary movement is rapid around roots

(d) No hard pan is present

148. The difference between a shallow tube-well and a deep tube well is made on the basis of

(a) Depth of aquifer

(b) Depth of tube-well

(c) Position of water table

(d) Type of aquifer

149. The brake horse power of a centrifugal pump has a direct relationship with

(a) The speed of the impeller

(b) The square of the speed of impeller

(c) The cube of the speed of impeller

(d) None of these

150. Most common method for irrigating the potato crop is

(a) Sprinkler method (b) Check-basin method

(c) Furrow method (d) Border method

151. Chute spillway is superior to drop inlet spillway when

(a) Large discharge is required

(b) No opportunity to provide temporary storage

(c) Channel is to be brought down a steep slope

(d) All of the above

Answers			
	146. (d)	148. (b)	150. (c)
	147. (c)	149. (c)	151. (d)

152. Sheet of water which overflows a weir is called

(a) Head (b) Static head

(c) Nappe (d) NOA

153. Infiltration rate during irrigation

(a) Increases (b) Decreases

(c) Both (a) and (b) (d) NOA

154. Darcy's law is valid under the condition of

(a) Laminar flow with Reynold's number > 10.0

(b) Reynold's number < 1.0

(c) Newtonian flow

(d) Steady uniform flow

155. The ratio of volume of voids to the total soil volume is called

(a) Porosity (b) Void ratio

(c) Dry bulk density (d) Wet bulk density

156. The sprinkler system operates at following pressure range

(a) 1 - 4 kg / cm^2 (b) 4 - 8 kg / cm^2

(c) 4 - 12 kg / cm^2 (d) 8 - 12 kg / cm^2

157. The wells in which the water levels remain at the water table level are

(a) Non-artesian wells (b) Artesian wells

(c) Confined wells (d) Tube wells

158. The soluble soil matters are

(a) Sand and silt

(b) Clay and organic matter

(c) Sand, silt, clay and organic matter

(d) NOA

Answers				
	152. (c)	**154. (a)**	**156. (a)**	**158. (c)**
	153. (c)	**155. (a)**	**157. (a)**	

159. The minimum wind velocity required to initiate movement of soil particles is knows as

(a) Critical velocity (b) Dynamic velocity
(c) Intrinsic velocity (d) Threshold velocity

160. The minimum water content at which the soil just begins to crumble when rolled into threads is known as

(a) Liquid limit (b) Plastic limit
(c) Shrinkage limit (d) Permeability limit

161. A soil has hydraulic conductivity in horizontal and vertical directions as K1 and K2, and then its effective hydraulic conductivity would be

(a) K1 + K2 (b) K1 / K2
(c) K1 × K2 (d) $(K1 \times K2)^{1/2}$

162. If a fourth order watershed has bifurcation ratio as 4, the number of second order streams

would be

(a) 4 (b) 8
(c) 16 (d) 32

163. The average water extraction of plants from the first 25% of soil depth is

(a) 50% (b) 45%
(c) 40% (d) 35%

164. The value of recession constant (kr) is

(a) 1 (b) <1
(c) >1 (d) -1

165. In treatment of catchment area of gullies, contour bunds are recommended for lands with slopes upto

(a) 4 % (b) 6 %
(c) 8 % (d) 10 %

Answers	159. (d)	161. (d)	163. (c)	165. (b)
	160. (b)	162. (c)	164. (b)	

166. **At field capacity, soil moisture tension is**
(a) 10 - 30 centi bar (b) 10 - 30 bar
(c) 7 - 32 centi bar (d) 7 - 32 bar

167. **Power developed by an average pair of bullocks is about**
(a) 750 kW (b) 75 kW
(c) 750 W (d) 75 W

168. **Soil formation that have the maximum specific yield is**
(a) Clay (b) Sand
(c) Gravel (d) Sand stone

169. **Runoff coefficient will be higher in**
(a) Sandy soil (b) Sandy loam soil
(c) Clay and silt loam (d) Stiff clay

170. **Froude's number is the ratio of the**
(a) Inertia force to the shear force
(b) Inertia force to the viscous force
(c) Inertia force to the gravity force
(d) Viscous force to the gravity force

171. **The ratio of the basin area to the area of circle having the same perimeter as the basin is known as**
(a) Circulatory ratio
(b) Elongation ratio
(c) Compactness coefficient
(d) Farm factor

172. **A practical method of reducing sheet erosion from slopy land is**
(a) Keep the land fallow
(b) Farming on contour strips
(c) Construction of small reservoir
(d) Use plastic sheet

Answers	166. (a) 167. (c)	168. (c) 169. (d)	170. (c) 171. (a)	172. (b)

173. **The percentage of soil particles transported by saltation process in case of wind erosion varies from**

(a) 3 to 40 % (b) 50 to 75 %
(c) 80 to 90 % (d) 5 to 25 %

174. **The dimensions of transmissibility of an aquifer will be**

(a) L/T (b) L^2/T
(c) L/T^2 (d) NOA

175. **The drip irrigation is very effective for**

(a) Water conservation
(b) Management of large cultivable land for high production
(c) Energy conservation
(d) All of the above

176. **Irrigation interval of drip irrigation varies from**

(a) 3 - 4 days (b) 1 - 3 days
(c) 7 days (d) 15 days

177. **Emitters are used in**

(a) Sprinkler irrigation (b) Surface irrigation
(c) Drip irrigation (d) Sub-surface irrigation

178. **The form of water which is not available to plants, is**

(a) Unavailable water (b) Hygroscopic water
(c) Capillary water (d) Free water

179. **In irrigation, tensiometer is used for**

(a) The measurement of soil moisture content
(b) The measurement of soil moisture tension
(c) Irrigation scheduling
(d) Both (b) and (c) are correct

Answers				
	173. (b)	175. (d)	177. (c)	179. (d)
	174. (b)	176. (b)	178. (b)	

180. 20-40 rule is used to compute

(a) Head loss in a drainage pipe
(b) Slope of drainage ditch
(c) Design discharge below the junction point of ditches
(d) Hydraulic radius of drainage ditch

181. A geological formation, which has more water holding capacity but impermeable for flow of water, is known as

(a) Aquifer (b) Aquifuge
(c) Aquitard (d) Aquiclude

182. To ensure surface drainage, a minimum furrow grade needed is

(a) 0.5% (b) 0.05%
(c) 5% (d) 10%

183. If all other parameters are fixed, then doubling the diameter of a tubewell increases the discharge by

(a) 75% (b) 50%
(c) 20% (d) 10%

184. The distance between the centre of a well and the outer point of the cone of depression is called

(a) Well radius (b) Aquifer radius
(c) Radius of draw down (d) Radius of influence

185. The boundary line along a topographic ridge separating two adjacent drainage basins is called as

(a) Contour line (b) Drainage divide
(c) Isobath (d) Isochrone

186. The sum of static suction head and static discharge head is called

(a) Pressure head (b) Velocity head
(c) Total static head (d) Total discharge head

Answers				
	180. (c)	182. (b)	184. (d)	186. (c)
	181. (d)	183. (d)	185. (b)	

187. For a given condition, a high intensity rain produces

(a) Less splash (b) More infiltration
(c) More splash (d) Crusting of soil

188. At optimum moisture content, the dry density of soil will be

(a) Minimum (b) Maximum
(c) Average (d) Zero

189. Soil degradation takes place due to

(a) Geological erosion (b) Accelerated erosion
(c) Glacial erosion (d) Tidal erosion

190. Steady infiltration rate is called

(a) Basic intake rate
(b) Seepage rate
(c) Percolation rate
(d) Cumulative infiltration rate

191. Which soil has a higher angle of repose ?

(a) Sandy soil (b) Clay soil
(c) Sandy loam soil (d) Clay loam soil

192. In terms of discharge 'D' the well loss will be proportional to

(a) D (b) $D^{1/2}$ (c) D^2 (d) D^{-2}

193. In a watershed, when the streams of second and third order meet, the resulting stream is of order

(a) Second (b) Third
(c) Fourth (d) Fifth

194. The product of hydraulic conductivity and aquifer thickness is called

(a) Storage coefficient (b) Specific yield
(c) Transmissibility (d) Drainable porosity

Answers				
	187. (c)	189. (b)	191. (a)	193. (b)
	188. (b)	190. (a)	192. (a)	194. (c)

195. Line joining equal depths of water table are called

(a) Isobath lines (b) Isohyete lines
(c) Isobar lines (d) NOA

196. Movement of irrigation water from the soil surface into the soil is called

(a) Percolation (b) Interflow
(c) Infiltration (d) Water intake

197. In general, the contour bunding practice is not recommended for the following type of soil

(a) Loamy soil (b) Deep black soil
(c) Sandy soil (d) Highly permeable soil

198. Most efficient rectangular cross section of a channel is defined as follows when hydraulic radium is 'R' and flow depth is 'd'

(a) R = d (b) R = d/2
(c) R = 2d (d) R = 4d

199. The nature of Hougoudt's equation for drain spacing is

(a) Parabolic (b) Hyperbolic
(c) Elliptical (d) Circular

200. The empirical method for computing consumptive use of a crop using the mean monthly temperature and day light hours is

(a) Thornthwaite (b) Blaney-Criddle
(c) Hargreaves (d) Lowry Johnson

201. Permissible flow velocity for design of grassed waterway to be under a good grass cover is taken as

(a) 1 – 1.5 m/s (b) 1.5 – 1.8 m/s
(c) 2 – 2.5 m/s (d) 2.5 – 3.0 m/s

Answers				
	195. (a)	197. (b)	199. (a)	201. (b)
	196. (c)	198. (b)	200. (b)	

202. If the Froude's number during a hydraulic jump is 1-1.7, then it is called

(a) Oscillating jump (b) Weak jump
(c) Steady jump (d) Undular jump

203. The flow velocity of water is measured by

(a) Anemometer (b) Current meter
(c) Tensiometer (d) NOA

204. The capacity of a centrifugal pump varies with its speed 'N' as

(a) N^2 (b) N (c) N (d) N^{-1}

205. If 'H' is the head over the crest of a triangular weir, the discharge will be proportional to

(a) $H^{1/2}$ (b) $H^{3/2}$ (c) $H^{5/2}$ (d) H2

206. For a well, yield per unit of draw down is called

(a) Specific yield (b) Specific capacity
(c) Well yield (d) Safe yield

207. The number of stream segments per unit area of water shed is known as

(a) Watershed density (b) Stream density
(c) Stream order (d) Basin relief

208. Usually, the discharge capacity of minor distributary in India is

(a) > 1000 lit/sec (b) < 750 lit/sec
(c) 0.75 – 5.5 cumec (d) 4 – 8.5 cumec

209. The unit of infiltration rate is

(a) mm/hr (b) cm^3/hr
(c) m^2/hr (d) NOA

OOOOO

Answers				
	202. (d)	204. (b)	206. (b)	208. (b)
	203. (b)	205. (c)	207. (b)	209. (a)

Sikkim Public Service Commission (AE) Exam - 2017 Agricultural Engineering (SWCE)

1. **Interception loss is solely due to**
   (a) evaporation (b) transpiration
   (c) through fall (d) stream flow

2. **Indirect runoff includes**
   (a) Interflow and base flow
   (b) Tnterflow and channel flow
   (c) Base flow only
   (d) Quick return flow

3. **Barlow's table is associated to the computation of**
   (a) Evaporation (b) Hydraulic roughness
   (c) Runoff coefficient (d) Runoff

4. **Line joining the points of equal time of concentration is called as**
   (a) isochrone (b) isocells
   (c) isobar (d) isohyel

5. **Unit of erosion intensity of long term erosion is given by**
   (a) mm per annum (b) m^3/s
   (c) $m^3/$ ha (d) tons/ha

Answers	**1. (a) 3. (c) 5. (d)** **2. (a) 4. (a)**

6. **Masonary spurs are located at the point, where**
   (a) Immediate control is needed
   (b) Sharp bend takes place
   (c) Stream current is swift
   (d) NOA

7. **Basedon construction of materials, the spurs are classified as**
   (a) vegetative, permanent and semi-permanent spurs
   (b) T & L shaped spurs
   (c) masonary, wooden and vegetative spurs
   (d) NOA

8. **Specific capacity of well denotes**
   (a) discharge per unit time
   (b) discharge per unit drawdown
   (c) drawdown per unit time
   (d) NOA

9. **In saltation process of soil movement, The movement takes place in the form**
   (a) suspension in wind
   (b) surface creep
   (c) low bounces over the land surface
   (d) NOA

10. **Shelterbelts are composed of**
    (a) one row of vegetative materials only
    (b) more than two rows of vegetative materials only
    (c) two rows of non - vegetative materials only
    (d) one row of non - vegetative materials only

Answers	**6. (c)**	**8. (b)**	**10. (b)**
	7. (a)	**9. (c)**	

11. **Parabolic dunes are formed on**
    (a) uniform sloppy ground surface
    (b) undulated ground surface
    (c) level ground surface
    (d) sloppy vegetative ground surface

12. **Plastic mulching is not suitable for**
    (a) erosion control (b) taller vegetation
    (c) moisture conservation (d) soil loss control

13. **For the design of grassed waterway, the average grade is used as**
    (a) 5% (b) 10% (c) 16% (d) 1%

14. **The most suitable shape of grassed way for use is**
    (a) Triangular (b) parabolic
    (c) Trapezoidal (d) rectangular

15. **In embankment of pond, the burrowing problem is more common**
    (a) at middle
    (b) at the bottom
    (c) around the spillway section
    (d) throughout the length

16. **A best site for pond construction is**
    (a) narrow valley with steep sides
    (b) a clay formation
    (c) a depressed part with pervious layer below
    (d) all of the above

17. **Laplace equation used for seepage analysis is valid for**
    (a) isotropic soil (b) anisotropic soil
    (c) sandy soil (d) clay soil

Answers	**11. (d)**	**13. (a)**	**15. (b)**	**17. (a)**
	12. (a)	**14. (b)**	**16. (d)**	

18. A rectangular channel would be hydraulically most efficient, if the flow depth is equal to

(a) bottom width (b) half of bottom width

(c) half of top width (d) NOA

19. Manning's n for a straight concrete channel is equal to

(a) 0.015 (b) 0.018

(c) 0.014 (d) 0.019

20. In rivers and canals the average flow velocity occurs at the depth of

(a) 0.4 d from the free surface

(b) 0.6 d from the free surface

(c) 0.4 d to 0.8 d from the free surface

(d) NOA

21. A channel with constant cross-sectional shape, size and bottom slope is called as

(a) natural channel (b) prismatic channel

(c) ideal channel (d) all of the above

22. Hydraulic jump below a spillway or a sluice gate is an example of

(a) Steady rapidly varied flow

(b) Unsteady rapidly varied flow

(c) Steady gradually-varied flow

(d) NOA

23. In laminar flow, the

(a) viscous forces are strong

(b) inertia forces are strong

(c) viscous forces are week

(d) NOA

Answers	
	18. (b) 20. (b) 22. (a)
	19. (c) 21. (b) 23. (a)

24. **Time of concentration is the function of**
   (a) Channel length and its slope
   (b) Channel length and watershed slope
   (c) Channel slope and elongated length of watershed
   (d) NOA

25. **For a given cross-sectional area of channel, the hydraulic radius decreases with**
   (a) decrease in wetted perimeter
   (b) increase in wetted perimeter
   (c) decrease in flow depth
   (d) NOA

26. **Spiles are used for the purpose of**
   (a) conveyance of water in a channel
   (b) erosion control at outlet
   (c) diversion of water
   (d) NOA

27. **The depth of water flowing over the weir is called as**
   (a) weir crest (b) water depth
   (c) flow head (d) NOA

28. **Parshall flumes allow reasonably accurate measurement of flow, even when**
   (a) partially submerged (b) fully submerged
   (c) not smoothly installed (d) NOA

29. **Irrigation frequency is the functions of**
   (a) crop and soil
   (b) soil and climate
   (c) crop, soil and climate
   (d) all of the above

Answers	24. (c)	26. (c)	28. (a)
	25. (b)	27. (a)	29. (d)

30. Consumptive use will be less in

(a) poorly planted crop but water is efficiently applied as per requirement
(b) poorly planted crop with inefficient water application
(c) density planted crops
(d) NOA

31. The value of crop coefficient (K_c) during maximum canopy coverage and root system, is usually

(a) 0.5 (b) 1.5 (c) 1.0 (d) 0.2

32. Sorption refers to

(a) Rising of water content in the soil
(b) reduction of water content in soil
(c) decrease in infiltration
(d) all of the above

33. Dimension of USWB class-A pan is

(a) 120 cm diameter and 50 cm depth
(b) 120 cm diameter and 25 cm depth
(c) 100 cm diameter and 50 cm depth
(d) NOA

34. Quantity of water, exclusive of precipitation, required for crop production is called as

(a) Irrigation requirement
(b) net irrigation requirement
(c) Gross water requirement
(d) NOA

35. In furrow irrigation method, the furrows are constructed

(a) along the field boundary
(b) across the land slope
(c) along the general land slope
(d) NOA

Answers	30. (b)	32. (d)	34. (b)
	31. (b)	33. (b)	35. (b)

36. Formation that contains water but transmits water at slow rate, is called as

(a) Aquiclude (b) aquifer
(c) Aquifuge (d) hard pan

37. The drip system was firstly used in

(a) America (b) Israel
(c) USSR (d) India

38. Operating pressure of sprinkler system is

(a) 1 to 4 kg/cm^2 (b) 10 to 15 kg/cm^2
(c) 0.15 to 0.5 kg/cm^2 (d) NOA

39. Check basin method of irrigation is most suitable in

(a) heavy soils (b) coarse soils
(c) loamy soils (d) sandy soils

40. Sichardt equation is associated to compute

(a) radius of influence in ground water flow
(b) friction factor
(c) grain size
(d) NOA

41. Border irrigation is most commonly used in

(a) Row crops
(b) All close growing grain crops
(c) Horticultural crops
(d) Vegetable crops

42. Tensiometer measures the moisture content indirectly, by measuring

(a) Matrix potential (b) Hydrostatic potential
(c) Osmotic potential (d) NOA

Answers	
	36. (a) 38. (a) 40. (a) 42. (a) 37. (b) 39. (a) 41. (b)

43. Water held in interstices or small pores of soil is called as

(a) Structural water (b) capillary water

(c) Adsorbed water (d) NOA

44. Soil water that is not available for plant growth is the

(a) capillary water

(b) gravitational water

(c) hygroscopic water

(d) vadose water

45. To retain 90% of gravel pack material, the slot size of screen should be equal to

(a) d_{10} of pack material

(b) d_{50} of pack material

(c) d_{60} of pack material

(d) NOA

46. Darcy's law is applicable to the

(a) viscous flow of water in the soil

(b) viscous flow of water in the conduit

(c) ideal flow in the pipe

(d) all of the above

47. The force, to keep the soil and water together during wet condition is the

(a) adhesion force (b) suction

(c) soil water potential (d) surface tension

48. Crop coefficient is the ratio of

(a) ET crop and reference crop ET

(b) reference crop ET and ET crop

(c) actual ET and pan evaporation

(d) NOA

Answers	43. (b)	45. (a)	47. (d)
	44. (c)	46. (d)	48. (a)

49. Jacob method for evaluation of aquifer parameters, is valid for the value of u

(a) less than 0.001 (b) 1

(c) more than 0.41 (d) NOA

50. For a well construction in a aquifer with coefficient of permeability less than 20 m/day, the optimum value of screen entrance velocity for screen design should be

(a) 20 cm/s (b) 10.0 cm/s

(c) 11.5 cm/s (d) 5.0 cm/s

OOOOO

Answers	49. (a) 50. (d)

Andhra Pradesh Public Service Commission (AEE) Exam - 2016

Agricultural Engineering (SWCE)

1. **The velocity of a fluid in a pipe of diameter D is V. The pipe is connected to another pipe of diameter 2D. Reynolds number in the pipe of diameter D in relation to the pipe of diameter 2D is**

   (a) Double (b) Four times
   (c) Half (d) Same

2. **Which of the following mineral particle size is classified as silt according to ISSS**

   (a) 0.05 to 0.1 mm (b) 0.002 to 0.05 mm
   (c) 0.002 to 0.02 mm (d) NOA

3. **Maize is a**

   (a) Soil maintaining crop (b) Soil building crop
   (c) Soil depleting crop (d) NOA

4. **Class IV type lands are**

   (a) Suitable for cultivation
   (b) Not suitable for cultivation
   (c) Partly suitable for cultivation
   (d) NOA

5. **Length of the surveyor's chain is**

   (a) 33 ft. (b) 66 ft. (c) 100 ft. (d) 150 ft.

Answers	**1. (a)**	**3. (a)**	**5. (b)**
	2. (b)	**4. (a)**	

6. **Soil degradation takes place due to**
   (a) Glacial erosion (b) Geologic erosion
   (c) Accelerated erosion (d) All of the above

7. **Darcy's Law is valid for**
   (a) Laminar and turbulent flow
   (b) Turbulent flow
   (c) Laminar flow
   (d) Transient flow

8. **The ratio of water stored in the root zone of the plants to water delivered to the field is termed as**
   (a) Water application efficiency
   (b) Water storage efficiency
   (c) Water distribution efficiency
   (d) Water use efficiency

9. **The ratio of the volume of voids to the total soil volume is called**
   (a) Void ratio (b) Porosity
   (c) Dry bulk density (d) Wet bulk density

10. **Penman method is used to compute**
    (a) Consumptive use of crops
    (b) Potential evapotranspiration of crops
    (c) Water requirement of crops
    (d) Irrigation water requirement of crops

11. **Quick sand condition is created due to**
    (a) frictionless nature of soil
    (b) low value of cohesion of soil
    (c) upward seepage force greater than submerged weight of soil
    (d) downward seepage pressure

Answers	6. (d)	8. (b)	10. (b)
	7. (c)	9. (b)	11. (c)

12. **At field capacity, soil moisture tension of sandy soil is approximately equal to**

(a) 0.1 bar (b) 1.0 bar
(c) 10 bar (d) NOA

13. **Evapotranspiration in a crop field surrounded by dry fallow land will be higher than that surrounded by vegetation due to**

(a) conduction of heat (b) oasis effect
(c) clothesline effect (d) convection of heat

14. **For a watershed, the universal soil-loss equation computes**

(a) annual runoff
(b) average annual soil loss
(c) erodibility factor
(d) average annual rainfall

15. **The porosity of sandy soil usually ranges from**

(a) 30 to 35% (b) 35 to 50%
(c) 40 to 60% (d) 50 to 60%

16. **The indicator plant used for determining the permanent wilting percentage**

(a) Wheat (b) Safflower
(c) Sunflower (d) Paddy

17. **When the soil moisture and rainfall are inadequate during the growing season to support healthy crop growth to maturity is called**

(a) Metrological drought (b) Hydrological drought
(c) Agricultural drought (d) NOA

18. **Soil strength is determined by**

(a) Penetrometer (b) Micrometer
(c) Hydrometer (d) Dynamometer

Answers	12. (a)	14. (b)	16. (c)	18. (a)
	13. (b)	15. (b)	17. (c)	

19. Lysimeter is used to measure

(a) Infiltration (b) Evaporation

(c) Evapotranspiration (d) Vapour pressure

20. Atterberg's limits are related to the soil property

(a) Structure (b) Plasticity

(c) Density (d) Strength

21. The discharge rate of drip emitters usually ranges from

(a) 2-10 liters/day (b) 2-10 liters/hr

(c) 2-10 liters/min (d) 2-10 liters/sec

22. Sprinkler irrigation is recommended in

(a) Highly undulating area

(b) Soils having high infiltration rate

(c) Irrigation source is a tube well

(d) all of the above

23. Mole drains are suitable for

(a) Very coarse soil

(b) Medium coarse soil

(c) Sandy loam soil

(d) Fine texture soil

24. Hydraulically most efficient cross-section of an open channel is

(a) Triangular (b) Rectangular

(c) Semi-circular (d) Trapezoidal

25. Sediment yield is the

(a) Total soil loss from an area

(b) Product of gross erosion and delivery ratio

(c) Both (a) and (b)

(d) NOA

Answers	**19. (c)**	**21. (b)**	**23. (d)**	**25. (c)**
	20. (d)	**22. (d)**	**24. (c)**	

26. Chute spillway is used in control a drop of

(a) 0-3 m (b) 1-4 m

(c) 2-4 m (d) 3-6 m

27. Soil loss in geologic erosion is

(a) Les than accelerated erosion

(b) Greater than accelerated erosion

(c) Medium

(d) NOA

OOOOO

Answers	26. (d) 27. (a)

Rajasthan Public Service Commission (AEE) Exam - 2018 Agricultural Engineering (SWCE)

1. **Hydrographic Survey deals with the mapping of**
   (a) Large water bodies (b) Canal system
   (c) Watershed (d) Movements of clouds
2. **A precise method of computing the volume of earthwork in land levelling can be computed by**
   (a) Volumetric method
   (b) Prismoidal method
   (c) End-area method
   (d) Arithmetic mean method
3. **The ratio of the map distance to the corresponding distance of the ground is called as**
   (a) Scale (b) Unit fraction
   (c) Plan factor (d) Representative factor
4. **Which method of survey is the most accurate ?**
   (a) Plane table method (b) Grid method
   (c) Transit method (d) Chain survey method
5. **The accuracy of measurement in chain surveying does not depend upon**
   (a) Length of the offset
   (b) Importance of the features

Answers	1. (a)	3. (a)	5. (d)
	2. (b)	4. (c)	

(c) Scale of the plotting

(d) General layout of the chain lines

6. **An ideal vertical curve to join two gradients is**

(a) Circular (b) Parabolic

(c) Elliptical (d) Hyperbolic

7. **The time of concentration of a watershed is proportional to**

(a) $L^{1.77}$ (b) $L^{1.77}\ S^{0.385}$

(c) $S^{-0.385}$ (d) $S^{1.77}$

8. **The current sequence of water erosion is**

(a) Splash, Sheet, Rill, Gully

(b) Gully, Splash, Sheet, Rill

(c) Sheet, Gully, Rill, Splash

(d) Rill, Splash, Sheet, Gully

9. **The line which separates the catchment basin from the rest of the area is**

(a) Ridge line (b) Dam line

(c) Catchment line (d) Watershed line

10. **A combination of contouring and crop rotation, in which alternate rows are constructed perpendicular to the direction of wind and water flow, to prevent soil erosion, is called**

(a) Strip cropping (b) Mulching

(c) Vegetated waterways (d) Terracing

11. **What will be the height of an overflow spillway section for a design discharge of $1500 m^3/s$, given that the upstream water surface level is at elevation of 240 m and the upstream channel floor is at 200 m; the spillway, having a vertical face, is 50 m long.**

(a) 3.45 m (b) 4.55 m (c) 100 m (d) 5.76 m

Answers	**6. (b)**	**8. (a)**	**10. (a)**
	7. (c)	**9. (d)**	**11. (d)**

12. **A meter suitable for total flow measurement is**

(a) Turbine flow meter (b) Venturimeter

(c) Rotameter (d) Orifice meter

13. **The Water Horse Power (WHP) for centrifugal water pump for given flow rate of 4500 liter/h and 10 m head added to the flow is**

(a) 14.26 (b) 16.26

(c) 15.26 (d) 12.26

14. **Calculate the discharge of reciprocating pump (single cutting) if area of cylinder is 0.25 m^2, length of stroke is 0.15 m, number of cylinder = 1 and speed of pump is 50 rpm.**

(a) 0.01125 m^3/s (b) 0.02125 m^3/s

(c) 0.03125 m^3/s (d) 0.04125 m^3/s

15. **A spillway has been designed for a head of 2.80 m with a length 200 m. The discharge coefficient is C= 0.49. The discharge for this head will be**

(a) 2034 m^3/s (b) 2234 m^3/s

(c) 2434 m^3/s (d) 2634 m^3/s

16. **Contour bunding is done to check**

(a) Sheet erosion (b) Rill erosion

(c) Gully erosion (d) Ravine formation

17. **From the hydraulic efficiency point of view, the most efficient cross-section of an open channel is**

(a) Parabolic (b) Trapezoidal

(c) Semi-circular (d) Rectangular

18. **Watershed is a**

(a) Hydrological entity contributing runoff to a common point.

Answers	12. (a)	14. (c)	16. (a)	18. (b)
	13. (d)	15. (a)	17. (c)	

(c) Hydrological entity receiving runoff from multi-inlet.

(b) Hydrological entity receiving runoff to a single point.

(d) Hydrological entity distributing runoff from common inlet.

19. The depth of flow over a sharp crested rectangular weir should not be more than about

(a) half the crest width

(b) two-third of the crest width

(c) three-fourth of the crest width

(d) the width of the weir

20. Water horse power of centrifugal pump of 15 liters/sec capacity and 30m total head will be equal to

(a) 3.0 (b) 4.0 (c) 5.0 (d) 6.0

21. Interceptor drain helps to control water logging by

(a) Lowering the water table

(b) Draining out excess water to the natural drain

(c) Preventing subsoil water from reaching the area

(d) NOA

22. The actual area irrigated in a year from an outlet is

(a) Irrigation period (b) Irrigation frequency

(c) Intensity of irrigation (d) Irrigation efficiency

23. Interception loss is

(a) High in the beginning of storm and gradually decreases

(b) Low in the beginning of storm and gradually decreases

(c) High in the ending of storm and gradually decreases

(d) High in the beginning of storm and gradually increases

Answers	**19. (b)**	**21. (c)**	**23. (a)**
	20. (d)	**22. (c)**	

24. **When the speed of a centrifugal pump is changed the head varies as**
   (a) The speed
   (b) Square root of the speed
   (c) Square of the speed
   (d) Cube of the speed

25. **Ditch conduit formula is used for**
   (a) Sand bearing test (b) Size of tile drain
   (c) Grade of tile drain (d) Loads on drain pipes

26. **The maximum size of the raindrop is**
   (a) 6 mm (b) 2 mm
   (c) 10 mm (d) 0.5 mm

27. **An aquifer which is bounded by an impermeable layer at the bottom and semi-pervious layer at the top is known as**
   (a) Artesian aquifer (b) Confined aquifer
   (c) Semi-confined aquifer (d) Unconfined aquifer

28. **The drainage density is**
   (a) Length of streams per drainage area within basin
   (b) Stream discharge per unit drainage area
   (c) Drainage area per unit stream length
   (d) Number of streams per unit drainage area

29. **Value of drainage coefficient for small drainage projects is taken as**
   (a) 10 to 15 mm/day (b) 6 to 25 mm/day
   (c) 5 to 10 mm/day (d) 15 to 20 mm/day

30. **Which of the erosion is extremely harmful for the land ?**
   (a) Raindrop erosion (b) Gully erosion
   (c) Rill erosion (d) Sheet erosion

Answers	**24. (c)**	**26. (a)**	**28. (a)**	**30. (b)**
	25. (d)	**27. (c)**	**29. (b)**	

31. In the Universal Soil Loss Equation (USLE), the soil erodability factor K is

(a) Measure of the susceptibility of soil particles to detachment and transport

(b) Slope length gradient factor

(c) Crop management factor

(d) Rainfall-runoff factor

OOOOO

Answers	**31. (a)**

Maharashtra Public Service Exam. Agricultural Service Exam. - 2017 Agricultural Engineering (SWCE)

1. **Which equation is used to estimate the velocity of flow through a channel in designing grass waterways ?**
   (a) Rancer's equation (b) Israelson equation
   (c) Rational equation (d) Manning's equation

2. **Which one of the following is not a type of bench terrace ?**
   (a) Level (b) Outwardly slopping
   (c) Inwardly slopping (d) Along contour

3. **Erosivity is defined as**
   (a) Capacity of wind to cause erosion
   (b) Capacity of rain to cause erosion
   (c) Vulnerability of soil susceptible for erosion
   (d) NOA

4. **Saltation, suspension and surface creep forms of movement of soil particles is associated with which type of soil erosion from the following?**
   (a) Gully erosion (b) Wind erosion
   (c) Rill erosion (d) NOA

5. **What will be the vertical interval between two consecutive contour bunds if the land slope is 3% ?**
   (a) 0.90 m (b) 3.00 m (c) 0.30 m (d) 1.20 m

Answers	1. (d) 3. (b) 5. (a) 2. (d) 4. (b)

6. **Which one of the following is not a permanent gully control structure ?**

(a)	Drop spillway	(b)	Chute spillway
(c)	Drop inlet spillway	(d)	Brushwood dam

7. **Soil erosion which results in the form of uniform removal of land surface is termed as**

(a)	Splash erosion	(b)	Sheet erosion
(c)	Rill erosion	(d)	Gully erosion

8. **In case of streams, stream bank erosion generally takes place on the side of the stream.**

(a)	convex	(b)	downstream
(c)	concave	(d)	top

9. **The damaging effect of flood depends on their super criticality which is measured by the Froude number (Fr). The flow is said to be supercritical, if**

(a)	$Fr < 1$	(b)	$Fr > 1$
(c)	$Fr = 1$	(d)	$Fr \leq 1$

10. **Threshold rainfall is defined as**

(a) Cumulative rainfall before initiation of runoff

(b) Cumulative rainfall of storm

(c) Total daily rainfall

(d) NOA

11. **Which one of the following is not an artificial Rainwater Harvesting technique ?**

(a) Rock fracturing

(b) Afforestation

(c) Bore blast technique

(d) Construction of jacket around the well

Answers	6. (d)	8. (c)	10. (b)
	7. (b)	9. (b)	11. (b)

12. **Which of the following equations is used for water balance studies of a watershed ?**
    (a) P = R + E + dS = dSg
    (b) P = R + ET + U + dS
    (c) P = R + ET + U + dS + dSg
    (d) NOA

13. **Which one of the following options cannot be included in the concept of watershed development ?**
    (a) Construction of major dams
    (b) Optimal management of land water resources
    (c) Socio-economic and institutional development
    (d) Biodiversity protection

14. **Delineation of a watershed is an exercise of**
    (a) Area wise delineation
    (b) Land use wise delineation
    (c) Topographically drainage stream wise delineation
    (d) NOA

15. **Out of different biological measures used to control erosion in a watershed, which one of the following is not a biological measure ?**
    (a) Contour strip cropping
    (b) Buffer strip cropping
    (c) Mixed cropping
    (d) Field strip cropping

16. **Which of the following types of farm ponds should be selected where ground water table rise is within a few meters from the ground surface ?**
    (a) Embankment type
    (b) Polythene lined dugout type

Answers	12. (c) 13. (a)	14. (c) 15. (c)	16. (d)

(c) Dugout type

(d) Cement concrete lined embankment type

17. Which one of the following options is not a geomorphological characteristic of a watershed ?

(a) Total area of watershed

(b) Circulatory ratio

(c) Form factor

(d) Compaction factor

18. Triangular V-notch (90° triangular weir) is a simple flow measuring instrument used for evaluation of watershed development programme. Which is the discharge formula for this instrument ?

(a) $Q = 0.0138\ H^{3/2}$ (b) $Q = 0.0138\ LH^{3/2}$

(c) $Q = 0.0184\ H^{3/2}$ (d) $Q = 0.0138\ H^{5/2}$

19. For land use planning, land capability classification maps are prepared. Which type of land capability class the area demarked with green colour represent ?

(a) Class I (b) Class VI

(c) Class II (d) Class VIII

20. The surface of a channel that is in contact with water is called

(a) Hydraulic radius (b) Wetted area

(c) Wetted perimeter (d) NOA

21. The drainage density of any catchment/watershed varies inversely with the

(a) area of the basin

(b) width of the basin

(c) length of the basin

(d) average depth of the basin

Answers	**17. (a)** **18. (d)**	**19. (a)** **20. (c)**	**21. (a)**

22. The type of flow in which the fluid characteristics like velocity, pressure, density, etc. at a point do not change with time, is called

(a) Steady flow (b) Uniform flow

(c) Unsteady flow (d) Non-uniform flow

23. Infiltration rate of any soil is generally expressed by the following form of equation

(a) $y = mx + c$ (b) $y = at^{\alpha} + b$

(c) $y = at + b$ (d) $y = 4ax + c$

24. The typical characteristic curves of a centrifugal pump show the relationship amongst

A. Discharge B. Total head

C. Brake horse power D. Efficiency

Answer options

(a) A, B and C (b) A, B and D

(c) B, C and D (d) A, B, C and D

25. A canal aligned at right angles to the contours is a

(a) Watershed canal (b) Side slope canal

(c) Contour canal (d) Distributary canal

26. The bedding system of surface drainage is mostly used for

A. Flat soils

B. Steep slopy soils

C. Poorly drained soils with low permeability

D. Sandy soils with high permeability

Answer options

(a) A and B only (b) A and C only

(c) C and D only (d) B and D only

Answers	22. (a) 24. (a) 26. (b) 23. (b) 25. (b)

27. **Cover material is applied to pipe drains**

A. to facilitate water flow into the drain.

B. to prevent the entry of soil particles into the drain.

(a) A only (b) Both A and B

(c) B only (d) None of the above

28. **A 36 hectare catchment area having a drainage coefficient of 2.40 cm, will yield a discharge of**

(a) 100 lit/sec (b) 10 m^3/hr

(c) 10 lit/sec (d) 0.01 m^3/sec

29. **Which one of the following formulae is used to design drain spacing under unsteady state condition ?**

(a) Dupit-Forchheimer (b) Ernst

(c) Hooghoudt (d) Glover-Dumm

30. **Which of the following operations requires moving large quantities of earth over considerable distances ?**

A. Rough grading B. Land leveling

C. Land smoothening D. Land planning

(a) A only (b) A and B only

(c) B only (d) All of the above

31. **Which of the following statements is true ?**

(a) Specific yield + Specific retention = Porosity

(b) Specific retention - Specific yield = Porosity

(c) Porosity + Specific yield = Specific retention

(d) Porosity + Specific retention = Specific yield

32. **The recommended safe limits of land slope (longitudinal slope, %) for efficient irrigation for heavy clay soils is**

(a) 0.05 to 0.20 (b) 0.65 to 1.00

(c) 0.25 to 0.65 (d) 0.20 to 0.40

OOOOO

Answers	27. (b)	29. (d)	31. (a)
	28. (a)	30. (c)	32. (a)

Maharashtra Public Service Exam. Agricultural Service Exam. - 2018 Agricultural Engineering (SWCE)

1. **Which one of the following structures is not cross drainage work constructed on canal system ?**
   (a) Cantilever skimming platform
   (b) Super passages
   (c) Level crossing
   (d) Syphon

2. **The capacity of diversion channel should be estimated based on peak runoff for years recurrence interval.**
   (a) 5 (b) 15 (c) 10 (d) 20

3. **In case of grassed waterway, velocity of flow does not exceed**
   (a) 3.2 m/s (b) 1.8 m/s
   (c) 1.0 m/s (d) 4.0 m/s

4. **For a watershed having 5% land slope and 15 m horizontal interval, the vertical interval will be**
   (a) 0.50 m (b) 1.00 m
   (c) 0.75 m (d) 1.25 m

5. **The length of contour bund per ha having horizontal interval 25 m is**
   (a) 400 m (b) 1000 m (c) 500 m (d) 200 m

Answers	1. (c) 3. (b) 5. (a) 2. (c) 4. (c)

6. **The consistency of rainfall is determined by**
   (a) Mass-curve (b) Flow-duration curve
   (c) Hyetograph (d) Double-mass curve

7. **The nature of hydrograph depends on the characteristics of**
   (a) Rainfall and watershed
   (b) Watershed only
   (c) Rainfall only
   (d) NOA

8. **The assumptions of unit hydrograph are**
   (a) Linear response and time invariant
   (b) Non-linear time variance only
   (c) Non-linear response of time
   (d) NOA

9. **Snyder's method is used to derive the**
   (a) Unit hydrograph
   (b) Dimensionless unit hydrograph
   (c) Synthetic unit hydrograph
   (d) Distribution graph

10. **In the land capability Class I type soils, the slope of land is ....%.**
   (a) 3 to 5 (b) 5 to 8
   (c) 8 to 12 (d) 0 to 1

11. **Which of the following is not sediment load ?**
   (a) Bed load (b) Saltation load
   (c) Siltation load (d) Suspended load

12. **The K-factor in USLE is measured on unit plot of size**
   (a) 22 m long with 9% slope
   (b) 50 m long with 15% slope

Answers	**6. (d)**	**8. (a)**	**10. (d)**	**12. (a)**
	7. (a)	**9. (c)**	**11. (a)**	

(c) 44 m long with 12% slope

(d) 60 m long with 20% slope

13. .... type of gullies are generally found in the alluvial plains, where surface and sub-surface soils are easily erodible.

(a) U-shaped (b) V-shaped

(c) L-shape (d) W-shape

14. Nash model is associated to

(a) IUH (b) SUHG

(c) Distribution HHG (d) All of the above

15. .... is the material bouncing along the bed or moving directly or indirectly by the impact of bouncing particles with each other.

(a) Contact load (b) Suspended load

(c) Saltation load (d) Bed load

16. .... of the watershed represents the yield of sediment rate thorn the entire watershed area.

(a) The outlet

(b) The ridge line

(c) The high elevation point

(d) NOA

17. The sediment sampler should be kept in .... position from the stream bed.

(a) Horizontal (b) Vertical

(c) Parallel (d) NOA

18. Unit hydrograph method is not suitable for the estimation of surface runoff from a watershed area of

(a) < 25 km^2 and > 5000 km^2

(b) < 25 ha and > 5000 ha

Answers	**13. (a)**	**15. (a)**	**17. (b)**
	14. (a)	**16. (d)**	**18. (a)**

(c) < 25 acre and > 5000 acre

(d) < 15 km^2 and > 10,000 km^2

19. The intensity of moderate rainfall is

(a) 2.5 cm to 7.5 cm/hr (b) 2.5 mm to 7.5 mm/hr

(c) 7.5 mm to 10 mm/hr (d) 7.5 cm to 10 cm/hr

20. .... is the most successful method for controlling the stream bank erosion, when the stream takes a sharp bend and bed scour is not deep.

(a) Brushwood edging (b) Stone revetment

(c) Brushwood rollers (d) NOA

21. As per IMD norms, in plain area rain gauge station is necessary for an area of

(a) 250 km^2 (b) 520 km^2

(c) 450 km^2 (d) 1200 km^2

22. The kinetic energy of raindrop depends on

(a) Drop size (b) Rainfall intensity

(c) Both (a) and (b) (d) NOA

23. Chute spillways are located at the drop height of

(a) 1 to 2 m (b) 5 to 6 m

(c) 0.5 to 1 m (d) All of the above

24. USLE is

(a) An empirical equation

(b) A theoretical equation

(c) Both (a) and (b)

(d) NOA

25. Broad-base terraces are made on lands upto .... percent land grade only.

(a) 10 (b) 20 (c) 15 (d) 22

Answers				
	19. (b)	21. (b)	23. (b)	25. (a)
	20. (b)	22. (c)	24. (a)	

26. **Which of the following terms is not related to basin shape ?**

(a) Form factor (b) Elongation ratio

(c) Circulatory ratio (d) Drainage density

27. **For estimating erosivity from rainfall data .... method/s is/are used.**

(a) EI_{30} index method

(b) KE > 25 index method

(c) Both (a) and (b)

(d) Rational

28. **Soil erodibility (E) is estimated by**

(a) E = (% Sand + % Silt) / % Clay

(b) E= (% Clay + % Silt) / % Sand

(c) E= % Clay/ (% Sand + % Silt)

(d) E = % Sand / % Clay

29. **In the process of sedimentation, which types of particles are transported by bed load ?**

(a) Silt, clay and sand

(b) Only clay

(c) Only silt

(d) Sand, gravel and rock particles

30. **For design of grassed waterways the value of roughness coefficient 'n' is usually taken as**

(a) 0.04 (b) 0.02

(c) 0.08 (d) All of the above

31. **The National Watershed Development Project for Rainfed Areas (NWDPRA) was initiated in**

(a) 1973 - 74 (b) 1990 – 91

(c) 1977 - 78 (d) 1983 – 84

Answers	**26. (d)**	**28. (a)**	**30. (a)**
	27. (c)	**29. (d)**	**31. (b)**

32. The hydrostatic law states that the rate of increase of fluid pressure in a vertically downward direction is equal to at that point.

(a) Density of the fluid

(b) Weight of the fluid

(c) Specific weight of the fluid

(d) Volume of the fluid

33. Which one of the following discharge measuring devices operates efficiently on very small drop in head ?

(a) V-notch (b) H-flume

(c) Cut-throat flume (d) Parshall flume

34. The parallelism of advance and recession curves denote

(a) Less depth of application of water along the length of furrow

(b) Uniform distribution of water throughout the length of the border

(c) Appropriate design of check basin

(d) NOA

35. The critical parameter(s) related to clogging susceptibility of drippers is/are

(a) Size of the flow passage

(b) Velocity of water through the flow passage

(c) Both (a) and (b)

(d) NOA

36. In Kennedy's regime equation, $V = 0.55\ mD^{0.64}$ where m represents

(a) Side slope of channel

(b) Hydraulic radius of channel

(c) Bed slope of channel

(d) Critical velocity ratio

Answers	32. (c)	34. (b)	36. (d)
	33. (d)	35. (c)	

37. Drawdown at any instant is the difference between

(a) Static water level and ground level

(b) Pumping water level and ground level

(c) Pumping water level and impermeable level

(d) Static water level and pumping water level

38. A permeable bed, only partly filled with water and overlying a relatively impervious layer is called

(a) Semi - confined aquifer

(b) Confined aquifer

(c) Unconfined aquifer

(d) Artesian aquifer

OOOOO

Answers	37. (d) 38. (c)

Uttarakhand Public Service Exam. (JE) Exam. – 2013

Agricultural Engineering (SWCE)

1. Unit of Drainage coefficient is
   (a) kg (b) ton
   (c) cm (d) percent

2. Which of the following is not used for gully erosion control ?
   (a) Check dams (b) Brush dams
   (c) Loose rock dams (d) High dams

3. Which of the following is not a mechanical method of erosion control ?
   (a) Contour farming (b) Conservation tillage
   (c) Free cropping (d) Small dams

4. Which of the following is not a stage of gully development ?
   (a) Zero stage (b) Formation stage
   (c) Development stage (d) Healing stage

5. Which of the following is not a permanent gully control structure ?
   (a) Contour bund (b) Drop spillway
   (c) Permanent check dams (d) Drop (inlet) spillway

Answers	1. (c) 3. (c) 5. (a) 2. (d) 4. (a)

6. **Which of the following is not a type of soil erosion due to water ?**

(a) Raindrop erosion (b) Gully erosion
(c) Final erosion (d) Sheet erosion

7. **Which of the following is not a process of soil erosion ?**

(a) Detachment of soil particles
(b) Transportation of soil particles
(c) Both of the above
(d) Shining of soil particles

8. **Which of the following is not a type of soil erosion ?**

(a) Accelerated soil erosion
(b) Geological soil erosion
(c) Water erosion
(d) Single erosion

9. **Spacing of tile drains is generally kept as**

(a) 1 – 2 m (b) 4 – 5 m
(c) 9 – 60 m (d) 70 – 95 m

10. **The depth of tile drains in uniformly permeable soil is kept as**

(a) 0.25 to 0.5 m (b) 0.75 to 1.5 m
(c) 2.0 to 3.5 m (d) 4.0 to 5.5 m

11. **Which method should be used for irrigation in undulating fields ?**

(a) Flooding method of irrigation
(b) Furrow method of irrigation
(c) Check basin method of irrigation
(d) Sprinkler irrigation method

Answers	6. (c)	8. (d)	10. (b)
	7. (d)	9. (c)	11. (d)

12. Which of the following is not a method of surface irrigation?

(a) Free flooding irrigation

(b) Border irrigation

(c) Critical irrigation

(d) Check basin irrigation

13. Which of the following is not a method of irrigation ?

(a) Drip irrigation (b) Accelerated irrigation

(c) Sub-surface irrigation (d) Pitcher irrigation

14. Due to evaporation, the liquid water is transferred to

(a) Atmosphere (b) river

(c) Pond (d) well

15. Over-irrigation results in

(a) increasing crop yield

(b) maintaining soil fertility

(c) economic utilization of water

(d) NOA

16. Efficient irrigation to the crops will provide

(a) increased crop yield

(b) increased water logging

(c) increased salt accumulation

(d) NOA

17. Water conveyance efficiency is related to which of the following ?

(a) Water stored in the root zone

(b) Water needed in the root zone

(c) Uniformity of the water applied

(d) NOA

Answers	12. (c) 13. (b)	14. (a) 15. (d)	16. (a) 17. (a)

18. **Water distribution efficiency indicates**
   (a) water supplied at source
   (b) water delivered at field
   (c) average depth of water stored during irrigation
   (d) NOA

19. **To which of the following the 'duty' of water is related ?**
   (a) Quantity of water used
   (b) Area to the irrigated
   (c) Height of crop
   (d) NOA

20. **The Lysimeter is used to determine**
   (a) Sunshine hours (b) Wind velocity
   (c) Flow velocity (d) Evapotranspiration

21. **Discharge of water as vapour into atmosphere by leaves and stems of living plants is called**
   (a) Evaporation (b) consumptive use
   (c) Transpiration (d) NOA

22. **Evaporation pan is made of**
   (a) brass (b) cast iron
   (c) mild steel (d) NOA

23. **Diameter of a commonly used evaporation pan is**
   (a) 65 cm (b) 75 cm
   (c) 95 cm (d) 120 cm

24. **Which of the following is not related to wind erosion ?**
   (a) Speed of wind
   (b) Age of the soil
   (c) Moisture content of soil
   (d) Texture of soil

Answers	**18. (c)**	**20. (d)**	**22. (c)**	**24. (b)**
	19. (a)	**21. (c)**	**23. (d)**	

25. **Which of the following is not a drainage system ?**

(a) Drip system (b) Surface system

(c) Sub-surface system (d) All of the above

26. **Which of the following is not a component of a drip irrigation system ?**

(a) Head unit

(b) Perforated pipe

(c) Water conveyance and distribution pipes

(d) Drippers

27. **In which country the drip irrigation system was originally developed ?**

(a) India (b) Pakistan

(c) Israel (d) China

28. **Which of the following is not a component of a sprinkler irrigation system ?**

(a) Pump

(b) Sprinkler nozzle

(c) Main and lateral pipe lines

(d) Drip nozzles

29. **The rate of evaporation of water does not depend on**

(a) temperature of water

(b) temperature of air in contact with water

(c) humidity of air

(d) depth of water

30. **Evaporation process is a .... process.**

(a) chemical (b) biological

(c) physical (d) NOA

Answers	25. (a)	27. (c)	29. (d)
	26. (b)	28. (d)	30. (c)

31. **Evaporation is the process of**

(a) condensation (b) vaporization
(c) conduction (d) radiation

32. **Unit of 'delta' is**

(a) cubic meter (b) square meter
(c) hectare (d) meter

33. **The water requirement of a crop is mainly estimated for**

(a) Crop planning on the farm
(b) determining transpiration
(c) Determining water loss
(d) NOA

34. **The depth of a commonly used evaporation pan is**

(a) 20 cm (b) 50 cm
(c) 100 cm (d) 150 cm

35. **The permissible mean flow velocity in an earthen channel in sandy loam soil is**

(a) 40 cm/sec (b) 60 cm/sec
(c) 80 cm/sec (d) 100 cm/sec

36. **A significant soil building crops group is**

(a) Cereal crops (b) leguminous crops
(c) Fodder crops (d) fruit crops

37. **Border slope for clay to clay loam soils is kept generally**

(a) 0.05 to 0.20 % (b) 0.20 to 0.40 %
(c) 0.25 to 0.65 % (d) NOA

38. **The first step in planning a terrace system is the selection of**

(a) Inlet location (b) Terrace slope
(c) Watershed area (d) Outlet location

Answers	**31. (b)**	**33. (a)**	**35. (c)**	**37. (a)**
	32. (d)	**34. (a)**	**36. (b)**	**38. (d)**

39. **One hectare is equal to**
    (a) 1000 m^2 (b) 100 m^2
    (c) 10000 m^2 (d) 10 m^2

40. **Rational formula is used to estimate**
    (a) peak flow rate (b) average flow rate
    (c) uniform flow rate (d) free flow rate

41. **Mannings formula is used to determine**
    (a) peak flow rate (b) flow velocity
    (c) return period (d) time of peak

42. **Chezy's formula is used to determine**
    (a) flow direction (b) flow velocity
    (c) flow duration (d) NOA

43. **Temporary gully control structures are designed for a recurrence interval of**
    (a) upto 10 years (b) upto 8 years
    (c) upto 15 years (d) upto 20 years

44. **Primary cause of failure of permanent gully control structures is**
    (a) Insufficient hydraulic capacity
    (b) Insufficient flow velocity
    (c) Both of the above
    (d) NOA

45. **Spacing of mole drains ranges between ....**
    (a) 0.5 to 1.0 m (b) 20 to 25 m
    (c) 10 to 15 m (d) 1.5 to 9 m

46. **In heavy rainfall areas which type of bench terraces should be preferred ?**
    (a) Level benches

Answers	39. (c)	41. (b)	43. (a)	45. (d)
	40. (a)	42. (b)	44. (c)	46. (c)

(b) Slopping outward benches
(c) Sloping inward benches
(d) NOA

47. Drainage coefficient is defined as the depth of water in centimeter drained from any area in

(a) 12 hours (b) 18 hours
(c) 06 hours (d) 24 hours

48. Most important factor influencing the value of drainage coefficient is

(a) Crop (b) field size
(c) Rainfall (d) NOA

49. In an open channel when flow depth at a section changes with time, the flow is said to be

(a) uniform flow (b) unsteady flow
(c) irregular flow (d) critical flow

50. Sub-surface drainage system includes

(a) drainage outlet and collector drains only
(b) drainage outlet and laterals only
(c) drainage outlet, collectors and laterals
(d) NOA

51. Universal Soil Loss Equation (USLE) is used to calculate

(a) average annual soil loss
(b) average weekly soil loss
(c) average daily soil loss
(d) average monthly soil loss

52. The satisfactory operating pressure for a sprinkler system ranges between

(a) 1.0 – 1.5 kg/cm^2 (b) 1.5 – 2.5 kg/cm^2
(c) 2.5 – 3.5 kg/cm^2 (d) 3.5 – 4.0 kg/cm^2

Answers	47. (d)	49. (b)	51. (a)
	48. (a)	50. (a)	52. (b)

53. **The common size of screen opening for a tube well is**
   (a) less than 1.5 mm (b) 1.5 mm to 5.0 mm
   (c) 5.0 mm to 7.5 mm (d) 10.0 mm to 15.0 mm

54. **One cubic meter volume is equal to**
   (a) 10 litre (b) 1000 litre
   (c) 100 litre (d) 10000 litre

55. **The vertical interval of a terrace system does not depend on**
   (a) Land slope (b) crop height
   (c) Surface topography (d) soil type

56. **The longitudinal slope in a terrace is kept as**
   (a) 0.75 % (b) 1.50 %
   (c) 2.50 % (d) 10.0 %

57. **Weirs are classified based on ....**
   (a) shape of the notch only
   (b) type of the crest only
   (c) both (a) and (b)
   (d) NOA

58. **Minor irrigation schemes include**
   (a) Land reclamation schemes
   (b) surface water irrigation scheme
   (c) ground-water irrigation scheme
   (d) both (b) and (c)

59. **The flow rate from a canal outlet depends on**
   (a) Size of outlet opening only
   (b) head of water above outlet only
   (c) both (a) and (b)
   (d) NOA

Answers	53. (a)	55. (b)	57. (c)	59. (c)
	54. (b)	56. (c)	58. (d)	

60. **Ponds are small water storage structures used for**
(a) Water supply only
(b) Ground-water recharge only
(c) Irrigation only
(d) All of the above

61. **The water table in an unconfined aquifer depends on**
(a) permeability of soil only
(b) pumpage from well only
(c) area of recharge only
(d) all of the above

62. **Water required by the border strip is 42.86 cubic meter, if the discharge available is 36 m^3/hr, then the time required to irrigate the border will be**
(a) 4.19 hour (b) 3.19 hour
(c) 2.19 hour (d) 1.19 hour

63. **If the weight of moist soil is 1.18 kg and the weight of dry soil is 1 kg, then the moisture content of soil on dry weight basis will be,**
(a) 0.0018 % (b) 1.8 %
(c) 0.018 % (d) 18 %

64. **The amount of silt and clay in a sandy loam soil is**
(a) more than 30% (b) more than 20%
(c) more than 50% (d) more than 40%

65. **The average moisture extraction by plants from the first 25% of soil depth is**
(a) 50% (b) 45% (c) 40% (d) 35%

66. **The critical state of flow occurs when the value of Froude number is**
(a) more than 1 (b) less than 1
(c) equal to 1 (d) all of the above

Answers	
	60. (d) 62. (d) 64. (b) 66. (c)
	61. (d) 63. (d) 65. (c)

67. Emitter pipes are classified based on pressure rating into

(a) two classes (b) three classes

(c) four classes (d) five classes

68. The material of emitting pipes should be resistant to

(a) Fertilizers (b) Chemicals

(c) Both (a) and (b) (d) NOA

69. Water application rate from sprinkler system depends on

(a) discharge of sprinkler only

(b) sprinkler spacing only

(c) Lateral movement speed

(d) all of the above

70. The term "EROSIVITY" refers to

(a) erosive time of rain

(b) erosive potential of rain

(c) erosive resistance of rain

(d) NOA

Where, W = width of terrace, m; S = land slope, %

71. In irrigated regions, water logging of low lands is due to

(a) seepage from canals

(b) seepage from unlined irrigation channels

(c) both (a) and (b)

(d) NOA

72. Open drains have disadvantage because

(a) divide farm area into fragments.

(b) interfere with the movement of machinery.

(c) waste considerable area of the farm.

(d) all of the above

Answers	67. (b)	69. (d)	71. (c)
	68. (c)	70. (b)	72. (d)

73. **Depth of deep tube wells is kept as..................**

(a) 20 m (b) 40 m

(c) 60 m (d) 100 m or more

74. **The gully development is accomplished under how many stages ?**

(a) Only two stages (b) Only three stages

(c) Only four stages (d) Only five stages

75. **Which of the following is due to wind erosion ?**

(a) Delta (b) Sea coast

(c) Sedimentation (d) Sand dune

76. **Gully erosion is an advanced stage of**

(a) Sheet erosion (b) Channel erosion

(c) Splash erosion (d) Rill erosion

77. **Sprinklers are lubricated by**

(a) oil (b) grease

(c) oil and grease (d) water

78. **The Planimeter measures**

(a) area (b) volume

(c) density (d) land roughness

79. **A well screen is used in**

(a) open well (b) cavity well

(c) tube well (d) NOA

80. **The recorded description of materials encountered in sequence throughout drilling with reference to the distance from the ground surface is known as**

(a) well log (b) well casing

(c) well depth (d) well description

Answers				
	73. (d)	75. (d)	77. (d)	79. (b)
	74. (c)	76. (d)	78. (a)	80. (a)

81. Culturable command area for a minor irrigation project is

(a) more than 10000 hectare

(b) more than 5000 hectare

(c) upto 5000 hectare

(d) upto 2000 hectare

82. Small watershed is those in which

(a) runoff is predominant

(b) overland flow dominates the runoff

(c) base flow predominant

(d) all of the above

83. The difference in moisture content of the soil between field capacity and permanent wilting point is known as

(a) capillary water (b) hygroscopic water

(c) percolation water (d) available water

84. Sprinkler irrigation method can be preferably used

(a) in places with high wind velocity

(b) for clay soil with very low infiltration rate

(c) for soils with heavy texture and low infiltration rate

(d) for soils with light texture and high infiltration rate

85. Contour trenching should be done in

(a) Winter season (b) summer season

(c) Throughout the year (d) NOA

86. If the net amount of irrigation is 10 cm and the field irrigation efficiency is 80%, the gross amount of water applied is

(a) 10.66 cm (b) 12.50 cm

(c) 8.0 cm (d) 800 cm

Answers	**81. (d)**	**83. (d)**	**85. (b)**
	82. (b)	**84. (d)**	**86. (b)**

87. Mole drains are underground unlined circular or oval earthen channels formed by a mole plough in

(a) sandy-loam soils (b) non-cohesive soils

(c) sandy soils (d) cohesive soils

88. A drainage canal draining 250 hectare area has a discharge of 0.3 m³/s, the drainage coefficient of the area will be

(a) 0.7 cm (b) 1.036 cm

(c) 1.412 cm (d) 2.178 cm

89. Wind erosion is more in

(a) cohesive soils (b) non-cohesive soils

(c) rocky soils (d) wet soil

90. In splash erosion, the raindrop energy acts in the form of

(a) kinetic energy (b) potential energy

(c) chemical energy (d) NOA

91. The property of rainfall which mainly affects the soil erosion is

(a) direction of rainfall (b) time of rainfall

(c) form of rainfall (d) intensity of rainfall

92. Which of the following soil property is mainly affected by wind erosion ?

(a) Soil texture (b) Soil structure

(c) Soil temperature (d) Soil moisture

93. Chezy's formula is represented as

(a) $V = R(CS)^{0.5}$ (b) $V = C\,(RS)^{0.5}$

(c) $V = (CRS)^{0.5}$ (d) $V = S\,(RC)^{0.5}$

Where: V = Flow velocity, C = Coefficient, R = Hydraulic radius, S = Slope of land

Answers				
	87. (d)	89. (b)	91. (d)	93. (b)
	88. (b)	90. (a)	92. (a)	

94. **Up and down the slope farming results in**
    (a) minimizing soil erosion
    (b) increasing soil erosion
    (c) improving moisture conservation
    (d) NOA

95. **The 'gabion' is constructed by using which material ?**
    (a) Vegetative materials (b) R.C.C.
    (c) Brick mortar (d) Wire-net and stones

96. **To determine moisture content of a soil, the soil is kept in oven for 24 hours at the temperature of**
    (a) 100 °C (b) 105 °C
    (c) 110 °C (d) 120 °C

97. **Check dams help in _____.**
    (a) decrease in flow velocity
    (b) minimize channel erosion
    (c) increase infiltration of water
    (d) all of the above

98. **The depth of a most efficient rectangular channel is how many times of its width ?**
    (a) 2.0 times (b) 0.75 times
    (c) 0.5 times (d) 1.5 times

99. **Evapotranspiration can be measured by using which of the following instrument / equipment ?**
    (a) Current meter (b) Lysimeter
    (c) Coshocton wheel (d) Stage recorder

100. **The relation between the area irrigated and the quantity of water used to irrigate it for the purpose of maturing its crop is known as,**

Answers				
	94. (c)	96. (c)	98. (c)	100. (d)
	95. (d)	97. (d)	99. (b)	

(a) irrigation frequency (b) irrigation period
(c) irrigation requirement (d) duty of water

101. In contour cultivation tillage operations are performed

(a) normal to the contours of the field
(b) along the contours of the field
(c) across the contours of the field
(d) in any direction

102. The water which can be removed by drainage is

(a) hygroscopic water (b) gravitational water
(c) capillary water (d) perched water

103. Which of the following trees can be used for bio-drainage work ?

(a) Mango (b) Eucalyptus
(c) Guava (d) Sisal

104. In tile drain installation, the envelope material is required for

(a) increasing the flow rate
(b) increasing the life of tile drains
(c) Increasing the strength of tile drains
(d) decreasing the length of tile drains

105. Which of the following is the surface drain ?

(a) Mole drain (b) Tile drain
(c) Vertical drain (d) Open ditch drain

106. The prismoidal formula is used to determine ....

(a) runoff rate (b) earthwork volume
(c) land slope (d) infiltration rate

Answers			
	101. (b)	103. (b)	105. (d)
	102. (b)	104. (c)	106. (b)

107. Which of the following is not a land grading method ?

(a) Profile method (b) Laser method

(c) Trapezoidal method (d) Plane inspection method

108. Four point method is used to determine

(a) earthwork volume (b) cross slope

(c) longitudinal slope (d) volume of water

109. Water meter is used to measure

(a) flow rate in streams

(b) flow rate in pipes

(c) water volume storage

(d) water energy

110. One ha-cm volume of water is equal to

(a) 10 m^3 (b) 100 m^3

(c) 1000 m^3 (d) 10000 m^3

111. The pressure head in a sprinkler system is converted into velocity head at the

(a) sprinkler head (b) sprinkler jet

(c) nozzle (d) riser head

112. A soil solution with its pH value as 7.0 indicates that

(a) soil is saline (b) soil is acidic

(c) soil is alkaline (d) soil is neutral

113. The discharge of emitters in a drip irrigation system usually ranges between

(a) 2 to 10 litre/hour (b) 2 to 10 litre/second

(c) 120 to 200 litre/hour (d) 50 to 75 litre/hour

114. Estimation of design discharge is done in

(a) hydraulic design (b) structural design

(c) hydrologic design (d) final design

Answers	107. (c)	109. (b)	111. (c)	113. (a)
	108. (a)	110. (b)	112. (d)	114. (a)

115. In water logged lands, the soil pores are saturated

(a) within a depth of 30 cm
(b) within a depth of 40 cm
(c) within a depth of 60 cm
(d) beyond root zone of a crop

116. Removal of thin and fairly uniform layer of the soil from the land surface by runoff water is called as,

(a) torrent erosion (b) sheet erosion
(c) glacial erosion (d) uniform erosion

117. A high intensity rainfall causes severe erosion because of

(a) greater detachment of soil particles only
(b) more runoff generation only
(c) better transportation of eroded soil only
(d) all of the above

118. Which of the following aspects are kept in consideration while designing a drop structure ?

(a) Hydrologic (b) Hydraulic
(c) Structural (d) All of the above

119. Contour bunds are recommended in the areas where

(a) rainfall is low (b) rainfall is high
(c) soil is heavy (d) NOA

120. The period for which water is supplied from canal to a crop is called

(a) base (b) duty
(c) delta (d) irrigation period

121. Arrangement of soil particles in a soil mass is called

(a) soil texture (b) soil structure
(c) infiltration (d) particle density

Answers	**115. (d)**	**117. (d)**	**119. (a)**	**121. (b)**
	116. (b)	**118. (d)**	**120. (a)**	

122. **The factor which affects irrigation efficiency is**
   (a) Design of irrigation system
   (b) degree of land preparation
   (c) skill and ease of irrigation
   (d) all of the above

123. **To carry irrigation channels across the road, the appropriate structure is**
   (a) culvert (b) siphon
   (c) spillway (d) all of the above

124. **In an open channel water flows under the influence of**
   (a) gravity force (b) inertia force
   (c) suction force (d) NOA

125. **In open channels, the flow is due to**
   (a) pressure difference (b) elevation difference
   (c) velocity difference (d) all of the above

126. **For a given cross sectional area of channel, the hydraulic radius decreases with**
   (a) increase in wetted perimeter
   (b) decrease in wetted perimeter
   (c) decrease in flow velocity
   (d) increase in flow velocity

127. **The most efficient section of open channel is**
   (a) semicircular (b) triangular
   (c) trapezoidal (d) parabolic

128. **Tensiometers are used to measure**
   (a) soil organic matter (b) flow depth
   (c) flow velocity (d) soil moisture

Answers				
	122. (d)	124. (a)	126. (b)	128. (d)
	123. (a)	125. (b)	127. (a)	

129. The common water distribution pattern used in canal command areas of northern India is

(a) shejpali system (b) tail to tail system

(c) warabandi system (d) all of the above

130. Runoff coefficient depends on

(a) nature of soil surface (b) type of land use

(c) rainfall intensity (d) all of the above

131. Free board is provided to prevent the embankment against

(a) overtopping (b) sliding

(c) overturning (d) all of the above

132. The agronomic measures increase infiltration rate and thereby there is

(a) reduction in runoff (b) increase in soil erosion

(c) formation of gullies (d) NOA

133. Rate of increase in crop yield per unit increase in water application is known as

(a) water use efficiency (b) irrigation response

(c) project efficiency (d) gross water requirement

134. Straight and parallel contour lines represent

(a) uniformly sloping undulating surface

(b) uniformly sloping plane surface

(c) undulating surface

(d) NOA

135. The removal of excess water from the ground surface is called

(a) ground water flow

(b) surface drainage

(c) sub-surface drainage

(d) water table control

Answers	129. (c)	131. (a)	133. (b)	135. (b)
	130. (d)	132. (a)	134. (b)	

136. According to U.S. Dept. of Agriculture, the size of particles of coarse sand varies between

(a) 1.0 to 2.0 mm (b) 0.5 to 1.0 mm
(c) 0.25 to 0.5 mm (d) NOA

137. The drip irrigation system is very effective in case of

(a) paddy fields (b) sugarcane fields
(c) orchards (d) all of the above

138. Which of the following is not a permanent structure ?

(a) Drop spillway (b) Chute spillway
(c) Drop inlet spillway (d) Contour bund

139. If the depth of flow in a river is 'd', then the average flow velocity occurs at a depth equal to

(a) 0.4 d from free surface
(b) 0.6 d from free surface
(c) 0.2 d from free surface
(d) at the free surface

140. Graded bunds are useful in areas where

(a) rainfall is very low (b) rainfall is low
(c) rainfall is high (d) NOA

141. Due to shrinkage of soil during land grading, the cut-fill ratio should be

(a) greater than one (b) less than one
(c) either of (a) and (b) (d) NOA

142. Advantages of minor irrigation projects are

(a) low cost
(b) easily manageable
(c) higher irrigation efficiency
(d) all of the above

Answers				
	136. (b)	138. (d)	140. (c)	142. (d)
	137. (c)	139. (b)	141. (a)	

143. The desired cut or fill at any point can be obtained by comparing

(a) original and proposed elevations
(b) original and surrounding elevations
(c) proposed and surrounding elevations
(d) all of the above

144. Control of soil erosion is vital for

(a) sustenance of agriculture
(b) maintaining crop productivity
(c) control of sedimentation
(d) all of the above

145. Mulching helps in

(a) controlling soil erosion
(b) maintaining soil moisture
(c) controlling weeds
(d) all of the above

146. The drop in case of a straight drop spillway should not exceed to

(a) 5 m (b) 3 m (c) 10 m (d) 8 m

147. In drip irrigation system, the drippers are equipped on

(a) main line (b) sub-main line
(c) lateral line (d) all of the above

148. Drip irrigation is also known as

(a) sub-surface irrigation (b) complete irrigation
(c) trickle irrigation (d) surge irrigation

149. Void ratio of soil is also known as

(a) relative density (b) relative porosity
(c) specific gravity (d) NOA

Answers	143. (a)	145. (d)	147. (c)	149. (b)
	144. (d)	146. (b)	148. (c)	

150. The part of rainfall which becomes part of the water requirement of crops is known as

(a) gross rainfall (b) efficient rainfall

(c) effective rainfall (d) true rainfall

151. The method which estimates evaporation from a free water surface by examining energy balance at the water surface is

(a) Blaney - Criddle method

(b) Dalton method

(c) Penman method

(d) NOA

152. The term extensively used to express the performance of a complete irrigation system or components of the system is called

(a) irrigation effect (b) irrigation efficiency

(c) irrigation facility (d) irrigation availability

153. Uniformity of water application in sprinkler irrigation is affected by

(a) water temperature (b) wind velocity

(c) soil characteristics (d) time of irrigation

154. Which of the following is a measure for reclamation of alkali soil ?

(a) Green manuring with dhaincha in summer

(b) Use of gypsum

(c) Provision of drainage system

(d) All of the above

155. The primary purpose of contour farming in low rainfall areas is

(a) to increase runoff

(b) to increase soil loss

Answers	150. (c)	152. (b)	154. (b)
	151. (c)	153. (b)	155. (d)

(c) to conserve flow energy

(d) to conserve rain water

156. Which major nutrient is very soluble and can be expected in drainage effluent ?

(a) Nitrogen (b) Phosphorous

(c) Potash (d) NOA

157. In water - logged areas, when organic matter accumulates in the soil ?

(a) Before water logging

(b) After water logging

(c) During water logging

(d) NOA

158. One atmospheric pressure is equal to how many cm of water column ?

(a) 1000 cm (b) 1050 cm

(c) 1023 cm (d) 1036 cm

159. In which type of soil, the drainage will be poor ?

(a) Sandy soils (b) Clayey soils

(c) Silty soils (d) Loamy soils

160. Which of the following is not a salt tolerant crop ?

(a) Barley (b) Dhaincha

(c) Gram (d) Spinach

161. Which of the following is not a water lift ?

(a) Persian wheel (b) Swing basket

(c) Counterpoise (d) Turbine

162. One horse power is equal to

(a) 724 watts (b) 746 watts

(c) 714 watts (d) 764 watts

Answers	156. (b)	158. (d)	160. (c)	162. (b)
	157. (b)	159. (b)	161. (d)	

163. Soil taxonomy deals with which of the following ?

(a) Principles of soil productivity
(b) Principles of soil erosivity
(c) Principles of soil classification
(d) Principles of soil formation

164. Under irregular topographic field conditions which of the following strip cropping system is preferred ?

(a) Contour strip cropping system
(b) Field strip cropping system
(c) Buffer strip cropping system
(d) Either of the above

165. The value of runoff coefficient normally is

(a) always more than one
(b) always equal to one
(c) always less than one
(d) all of the above

166. In a field contour lines are obtained by joining the points of

(a) same rainfall (b) same elevation
(c) same erosion (d) same infiltration

167. Gully plugs help in

(a) reducing infiltration
(b) reducing flow velocity
(c) reducing sediment deposition
(d) reducing percolation

168. Hygrophilic soils are those which

(a) condense water (b) repulse water
(c) release water (d) attract water

Answers			
	163. (c)	165. (b)	167. (b)
	164. (c)	166. (b)	168. (b)

169. Seepage force always acts in

(a) only in upward direction

(b) opposite direction to flow

(c) in the direction of flow

(d) only in the downward direction

170. In the design of a drop structure which of the following force is considered ?

(a) Gravitational forces (b) Viscous forces

(c) Frictional forces (d) Drag forces

OOOOO

Answers	169. (c) 170. (c)

Uttarakhand Public Service Exam. (AE) Exam. – 2022

Agricultural Engineering (SWCE)

1. **Plane table survey requires**

1.	Drawing board	2.	Alidade
3.	Plumb bob	4.	Spirit level
(a)	1 only	(b)	1, 2, 4
(c)	1, 2, 3, 4	(d)	1, 2, 3

2. **If the RPM of the pump is increased by 50%, the required BHP will increase by**

(a)	50 %	(b)	1.75 times
(c)	2.25 times	(d)	3.38 times

3. **Irrotational flow is such that**
   (a) Velocity may not be zero.
   (b) Circulation is zero
   (c) 2-Dimensional flow in X-Z plane in the presence of gravitational forces
   (d) The particles cannot go in circular motion

4. **Staff reading taken on a point of known elevation**

(a)	Fore sight	(b)	Back sight
(c)	Intermediate sight	(d)	Turning point

Answers	**1. (c)**	**3. (b)**
	2. (d)	**4. (b)**

5. **As compared to volute centrifugal pumps, jet pumps are .... in efficiency.**

   (a) equal (b) high
   (c) low (d) None of the above

6. **Select the correct answer**

   (a) Back Bearing = Fore Bearing + 180°
   (b) Back Bearing = Fore Bearing – 180°
   (c) Back Bearing = Fore Bearing ± 180°
   (d) None of the above

7. **When the speed of centrifugal pump is changed, the performance of pump is changed as**

   1. The capacity varies inversely as speed.
   2. The head varies as square of the speed.
   3. The BHP varies as cube of the speed.

   (a) Only 1 is true (b) 2 & 3 are true
   (c) 1 & 2 are true (d) 1, 2 & 3 are true

8. **The particle density of agricultural produce is 1.95 g/cc. The porosity of produce is 36%. The bulk density of produce will be**

   (a) 1.00 g/cc (b) 1.25 g/cc
   (c) 1.50 g/cc (d) 1.75 g/cc

9. **Which of the following assumptions are made for deriving Bernoulli's equation ?**

   (a) Steady flow (b) Unsteady flow
   (c) Both (a) & (b) (d) None of the above

10. **The suction lift of the horizontal centrifugal pump should normally be between**

   (a) 2 to 4 m (b) 3 to 5 m
   (c) 7.5 to 10 m (d) 4.5 to 6.0 m

Answers	5. (b)	7. (b)	9. (a)
	6. (c)	8. (b)	10. (c)

11. **In the International Standard atmosphere**
    (a) Pressure stays constant with altitude
    (b) The lapse rate varies linearly with altitude
    (c) The rate of drop of pressure is over five times the rate of temperature with the altitude
    (d) None of the above

12. **The main purpose of the foot valve in a pump is to ....**
    (a) to prevent any foreign material from entering to the suction pipe
    (b) to hold suction pipe
    (c) retain primed water so as to avoid priming every time
    (d) (a) & (c)

13. **The main purpose of the foot valve in a pump is to ....**
    (a) to prevent any foreign material from entering to the suction pipe
    (b) to hold suction pipe
    (c) retain primed water so as to avoid priming every time
    (d) (a) & (c)

14. **Weirs used to measure comparatively large discharges and whose crest is horizontal and sides are perpendicular are called**
    (a) Parshall flumes (b) V notch weirs
    (c) Rectangular weirs (d) None of the above

15. **If the contour lines are seen very near to each other, it denotes .... slope.**
    (a) level land (b) lower land slope
    (c) higher land slope (d) none of the above

Answers	11. (b)	13. (d)	15. (c)
	12. (d)	14. (b)	

16. Deep well turbine pump is also called as a

(a) Diffusion pump (b) Deep pump

(c) Volute pump (d) Vertical pump

17. Flow measuring device having the advantages of weir and submerged orifice are called

(a) rectangular weir (b) submerged orifice

(c) Both (a) & (b) (d) parshall flume

18. The sum of elevations of 20 stations of a field is 220 m. The elevation of centroid will be .... m.

(a) 10.5 (b) 11.0

(c) 11.5 (d) 12.0

19. In a centrifugal pumping system, the foot valve

(a) pumps water into pump

(b) retains water in the pump and suction pump

(c) provide over flow passage

(d) None of the above

20. When the crust length is less than the width of the approach section of up-stream channel,

the weir is called

(a) Broad crested weirs (b) Suppressed weirs

(c) Contracted weirs (d) Both (b) and (c)

21. The viscosity of a fluid is primarily a function of

(a) Pressure (b) Temperature

(c) Both (a) & (b) (d) None of these

22. Continuity equation is applicable for the following :

(a) Steady & unsteady flow

(b) Uniform and non-uniform flow

(c) Compressible and incompressible fluids

(d) All of these

Answers				
	16. (d)	18. (b)	20. (c)	22. (d)
	17. (d)	19. (b)	21. (b)	

23. If the fluid characteristics at any given time remain the same at different points in the direction of flow, the flow is known as

(a) uniform flow (b) non-uniform flow

(c) steady flow (d) unsteady flow

24. If the ratios of the corresponding length dimensions between the model and the prototype are same, then it will be

(a) Geometric similarity (b) Kinematic similarity

(c) Dynamic similarity (d) None of the above

25. In which type of flows, velocity potential exists ?

(a) Rotational flow (b) Irrotational flow

(c) Both (a) & (b) (d) None of the above

26. Stream function has been defined for a

(a) one dimensional case

(b) two dimensional case

(c) three dimensional case

(d) None of the above

27. When two flows are geometrically, kinematically and dynamically similar, then they are said to be

(a) dynamically similar (b) non-similar

(c) partially similar (d) completely similar

28. Most common water meters available for installation in pipe lines

(a) Propeller type water meter

(b) Indicator type water meter

(c) Both (a) & (b)

(d) None of the above

Answers	**23. (c)**	**25. (c)**	**27. (a)**
	24. (a)	**26. (c)**	**28. (c)**

29. **Saturation capacity of soil is also termed as**
   (a) Moisture capacity
   (b) Minimum water holding capacity
   (c) Maximum water holding capacity
   (d) None of the above

30. **What is the function of air vent in a pipe line ?**
   (a) To take out water from the pipe line
   (b) To fill the water in the pipe line
   (c) To balance the pipe line
   (d) To release entrapped air

31. **Bernoulli's theorem is the application of law of conservation of**
   (a) Mass (b) Energy to fluid flow
   (c) Both (a) & (b) (d) None of the above

32. **V-notch weir is normally used to measure discharge from .... and .... streams.**
   (a) large, medium (b) small, large
   (c) medium, large (d) small, medium

33. **Venturimeter is used for measurement of**
   (a) velocity at a point (b) average velocity
   (c) discharge (d) None of these

34. **When fluid is flowing through a pipe, the velocity of flow over the cross-section is**
   (a) uniform
   (b) non-uniform
   (c) slower towards the side of passage
   (d) Both (b) & (c)

Answers	29. (c)	31. (b)	33. (c)
	30. (d)	32. (d)	34. (c)

35. **The normally adopted norm for longitudinal slope of an irrigation channel is**

(a) 0.1 % (b) 0.6 % (c) 0.3 % (d) 0.4 %

36. **What is the minimum measurement taken by levelling staff ?**

(a) 5 mm (b) 10 mm (c) 15 mm (d) 20 mm

37. **Abney level can be used for**

(a) measuring land slope
(b) measuring height of tree
(c) marking contour line
(d) All of these

38. **Plumb bob is used for**

(a) marking perpendicular line
(b) locating points directly below or above another point
(c) marking straight line
(d) demarcating triangle

39. **Cross-staff has _____ sides.**

(a) 1 (b) 3
(c) 4 (d) None of these

40. **When two centrifugal pumps are operated in series, the discharge**

(a) remain constant (b) increases
(c) decreases (d) None of these

41. **Oblique offset is known as**

(a) lateral measurement perpendicular to chain line.
(b) lateral measurement at an angle other than 90° to chain line.
(c) Both (a) & (b)
(d) None of these

Answers	**35. (c)**	**37. (d)**	**39. (c)**	**41. (b)**
	36. (a)	**38. (b)**	**40. (a)**	

42. **The functions of a theodolite are to measure the following quantities**
(a) The horizontal angle
(b) The vertical angle
(c) The horizontal distance
(d) All of the above

43. **Open traverse is suitable in surveying of**
(a) ponds (b) rivers
(c) estates (d) None of the above

44. **Plane table survey is particularly suitable for preparation of**
(a) all types of maps (b) small scale maps
(c) large scale maps (d) None of the above

45. **The earth work from a field of one hectare with a soil cut of the depth of 7.5 mm is equal to .... m^3.**
(a) 750 (b) 0.75
(c) 75 (d) 7.5

46. **The operation of levelling across a river is termed as**
(a) plane table levelling (b) reciprocal levelling
(c) check levelling (d) None of the above

47. **The line joining points of equal elevation is known as**
(a) horizontal line (b) level line
(c) vertical line (d) contour line

48. **Instrument used for the computation of irregular area is known as**
(a) Planimeter (b) Speedometer
(c) Pentagraph (d) None of these

Answers	42. (d) 43. (d)	44. (b) 45. (c)	46. (d) 47. (b)	48. (a)

49. **The operation of levelling to determine the elevation between two points is known as**

(a) cross levelling (b) fly levelling

(c) check levelling (d) differential levelling

50. **A cross staff is used for setting**

(a) 60° angle (b) right angle

(c) 120° angle (d) None of the above

51. **A-frame is commonly used in ....**

(a) contour line demarcation over the land surface

(b) earth work computation

(c) chain surveying

(d) theodolite surveying

52. **Compass survey is based on**

(a) traversing (b) triangulation

(c) parallelism (d) None of the above

53. **A closed contour line with one or more higher values inside represents**

(a) valley (b) ridge

(c) hill (d) None of the above

54. **Method for calculating capacity of the reservoir**

(a) Prismoidal Rule (b) Traphazoidal Rule

(c) End-Area Method (d) Both (a) & (b)

55. **In case of direct method of chaining the uneven slope, steeper the slope, ... will be the interval.**

(a) higher (b) lesser

(c) uneven (d) None of the above

56. **Reciprocating pump develop**

(a) High head with low discharge capacity

Answers	49. (d)	51. (a)	53. (c)	55. (b)
	50. (b)	52. (a)	54. (d)	56. (c)

(b) Low head with high discharge capacity
(c) Constant head with low discharge capacity
(d) Constant head with high discharge capacity

57. The removal of air by filling the pump with water is called as

(a) Deaerating (b) Sterilizing
(c) Priming (d) All of these

58. Hydraulic Ram is specially suitable for hilly areas, where

(a) Water is at shallow depth
(b) Considerable slope in rivers
(c) Considerable slope in streams
(d) both (c) and (b)

59. Propeller pump is suitable for

(a) low discharge, low head
(b) low discharge, high head
(c) high discharge, low head
(d) high discharge, high head

60. A suitable pump for drainage pumping is

(a) Submersible pump (b) Propeller pump
(c) Mixed flow pump (d) both (b) and (c)

61. Which of the following is not a part of a centrifugal pump ?

(a) Rotar (b) Casing
(c) Compressor (d) Impeller

62. A 50 HP pump has power equal to

(a) 3.73 kW (b) 37.3 kW
(c) 373 kW (d) 5 kW

Answers			
	57. (c)	59. (c)	61. (c)
	58. (d)	60. (d)	62. (b)

63. The casing of a impeller wheel in a centrifugal pump is called

(a) Volute (b) Housing

(c) Cylinder (d) None of the above

64. The brake horse power of a centrifugal pump varies directly

(a) as the square root of speed of impeller

(b) as the speed of impeller

(c) as the square of the speed of impeller

(d) as the cube of the speed of impeller

65. Reciprocating pump compared to other pumps develops

(a) High heads (b) Low capacity

(c) both (a) & (b) (d) None of the above

66. The reflex valve is fitted on the

(a) suction side of pump (b) delivery side of pump

(c) at the bottom of pipe (d) None of the above

67. The rational formula is used to determine which of the following ?

(a) Daily runoff volume

(b) Average daily discharge rate

(c) Monthly discharge velocity

(d) Design discharge for a hydraulic structure

68. Nozzle and Venturi are the main components of

(a) Centrifugal pump (b) Submersible pump

(c) Propeller pump (d) Jet pump

69. The value of exponent for fully pressure compensating emitter in drip irrigation will be

(a) 0.0 (b) 0.5

(c) 0.75 (d) 1.0

Answers				
	63. (a)	65. (b)	67. (d)	69. (b)
	64. (d)	66. (b)	68. (d)	

70. **Leakage factor is related to which of the following ?**
   (a) Confined acquifer
   (b) Unconfined acquifer
   (c) Semi-confined acquifer
   (d) None of these

71. **Turbine pump when close-coupled to a .... is known as a submersible pump.**
   (a) Electric motor (b) Electric pump
   (c) Submerged electric motor (d) None of the above

72. **The pump operating on the principle of difference in specific weights in the water column of the wells is known as ....**
   (a) Hydraulic Ram (b) Centrifugal pumps
   (c) Air lift pumps (d) Jet pumps

73. **Which of the following is not a type of impeller of a centrifugal pump ?**
   (a) High speed (b) Open
   (c) Closed (d) Semi-open

74. **Current meter is used to measure which of the following ?**
   (a) Depth of flow in streams
   (b) Direction of flow in streams
   (c) Duration of flow in streams
   (d) Velocity of flow in streams

75. **Lysimeter is used to measure which of the following ?**
   (a) Vapour pressure (b) Evaporation
   (c) Transpiration (d) Evapotranspiration

76. **In case of ideal fluids, viscosity is _____**
   (a) unity (b) zero
   (c) greater than one (d) None of the above

Answers	
	70. (c) 72. (a) 74. (d) 76. (b) 71. (c) 73. (a) 75. (d)

77. The longest of the chain lines used in chain survey is generally regarded as

(a) Check line (b) Base line

(c) Tie line (d) None of the above

78. At critical stage of flow, the specific force of the flow will be

(a) maximum (b) zero

(c) minimum (d) None of the above

79. Frictional loss through a pipe implies

(a) Loss due to dynamic coefficient of friction

(b) Loss of flow rate in pipe due to surface roughness

(c) Loss of energy due to surface slip

(d) Loss of momentum due to surface roughness

80. Foot valve is placed at

(a) Foot of the pump

(b) End of the suction pipe

(c) In the middle of the suction pipe

(d) End of the delivery pipe

81. How many phase matter the soil is ?

(a) Four (b) Three (c) Two (d) One

82. Distance measured with Gunter Chain is 15.39 chains. How much would be this distance in metres ?

(a) 309.64 (b) 350.00

(c) 325.09 (d) None of the above

83. In a multistage pump, the specific speed is calculated on the basis of

(a) Total head (b) Head per stage

(c) Capacity per stage

(d) Head & capacity per stage

Answers	**77. (b)**	**79. (a)**	**81. (a)**	**83. (c)**
	78. (c)	**80. (b)**	**82. (a)**	

84. **Submersible pumps are**

(a) Jet pumps

(b) Multistage centrifugal pumps

(c) Mixed flow pumps

(d) Propeller pumps

85. **Viscosity of water ______ with increase in temperature.**

(a) increases (b) decreases

(c) remains unchanged (d) None of the above

86. **If the depth of flow before a hydraulic jump is 1.0 m with Froude number of flow as unity. What will be the sequent flow depth in rectangular channels ?**

(a) 0.8 m (b) 1.6 m

(c) 1.0 m (d) 1.8 m

87. **On which of the following the shape factor of a watershed does not depend ?**

(a) Shape of the watershed

(b) Area of the watershed

(c) Order of the watershed

(d) length of the watershed

88. **A soil sample has porosity of 40%, then its void ratio will be**

(a) 0.66 (b) 0.40

(c) 0.28 (d) 0.06

89. **Which of the following is the fastest method of drilling in alluvial formulations ?**

(a) Cable tool percussion drilling

(b) Rotary drilling

(c) Hammer drilling

(d) None of the above

Answers	84. (c)	86. (c)	88. (a)
	85. (b)	87. (c)	89. (a)

90. The water application efficiency will be highest in which of the following irrigation methods ?

(a) Border irrigation method

(b) Furrow irrigation method

(c) Drip irrigation method

(d) Sprinkler irrigation method

91. When two wells are located within their radii of influences, the discharge of each of these wells is affected. This phenomenon is called as

(a) Well failure (b) Well surging

(c) Well interference (d) Well development

92. Antecedent Moisture Condition (AMC) of a drainage basin is determined based on

(a) Preceding 2-days total rainfall

(b) Preceding 3 days total rainfall

(c) Preceding 4-days total rainfall

(d) Preceding 5-days total rainfall

93. Diameter of the open well is decided based on the concept of

(a) Specific drawdown (b) Specific yield

(c) Specific retention (d) None of the above

94. Herringbone and grid iron are the systems of layout of which of the following ?

(a) Surface drainage (b) Surface irrigation

(c) Tile drainage (d) None of the above

95. A drainage canal discharges 500 m^3/hr and drains 120 ha of the area. What will be the drainage coefficient of this land ?

(a) 10 mm (b) 20 mm

(c) 30 mm (d) 40 mm

Answers			
	90. (c)	92. (d)	94. (c)
	91. (c)	93. (b)	95. (a)

96. The drains constructed from hill side of earthen dams, canals or at foot hills are called as

(a) Interceptor drains (b) Mole drains

(c) Vertical drains (d) None of the above

97. Which of the following is not related with the design of drop spillways ?

(a) Hydrologic design (b) Hydraulic design

(c) Regular design (d) Structural design

98. Plantation of high water consuming plants/trees for withdrawal of ground water is a form of which of the following ?

(a) Vertical drainage (b) Bio-drainage

(c) Natural drainage (d) Artificial drainage

99. In areas where soil is shallow and rainfall is also low which of the following type of bench terracing system should be preferred ?

(a) Outward sloping benches

(b) Inward sloping benches

(c) Any from (a) & (b)

(d) None of the above

100. The most appropriate method for irrigating land with more undulations is

(a) Check basin irrigation method

(b) Border irrigation method

(c) Sprinkler irrigation method

(d) Furrow irrigation method

101. Which of the following statements is correct ?

(a) Total porosity of Sandy soil is maximum.

(b) Total porosity of Clay soil in maximum.

Answers	**96. (a)**	**98. (b)**	**100. (c)**
	97. (c)	**99. (b)**	**101. (b)**

(c) Total porosity of Clay soil is minimum.

(d) Total porosity of Silty soil is maximum.

102. Soils having slow infiltration rate (2.5 – 12.5 mm/hr) when wetted are classified in which of the following groups ?

(a) Hydrologic soil group 'B'

(b) Hydrologic soil group 'A'

(c) Hydrologic soil group 'C'

(d) Hydrologic soil group 'D'

103. The maximum permissible mean velocity of flow in an earthen channel in sandy loam soil is

(a) 40 cm/sec (b) 60 cm/sec

(c) 80 cm/sec (d) 100 cm/sec

104. The most significant element which affects the discharge capacity of an underground pipe is

(a) Type of pipe (b) Head causing flow

(c) Friction in the pipe (d) Length of the pipe

105. At critical state of flow, the velocity head is equal to

(a) Half of the hydraulic depth

(b) Same as the hydraulic depth

(c) Three times the hydraulic depth

(d) Two times the hydraulic depth

106. All moisture that reaches to earth surface in liquid or solid form due to condensation of vapour is collectively called as

(a) Precipitation (b) Rainfall

(c) Snowfall (d) Drizzle

107. The process of computing the reservoir storage volume, water level and outflow rate with time corresponding to a particular inflow hydrograph is called as

Answers	102. (c)	104. (c)	106. (a)
	103. (c)	105. (a)	107. (b)

(a) Hydrograph analysis
(b) Flood routing
(c) Flood hydrograph
(d) Hydrograph development

108. Specific yield is a property of which of the following ?
(a) Perched acquifer
(b) Confined acquifer
(c) Semi-confined acquifer
(d) Unconfined acquifer

109. One Newton Force (N) is equal to which of the following?
(a) 10 kg–m/s^2 (b) 100 kg–m/s^2
(c) 1 kg–m/s^2 (d) None of the above

110. What measures are adopted to prevent seepage along the pipe spillways ?
(a) Construction of clay core
(b) Construction of horizontal wall
(c) Construction of vertical wall
(d) Construction of anti-seep collars

111. A significant soil building group of crops is
(a) Cereal crops (b) Leguminous crops
(c) Fodder crops (d) Fruit crops

112. Sub-surface drains remove water lies in which of the following form ?
(a) Capillary water (b) Gravitational water
(c) Hygroscopic water (d) All of the above

113. In Chute spillway, the channel section is always a
(a) Closed channel (b) Open channel
(c) V-Section channel (d) None of these

Answers	**108. (d)**	**110. (d)**	**112. (b)**
	109. (c)	**111. (b)**	**113. (b)**

114. Which of the following is not a form of precipitation ?

(a) Rainfall (b) Dew

(c) Frost (d) Avalanche

115. Which of the following is not a process of wind erosion ?

(a) Saltation (b) Suspension

(c) Surface creep (d) Radiation

116. Which of the following is the next stage of rill erosion ?

(a) Sheet erosion (b) Splash erosion

(c) Gully erosion (d) None of these

117. In universal soil loss equation, A = RKLSCP. What parameter is represented by 'K' ?

(a) Soil porosity (b) Soil density

(c) Soil erodibility (d) Rainfall erosivity

118. Construction of contour bunds is recommended upto a land slope of which of the following ?

(a) upto 2% (b) upto 4%

(c) upto 6% (d) upto 8%

119. Which of the following is not a watershed characteristic ?

(a) Shape factor (b) Elongation ratio

(c) Circularity ratio (d) Crop factor

120. The instrument used for continuous measurement of depth of flow of water in a stream is known as

(a) Current meter (b) Anemometer

(c) Water stage recorder (d) Turbidity meter

121. The most common structure used for controlling stream bank erosion is

(a) Retaining wall (b) Interceptor drain

(c) Drop spillways (d) Spur

Answers	**114. (d)**	**116. (c)**	**118. (c)**	**120. (c)**
	115. (d)	**117. (c)**	**119. (d)**	**121. (a)**

122. Construction of contour bunds is recommended in areas where

(a) Rainfall is high and soil is heavy
(b) Rainfall is high and soil is light
(c) Rainfall is low and soil is light
(d) None of the above

123. As per land use capability classification, the lands are classified in

(a) 3 classes (b) 5 classes
(c) 8 classes (d) 10 classes

124. The hand pump is an example of which of the following ?

(a) Reciprocating pump (b) Circular pump
(c) Centrifugal pump (d) Ideal pump

125. One micron is equal to which of the following ?

(a) 0.001 mm (b) 0.01 mm
(c) 0.10 mm (d) 0.0001 mm

126. Which of the following is not a type of storage in a dam ?

(a) Live storage or useful storage
(b) Temporary storage
(c) Dead storage or permanent storage
(d) Supreme storage

127. Theis' equation is used to determine which of the following ?

(a) Steady flow in a confined aquifer
(b) Steady flow in an unconfined aquifer
(c) Unsteady flow in a confined aquifer
(d) None of the above

Answers	122. (c)	124. (a)	126. (d)
	123. (c)	125. (a)	127. (c)

128. In uniform flow hydraulic grade line and energy grade lines are

(a) Parallel to each other

(b) Perpendicular to each other

(c) At an angle of 45° to each other

(d) At an angle of 60° to each other

129. One hectare-meter volume is not equal to which of the following ?

(a) 10,000 cubic metres (b) 10 million litres

(c) 100 hectare – cm (d) 1000 cubic metres

130. In a hydraulic jump flow velocity changes from

(a) Subcritical to Supercritical

(b) Subcritical to Critical

(c) Supercritical to Subcritical

(d) Critical to Subcritical

131. The day to day activities of watershed development projects are carried out by which of the following ?

(a) Watershed development team

(b) Watershed Committee

(c) Watershed association

(d) User group

132. Presently, the net area under irrigation in India is about

(a) 40 million hectare (b) 60 million hectare

(c) 80 million hectare (d) 100 million hectare

133. The total rainfed area in India is about

(a) 50 million ha (b) 72 million ha

(c) 46 million ha (d) 115 million ha

Answers	**128. (a)**	**130. (c)**	**132. (b)**
	129. (d)	**131. (b)**	**133. (b)**

134. **Each side of Cipolette weir has a side slope of**

(a) 1H : 2V (b) 1H : 3V
(c) 1H : 4V (d) 1H : 5V

135. **Which of the following is used to measure point or local velocity of fluid in a channel ?**

(a) Pitot-meter (b) Orifice meter
(c) Venturi meter (d) Rota meter

136. **Which of the following flow conditions are represented by a hydraulic jump ?**

(a) Steady & uniform flow
(b) Unsteady & uniform flow
(c) Steady & non-uniform flow
(d) Unsteady & non-uniform flow

137. **Estimation of design discharge is done under which of the following ?**

(a) Hydraulic design (b) Structural design
(c) Hydrologic design (d) None of these

138. **The water absorbed by plants is called as,**

(a) Capillary water (b) Gravitational water
(c) Hygroscopic water (d) Free water

139. **The units of dynamic viscosity are which of the following?**

(a) g/cm-s (b) g-s/cm
(c) cm/g-s (d) cm-s/g

140. **As per land capability classification class VIII lands are suitable for**

(a) Intensive cultivation (b) Wild life and recreation
(c) Proper crop rotation (d) None of these

Answers				
	134. (c)	136. (a)	138. (a)	140. (b)
	135. (a)	137. (a)	139. (a)	

141. While measuring infiltration by using double cylinder infiltration, measurements are made in

(a) Outer cylinder only

(b) Inner cylinder only

(c) Inner and outer cylinders both

(d) Either of these cylinders

142. Soils in hydrologic group 'A' exhibit

(a) High runoff potential

(b) Low runoff potential

(c) Very high runoff potential

(d) None of these

143. Seepage force acts in which of the following direction ?

(a) Only in upward direction

(b) Only in downward direction

(c) Opposite to the direction of flow

(d) In the direction of flow

144. Porosity of a soil mass is the ratio between

(a) Volume of voids and total volume

(b) Volume of solids and total volume

(c) Volume of voids and volume of solids

(d) Volume of solids and volume of voids

145. The value of Plasticity index for coarse sand is

(a) Ten (b) Five

(c) Zero (d) One

146. A line joining the points of equal elevation is called as

(a) Straight line (b) Contour line

(c) Artificial line (d) None of these

Answers	141. (b)	143. (b)	145. (c)
	142. (b)	144. (a)	146. (b)

147. Which of the following is the most appropriate device to measure flow on flat slopes under high degree of submergence ?

(a) Rectangular weir (b) Trapezoidal weir
(c) Parshall flume (d) H-Flume

148. Froud number is expressed as the ratio between

(a) Inertia forces to viscous forces
(b) Inertia forces to gravity forces
(c) Inertia forces to drag forces
(d) Inertia forces to friction forces

149. Susceptibility of soil towards erosion is represented by which of the following ?

(a) Erosivity (b) Erodibility
(c) Transportability (d) None of these

150. In Modified Soil Loss Equation (MUSLE), the rainfall factor of USLE is replaced by which of the following ?

(a) Energy factor (b) Runoff factor
(c) Crop factor (d) Wind factor

151. Which of the following weirs are most affected by end contraction ?

(a) Triangular weir (b) Rectangular weir
(c) Trapezoidal weir (d) Cipolletti weir

152. The value of runoff coefficient is generally remains

(a) less than one (b) more than one
(c) equal to one (d) None of the above

153. Flow condition when its specific energy is minimum is called as,

(a) Artificial flow (b) Controlled flow
(c) Critical flow (d) Ideal flow

Answers	147. (c) 148. (b)	149. (b) 150. (b)	151. (b) 152. (c)	153. (c)

154. The most efficient channel section is

(a) Rectangular (b) Semi-circular

(c) Triangular (d) Trapezoidal

155. At critical state of flow, the value of Froude number will be

(a) 0.0 (b) 1.0

(c) 2.0 (d) 4.0

156. Central Soil and Water Conservation, Research and Training Institute (CSWCRTI) is situated in which of the following cities in India ?

(a) New Delhi (b) Bhopal

(c) Dehradun (d) Hyderabad

157. Average precipitation over an area is determined by using which of the following method ?

(a) Cook's method

(b) Average elevation method

(c) Thissen polygon method

(d) Synders method

158. In hydraulically efficient rectangular channel section with B = bottom width and D = depth, which of the following conditions should be satisfied ?

(a) B = 4D (b) D = 2B

(c) B = 2D (d) B = D

159. Which of the following are units of transmissivity ?

(a) L^2T^{-1} (b) L^2T^{-2}

(c) L^3T^{-3} (d) LT^{-4}

160. One ppm is equal to which of the following ?

(a) 1000 mg per litre (b) 100 mg per litre

(c) 10 mg per litre (d) 1 mg per litre

Answers	**154. (b)**	**156. (c)**	**158. (c)**	**160. (d)**
	155. (b)	**157. (c)**	**159. (a)**	

161. **Under normal conditions, the specific gravity of mercury is**

(a) 13.8 (b) 13.6

(c) 13.4 (d) 13.2

162. **The use of a straight drop spillway is normally recommended for a drop up to**

(a) upto 1.0 m (b) upto 3.0 m

(c) upto 5.0 m (d) upto 8.0 m

163. **The pH value of saline soils is always**

(a) less than 4.5 (b) more than 10.5

(c) less than 8.5 (d) more than 8.5

164. **The ratio between sediment yield and gross generated erosion is known as**

(a) Sediment generation ratio

(b) Sediment deposition ratio

(c) Sediment delivery ratio

(d) None of the above

165. **How many are the stages of gully development ?**

(a) Five (b) Three

(c) Four (d) Eight

166. **The amount of water transpired by a crop in its growth to produce unit weight of dry matter is called**

(a) Transpiration ratio

(b) Evaporation ratio

(c) Transpiration coefficient

(d) Dry matter index

167. **To have maximum protection the wind break/shelter belts should be laid out in the direction of**

(a) In prevailing wind direction

Answers	161. (b)	163. (c)	165. (c)	167. (b)
	162. (b)	164. (c)	166. (a)	

(b) Normal to the wind direction

(c) 20 degree from the wind direction

(d) 10 degree from the wind direction

168. In case of open channels, flow takes place due to which of the following ?

(a) Pressure difference (b) Elevation difference

(c) Friction difference (d) None of the above

169. Which of the following is correct ?

(a) 1 Bar = 100 k Pa (b) 1 Bar = 10 k Pa

(c) 1 Bar = 1000 k Pa (d) 1 Bar = 1 k Pa

170. To obtain a unit hydrograph of 4-h duration, the intensity of rainfall excess will be

(a) 4.0 cm/hr (b) ¼ cm/hr

(c) 1.0 cm/hr (d) None of the above

171. Double mass curve is to check which of the following ?

(a) Consistency of rainfall data

(b) Variability of rainfall data

(c) Uniformity of rainfall data

(d) Intensity of rainfall data

172. Unique depth in uniform flow associated with each discharge is called as

(a) Critical depth (b) Normal depth

(c) Alternate depth (d) Sequent depth

173. In case of wind erosion, the maximum movement of soil particles takes place under which

of the following ?

(a) Suspension (b) Surface creep

(c) Saltation (d) Induction

Answers	168. (b)	170. (c)	172. (a)
	169. (a)	171. (a)	173. (c)

174. If soil moisture tension decreases, then the moisture content of the soil will

(a) decrease

(b) increase

(c) remain same

(d) either increase or decrease

OOOOO

Answers	**174. (b)**

Agriculture Research Service (ARS) Paper MAIN 2013 (Memory Based)

Objective Questions

1. If the speeds of rotor of pump changes from 1400 to 1500 rpm, the percentage changes in power will be ....
2. Specific storage of aquifer is the ratio of ....
3. The imaginary line joining hydraulic heads in confined aquifer is called as ....
4. The relationship between Chezy's and manning coefficient is...........
5. The value of Reynolds's number for partially turbulent flow is ....
6. The velocity of flow in clay soil is ....than sandy soil.
7. The slope of channel heavy soil (clay soil) is...........than light soil (sandy soil).
8. ....method of estimation of ET is based on temperature and sunshine duration.
9. The water advance front in relation to mean depth in border irrigation is described by scientist ....
10. The value of porosity of cubical arrangement of soil particle is ....
11. The value of uniformity coefficient of drip irrigation is about ....
12. The application efficiency of irrigation is defined as the ratio of ....
13. Tyson Weber groundwater flow model is used for ....
14. The average velocity of flow in grassed waterways is ....
15. The soil moisture pressure at field capacity is ....
16. The salt affected soil depends on ....

17. The cover management factors of USLE depend upon ....

Answers :

1. 70%
2. storage coefficient and thickness of aquifer
3. peizometric level or surface.
4. $C=1/n\ (R)^{1/6}$
5. 4000 to 10000
6. Lesser
7. Lesser
8. Blaney criddle's
9. Lewis and Milne
10. 48%.
11. 90-95%.
12. NIR to GIR.
13. detection of groundwater problems.
14. 1.5 to 2 m/s.
15. 1/10 to 1/3 atm.
16. soluble salt content and moisture content.
17. crop stages, density and types of crop.

Short Subjective Questions

18. Water is water hammer ? Write down the measures to prevent water hammer.
19. Write down the working principal of neutron moisture meter.
20. What is gully erosion ? Write down the process of gully formation and also enlist the different types of gullies.
21. Describe the design steps of sprinkler and drip irrigation system.
22. Explain the relationship between pressure and discharge in long path emitters, orifice tube emitter and pressure compensating emitter.

23. What is the water user association? Also write down its mandates.
24. Numerical based on the optimum number of stations in the catchment, if data of rainfall and error value is given.
25. Sketch the diagram of different types of water present in soil at different pressure.
26. Write down the importance of gravel pack envelope in tile drain.
27. Write down the factors of design of drain ditch.
28. What are the basic methods of leveling? Explain in detail the plane method of land grading or leveling.
29. Write down the process of plant water intake from soil. Also explain how it is measures?
30. Numerical based on flow through orifice.
31. Write down procedure for selection of centrifugal pumps by matching pump characteristics and system head curves.
32. What is flood routing? Explain the methods of reservoir routing, and measures to control flood.
33. What is the difference between saturated and unsaturated flow?
34. What is the most economical channel section? Derive the equation for most economical trapezoidal section b=2d tanQ/2.
35. Numerical based on specific energy and Froude number.

Long Subjective Questions

36. What do you understand by management of watersheds? Describe the objectives, present problem, rainfall-runoff and sediment data analysis, and benefit cost ration of watershed management.
37. Write down the assumption and derive the basic equation of steady state flow in an unconfined aquifer (Dupuit's equation).

38. 8 gm of sodium chloride (NaCl) has been dissolved 2 liters of water. Express salt concentration in ppm, mhos/cm, dS/m, meq/l.
39. Describe the S-curve method of developing a 6-hour Unit Hydrograph by using a 12 hour Unit Hydrograph of the catchment.
40. A stream of 150 liters/sec was diverted from a canal and 120 litres/sec was diverted to the field. An area of 2 ha was irrigated in 8 h. the effective root zone depth was 1.5 m. The depth of water penetration varied linearly from 1.6m at head end of the field to 1 m at the tail end. Available moisture holding capacity of the soil is 20 cm per meter depth of soil. If the runoff losses from field were 500 cubic meter and irrigation was provided at 50% moisture depletion level of available moisture, determine water conveyance, water application, water storage and water distribution efficiencies.

Agriculture Research Service (ARS) Paper

MAIN 2014 (Memory Based)

Objective Questions (2 Marks)

1. Riparian water right .... Canal water distribution is operated by ....
2. Perched aquifer is a special case of ....
3. The recommended land slope of medium (loam) soil is ....
4. ....is the method of water distribution system in India.
5. If 10 cm water is applied to field, 2 cm water lost as runoff and 1 cm as evaporation, the application efficiency is ....
6. Calculate vertical interval of terrace if side slope is 1:1, field slope is 2% and land width is 5 m.
7. If Q= 10 lps and H=76m then WHP=...........
8. Barley is less salt tolerant than wheat. (True/False)
9. The fertigation unit is installed before the filter unit. (True/False)
10. Time of concentration ....
11. If EC> 4 ds/m, pH >8.5 and ESP>15 the soil is known as ....
12. If the total length of watershed is 50 km and watershed area is 5 km^2 the drainage density is ....
13. $Q= C_d \times a \times (2gH)^{0.5}$ (Q is proportional to .... of head).
14. PRA is.......................
15. Nash models give.......................of outflow hydrograph.
16. Write down the formula of RSC index = ...

17. Diffusion of water vapour is caused by a ....as the driving force.
18. Clay particle found in subsurface is an example of...........
19. Stilling basin is used for ....
20. Shelterbelt is used for ....
21. Mole drainage is used in ....
22. The arrangement of soil particles in a specific pattern is called as ....
23. When two pumps are arranged in series the total discharge of the pump will be ....
24. The relationship between the soil moisture content and soil moisture tension is known as ....
25. For groundwater flow the value of Reynolds number is ....
26. The specific capacity of pump is the ratio of discharge per unit ....
27. The tension measurements by tensiometers are generally limited to metric suction values of below 1 atm.. (True/False)
28. The cipoletti weir is a trapezoidal weir having side slope ....
29. When a third order stream joins with second order then ....stream generated.
30. The large watershed is dominated by ....

Answers :

1. is a system for allocating water among those who possess land along its path, WUA and Irrigation Department
2. unconfined aquifer
3. 0.2 to 0.4
4. Osrabandi/warabandi, Shejpali and Satta (Bihar)
5. 70%
6. --
7. 10hp

8. (False)
9. (True).
10. is the time needed for water to flow from the most remote point in a watershed to the watershed outlet
11. saline alkali soil
12. 10 km^{-1}
13. square root
14. Participatory Rural Appraisal
15. cascade forms
16. $RSC = (CO_3^{-2} + HCO_3^{-}) - (Ca^{+2} + Mg^{+2})$.
17. vapour pressure gradient
18. aquiclude
19. dissipating the KE of flowing water
20. wind erosion control
21. soil containing more than 30% clay particle or Clay soil
22. soil structure
23. remain constant
24. soil moisture curve or characteristics curve
25. less than 1
26. drawdown
27. (True)
28. 1:4 (H: V)
29. third order
30. surface runoff

Short Subjective Questions (5 Marks)

31. What is Environmental Impact Assessment (EIA) and write down the various steps of EIA.
32. Explain the surge flow irrigation system.
33. What is irrigation scheduling and explain the various methods of irrigation scheduling?
34. Explain the erodibility and erosivity of soil of USLE equation.
35. Define soil less media and write down the component composition.

36. Define simulation modelling and list out various softwares used in watershed development programme.
37. Define hydrograph, unit hydrograph, synthetic hydrograph, instantaneous unit hydrograph and also write assumption of unit hydrograph.
38. What is most efficient cross section and write down the equation of most efficient cross section of trapezoidal and rectangular section with diagram.
39. What is critical flow and also write down the direct relationship between head of water flow and discharge through the channel section.
40. What is Froude number and explain the different types of flow based on these numbers.
41. What is effective size, uniformity coefficient and write down the criteria for non-gravel packing.
42. Calculate the head loss of pump .... data is given
43. Calculate the SAR values ...... data is given
44. Define RSC and also write down the criteria of RSC
45. Define hydraulic jump and write down the advantage of hydraulic jump.
46. What is blending and periodic use of canal water and GW for conjunctive use?
47. Determine the discharge in liter/second for a sprinkler operating at 2.8 Kg/cm^2 pressure and having 4x2.8mm diameter nozzle with discharge coefficient of 0.96
48. Draw graphically the advance curve, recession curve and the infiltration opportunity time for surface irrigation (border irrigation).
49. For a soil intake rate cm/hr, $I= 0.3t^{-0.6}$. Where t is in minutes. Determine accumulated depth of infiltration relation.
50. Write down the Dupuit's assumptions and also write the other assumptions.

Long Subjective Questions (10 Marks)

51. Derive the Dupuit's equation of steady state confined aquifer, and prove that $Q_1=1.1Q_2$.
52. Determine annual consumption of electrical energy of a motor driven centrifugal pump installed in a shallow tube well and operate for 3500 hour/year. The pump discharge is 16 liters/sec against a total head of 7m. The pump efficiency is 70%, motor efficiency is 84 5 and drive efficiency is assumed to 100%.
53. Write down the USLE and explain the various terms used in USLE, limitations of USLE and also write down the MUSLE equation and differentiate with USLE.
54. Enlist various moisture measuring technique and instrument and explain the principal and working of electrical resistivity methods and also write the limitations.
55. Define drip irrigation system, advantage, disadvantage, applicability and components.
56. Define salt affected soil and categorized this, and write down the reclamation procedure of alkali soil.

Agriculture Research Service (ARS) Paper MAIN 2015 (Memory Based)

Objective questions (2 Marks)

1. If CN = 25400/ (250+S), calculate the value of 'S' for paved surface.
2. A soil sample having EC< 4 ds/m, pH >8.5 and ESP>15 the soil is known as ....
3. A soil sample having EC>4, the soil is known as ....
4. Write down the SAR formula.
5. Darcy's law has been found to be valid for groundwater flow when the values of Reynolds number ....
6. Hyetograph refers to ....
7. In hydraulic structure the depth after hydraulic jump (increases/decreases).
8. The gross commanded area for an irrigation canal is 10,000 hectare and 80 percent of this land is cultivable commanded area. Actual Irrigated annually is 3200 hectare, what will be the Intensity of irrigation is ....
9. Tensiometer provide a .... measure of tenacity (tension) with which water is held by soil.
10. Permanent wilting point (PWP) or wilting point (WP) is defined as the water content at .... of suction pressure.
11. A leaky aquifer is an aquifer whose upper and lower boundaries are aquitards, or one boundary is an aquitards and the other is an aquiclude. (True/False)
12. Seepage line is also called as ....line
13. Canopy temperature of plant is measured by..............
14. If Q= 10 lps and H=32 m then WHP=..............

15. .... parts of hydraulic structure is used to dissipate the kinetic energy of water flowing.
16. An interceptor drain is a gravel trench that is excavated into a relatively impermeable soil layer and installed to collect and remove groundwater as it flows across the impermeable layer (True/False)
17. Uniformity coefficient for uniform material is...............
18. When a third order stream joins with second order then ....stream generated.
19. A cultivated area of 2 ha is irrigated by canal having salinity 3 ds/m and water drained from an area having salinity 6 ds/m. what will be leaching requirement?

Answers :

1. 4
2. Sodic (or alkali) Soil
3. Saline soil
4. $S.A.R = \frac{Na^+}{\sqrt{\frac{1}{2}(Ca^{2+}+Mg^{2+})}}$
5. Less than one (<1)
6. Graphical representation of the distribution of rainfall over time
7. Increases
8. 40 %
9. Direct
10. 15 atm
11. True
12. Phreatic/saturation
13. Infrared thermometer
14. 4.21 hp
15. Apron
16. True
17. Less than 2
18. Third order
19. 50%

Short Subjective Questions (5 Marks)

20. Discus in brief laser land leveling, its component and operation procedure.

21. What are the crop coefficients? What is the role of crop coefficient and how to calculate crop coefficient? Whether it is lesser or greater than one. If so explain why?

22. Describe the IUH for a watershed. How can you calculate constant k and n by Nash model in hydrograph?

23. What is irrigation scheduling and explain the various methods of irrigation scheduling.

24. What are the measure elements in irrigation water? Explain briefly : exchangeable sodium percentage (ESP), sodium adsorption ratio (SAR), electrical conductivity (EC), residual sodium carbonate (RSC).

25. Explain the four point method of earthwork volume measurement of land leveling. Why the cut fill ratio of earthwork is greater than one?

26. List the components of a drop spillway. State the functions of each component.

27. Explain the cutback in furrow irrigation.

28. Explain the procedures of KE>25 method of rainfall erosivity.

29. A 25 cm diameter well is pumped at a uniform rate of 3000 l/min. The drawdown observed at 1 m and 100 m distances from the center of the well are 8 m and 0.4 m, respectively. Determine the hydraulic conductivity and transmissibility of the water bearing strata, assuming the thickness of the saturated part of the aquifer as 25 m.

30. Derivation of infiltration equation by using Philip equation.

31. Explain the principle of use of venturimeter in drip fertigation.

32. Calculate the capacity of rectangular channel. (Data is provided)

33. Calculate the width of inward terrace. (Data is provided)

34. Calculate power consumption of centrifugal pump (Data is provided)

35. Calculate the size of irrigation stream in border irrigation. (Data is provided)

36. Calculate the discharge of drip irrigation.(Data is provided)

37. Calculate the discharge and head of centrifugal pump when the rotational speed of pump impeller (rpm) is given (affinity law of pump).

38. Calculate the discharge of drain for a given area and drainage coefficient.

Long Subjective Questions (10 Marks)

39. Explain any three parameters/factor of basin. A basin has an area of 26560 km^2, perimeter 965 km and length of 230 km. Determine (i) Form factor (ii) Compactness factor and (iii) elongation ratio.

40. Define sprinkler irrigation system, advantage, disadvantage, applicability and components.

41. Discus the effect and impacts of environmental management for irrigation project design. Also explain the role of NGO.

42. Explain and Classify different types of droughts according to National Commission on Agriculture. What is the aridity index and classify them and how can you calculate?

43. Discuss the remedial measure of following problem for given hydraulic structure.

    (a) Overturning, (b) piping, and (c) compression.

44. Write down procedure for selection of centrifugal pumps by matching pump characteristics and system head curves. Define the WHP, BHP, Pump Efficiency and Motor Efficiency.

ICAR National Eligibility Test (NET) - 2016 (Memory Based)

1. **Super passage" in canal irrigation system refers to**
   (a) Irrigation channel passes over drainage channel
   (b) Drainage channel passes over irrigation channel
   (c) Both a) and b)
   (d) None of the above

2. **Device placed over riser valve outlets as a means of connecting portable gated pipes to the pipeline.**
   (a) Hydrant (b) Gated pipes
   (c) Coupler (d) Air vent

3. **Most efficient hydraulic channel cross - section is**
   (a) Trapezoidal (b) Circular
   (c) Rectangular (d) Semi-circular

4. **If the electrical conductivity of irrigation and drainage water is 0.2 mmhos/cm and 0.4 mmhos/cm respectively, the leaching requirement will be equal to**
   (a) 80% (b) 50%
   (c) 40% (d) 20%

5. **If Na, Ca, and Mg added in water with quantity 4, 5 and 7 meq/lit respectively. What will be the salinity of water ?**
   (a) 1.6 dS/m (b) 0.6 dS/m
   (c) 2.6 dS/m (d) 4 dS/m

6. **Mole drain is the most suitable drainage system for**
   (a) Heavy clay soil (b) Loamy soil
   (c) Sandy soil (d) Silty soil

7. **Well development refers to**
   (a) Removal of well incrustation
   (b) Increase in well discharge
   (c) Removal of final particle from the area around the well screen
   (d) Well testing

8. **Perched aquifer is a special case of**

(a) Confined aquifer (b) Unconfined aquifer
(c) Leaky aquifer (d) False aquifer

9. **The head loss due to friction when water flow through pipe is proportional to**

(a) Square of velocity (b) Square root of velocity
(c) Fifth power of velocity (d) Velocity

10. **PRA stands for**

(a) Participatory Rural Appraisal
(b) Participatory Rural Approval
(c) Participatory Rural Agriculture
(d) Participatory Rainfed Agriculture

11. **The delta for a crop when its duty is 864 hectares/cumec in the field with base period of crop 120 days is**

(a) 12 cm (b) 1.20 cm
(c) 120 cm (d) None of the above

12. **If irrigation water diverted to field is 10m, and runoff and other losses is 2 m and 1 m respectively. The application efficiency is**

(a) 80% (b) 60%
(c) 70% (d) 100%

13. **The Cipoletti weir is contracted trapezoidal weir having side slope**

(a) 2 : 1 (b) 1 : 2
(c) 4 : 1 (d) 1 : 4

14. **Reynolds number is defined as the ratio of**

(a) Inertia to gravity force (b) Inertia to elastic force
(c) Inertia to viscous force (d) Viscous to inertia force

15. **A sheet of water, which overflows a weir is called as**

(a) Head (b) Nappe
(c) Crest (d) Notch

Answers :

1. B
2. A
3. D
4. B
5. A
6. A
7. C
8. B
9. A
10. A
11. C
12. C
13. D
14. C
15. B

□□□□□

ARS Mains (Model question paper)

1. On average, seawater in the world's oceans has a salinity of ....

2. In USLE A=RKLSCP, C refers to ....

3. Reynolds number refers to the ratio of ....

4. If kinematics viscosity is 20 m^2/s and density is 980 kg/m^3. The value of dynamic viscosity is.....................

5. For slow / tranquil flow the Froude number is equal ....

6. Time of concentration refers to ....

7. ....is a system for allocating water among those who possess land along its path.

8. In hydraulic jump water flow from supercritical to subcritical. (T/F)

9. Sediment delivery ratio (SDR) is defined as the sediment yield from an area divided by.........................

10. Channel order increases when two channels of similar order come together. (T/F)

11. Pattiseema, a lift irrigation project, interlinks ....and .... river through the polavaram right canal.

12. SAUNI stands for ...., SAUNI envisages filling 115 major dams of the arid Saurashtra region by diverting floodwaters overflowing from the Sardar Sarovar Dam across the Narmada in south Gujarat.

13. ...., ... and .... Irrigation projects are covered under Pradhan Mantri Krishi Sinchayee Yojana (PMKSY) was launched during the year 2015-16.

14. Major irrigation projects are those projects which have a Culturable Command Areas of More than 10,000 hectares. (T/F)

15. .... are devices used to control the discharge of water from the lateral to the plants.

16. If furrow slope in the direction of flow (%) is 2. Maximum non-erosive stream size (l/min) will be ....

17. At BMC surface irrigation schemes, it is assumed that E_c and E_b both are 90% for concrete lined canals continuous flow and that Ea is 50%. What is the overall irrigation efficiency?

18. If waters and soil extracts having electrical conductivity up to 5 dS/m. What will be value in ppm.

19. Date palm is highly salt tolerant crop. (T/F)

20. .... refers to growing alternate strips of different crops in the same field.

21. Cut-off drains are dug across a slope to intercept surface runoff while retention ditches dug along the contours to catch and retaining coming runoff. (T/F)

Subjective questions

1. What is interlinking of river project? Enlist different proposed or operationalized interlinking of rivers projects in India.

2. Discuss gulley erosion, its formation and different stages of its formation.

3. What is salt affected soil? What are the causes of salt problems in soil? Discuss in brief the causes and reclamation of saline and alkaline soils.

4. What do you mean by flood flouting? Also describes the elements of flood routing. Classify the flood routing and also explain any one method.

5. Define most economical channel section. Derive an equation for the most economical channel section for a rectangular cross section having bottom width "b", and depth "d".

6. Define sub-surface drainage. List benefits of sub surface drainage.

7. Describe Universal Soil Loss Equation, MUSLE, and RUSLE and also discuss its different factors and also discuss the applications of USLE.

8. Define integrated watershed development and also explain its objective. Discuss the importance of people's participation in watershed development.

9. Explain design procedure of a drip irrigation system. Also write the other name of drip irrigation. Write the advantages and disadvantages of drip irrigation systems.

10. Define various terms: Pf, Mole drain, Leaching requirement, Open Channel Flow, Specific energy curve, Cavitations and irrigation scheduling.

11. Write difference between

    I. Wind breaks and shelterbelts

    II. Diversions and waterways

    III. Hydraulic Conductivity and Intrinsic permeability

    IV. Conjunctive use and Consumptive use

    V. Active and passive remote sensing

    VI. Infiltration and Percolation

    VII. NIR and GIR

    VIII. Hyetograph and Mass Curve

    IX. PET and Reference ET

    X. Erosivity and Erodibility

12. Explain soil irrigability classification and soil capability classification.

13. What are hydrograph, unit hydrograph, synthetic hydrograph and S hydrograph? Explain the different components of hydrograph.

14. Differentiate between irrigation requirement and crop water requirement. Enlist the methods of evapotranspiration estimation. Also explain briefly.

15. How can NGOs, schools, banks, and industry help to carry out an afforestation programme?

16. Describe different textural classes of soil and the way they affect the plant growth.

17. What is weir and classify the weir? Discuss the guidelines for designing and operating the weir.

18. What is critical depth and critical flow? With the help of specific energy curve derive the criteria for critical flow.

19. The data on the ratio of subsurface drain discharge and hydraulic head plot as an approximate straight line on an arithmetic graph paper with a slope of 0.002 m^{-1} day^{-1}. The spacing (S) between the drains is 40 m. Assuming a steady state condition, calculate the value of saturated hydraulic conductivity.

20. Enlist different soil moisture constants and explain in brief. Draw a sketch showing the constants with their respective tensions.

21. Enlist and describe in brief the methods of irrigation scheduling. Write in brief the principle of neutron moisture meter.

22. A tube well is 0.46 m in diameter. The unconfined aquifer is of 18 m depth. After drawdown depth of water is 12 m in the well. Permeability of soil is 24.50 m/day. Radius of circle of

influence is 275 meters. Calculate discharge of the tube well (m^3/day and liters/sec).

23. Find the loss of head due to friction in a pipe of 500mm diameter and 1.5km long. The velocity of water in the pipe is 1.0 m/s. Take coefficient of friction as 0.005.

IARI Ph.D Subjective Questions (2011)

1. Why and how a tube well is developed ?

2. Draw and explain typical characteristic curve of a centrifugal pump.

3. Name the different the different components of a total hydrograph and explain with the help of a net sketches how are these components are found.

4. What is a critical flow ? Why is the critically of the flow is essential in developing head discharge relationship of flow in an open channel?

5. Estimate the specific surface area of a soil particle resembling the shape of a sphere with radius 0.03 mm contained in a cubical packing.

6. A canal is carrying 1 m^3/s flow and the electrical conductivity of the water is 0.2 dS/m.it is proposed to supplement the canal flow by pumping groundwater which has a salinity of 3 dS/m. If the maximum permissible salinity of mixed water is 0.5 dS/m, find the number of tube wells that may be commissioned, each with a capacity to discharge 20 L/s.

IARI Ph.D Subjective Questions - 2012 (Memory Based)

1. What is drainage ? Explain the different types of drainage and also describe the advantage of sub-surface drainage.
2. Explain in details the Universal Soil Loss equation (USLE) and also write its limitations.

IARI Ph.D Subjective Questions -2013

1. Explain FAO Penman-Monteith equation for calculation of reference evapotranspiration.
2. The data on the ratio of subsurface drain discharge and hydraulic head plot as an approximate straight line on an arithmetic graph paper with a slope of 0.002 m^{-1} day^{-1}. The spacing (S) between the drains is 40 m. Assuming a steady state condition, calculate the value of saturated hydraulic conductivity.
3. Explain the procedure to generate intensity duration frequency curves (IDF Curves) and give an example of use of IDF Curve.
4. Two pipes, one circular and one square, have the same cross-sectional area. Which has the larger hydraulic radius and by what percentage?
5. With the help of specific energy curve derive the criteria for critical flow.
6. (a) Show that for irrotational flow $\Delta^2\psi=0$.

   (b) If the stream function of a flow is $\psi=2xy$, what is the velocity at position x=2, y=5 ?

IARI Ph.D. Subjective Questions -2016 (Memory Based)

1. Define water storage efficiency and water application efficiency. Write differences between them.

2. Define unit hydrograph, synthetic hydrograph and instantaneous unit hydrograph. Also write their applicability.

3. Define the flow net. Write down the procedures to derive the flow net.

4. For a crop with effective rooting depth of 150 cm, calculate the irrigation interval. Given, field capacity = 14%, permissible depletion : 7 %, and crop evapotranspiration = 285 mm/ month.

IARI Ph.D. 2017question (Memory based)

1. Describe and Explain the NRCS Curve number method.

2. Describe the mechanism of water erosion and also explain the principal of water erosion.

3. Water flows through a rectangular channel 1m wide and 0.5m deep and then over a sharp triangular weir of crest length of 0.6m. If the water level in the channel is 0.225m above the weir crest, calculate the discharge over the weir. [Cd for rectangular and triangular weir is 0.62 and 0.59 respectively] (Assume necessary parameters).

Appendix-A

Table A-1. SI base units

Base quantity		**SI base unit**		
Name	**Symbol**	**Name**	**Symbol**	**Symbol for Dimension**
length	*l, x, r, etc.*	Meter	M	L
Mass	*m*	Kilogram	Kg	M
Time, duration	*t*	Second	S	T
Electric current	*I, i*	Ampere	A	I
Thermodynamic temperature	*T*	Kelvin	K	Θ
Amount of substance	*n*	Mole	mol	N
Luminous intensity	I_v	candela	cd	J

Source: THE INTERNATIONAL SYSTEM OF UNITS (SI) (2008). NIST Special Publication 330.

SI Derived units are products of powers of base units. Coherent derived units are products of powers of base units that include no numerical factor other than 1.

Table A-2. Examples of coherent derived units in the SI expressed in terms of base units

Derived quantity		SI coherent derived unit	
Name	Symbol	Name	Symbol
area	A	square meter	m^2
volume	V	cubic meter	m^3
speed, velocity	v	meter per second	m/s
acceleration	a	meter per second squared	m/s^2
Wave number	σ, v~	reciprocal meter	m^{-1}
density, mass density	ρ	kilogram per cubic meter	kg/m^3
surface density	ρ_A	kilogram per square meter	kg/m^2
specific volume	v	cubic meter per kilogram	m^3/kg
current density	j	ampere per square meter	A/m^2
magnetic field strength	H	ampere per meter	A/m
mass concentration	c	mole per cubic meter	mol/m^3
luminance	L_v	candela per square meter	cd/m^2

Source: THE INTERNATIONAL SYSTEM OF UNITS (SI) (2008).NIST Special Publication 330.

Table A-3. Coherent derived units in the SI with special names and symbols

Derived quantity	SI coherent derived unit			
	Name	Symbol	Expressed in terms of other SI terms	Expressed in terms of SI base units
plane angle	radian (a)	rad	1 (a)	m/m
solid angle	steradian (a)	sr (b)	1 (a)	m^2/m^2
frequency	hertz	Hz		s^{-1}
force	newton	N		$m\ kg\ s^{-2}$
pressure, stress	pascal	Pa	N/m^2	$m^{-1}\ kg\ s^{-2}$
energy, work, amount of heat	joule	J	N m	$m^2 kg\ s^{-2}$
power, radiant flux	watt	W	J/s	$m^2\ kg\ s^{-3}$
electric charge, amount of electricity	coulomb	C		s A
electric potential difference(e), electromotive force	volt	V	W/A	$m^2\ kg\ s^{-3}\ A^{-1}$
capacitance	farad	F	C/V	$m^{-2}\ kg^{-1}\ s^4\ A^2$
electric resistance	ohm	Ω	V/A	$m^2 kg\ s^{-3}\ A^{-2}$
electric conductance	siemens	S	A/V	$m^{-2}\ kg^{-1}\ s^3\ A^2$
magnetic flux	weber	Wb	V s	$m^2\ kg\ s^{-2}\ A^{-1}$
magnetic flux density	tesla	T	Wb/m^2	$kg\ s^{-2}\ A^{-1}$
inductance	henry	H	Wb/A	$m^2 kg\ s^{-2} A^{-2}$

Celsius temperature	degree Celsius	°C		K
luminous flux	lumen	lm	cd sr (b)	cd
illuminance	lux	lx	lm/m^2	m^{-2}cd

Source: THE INTERNATIONAL SYSTEM OF UNITS (SI) (2008).NIST Special Publication 330.

(*a*) The radian and steradian are special names for the number one that may be used to convey information about the quantity concerned. In practice the symbols rad and sr are used where appropriate, but the symbol for the derived unit one is generally omitted in specifying the values of dimensionless quantities.
(*b*) In photometry the name steradian and the symbol sr are usually retained in expressions for units.

TableA-4. Examples of SI coherent derived units whose names and symbols include SI coherent derived units with special names and symbols

Derived quantity	SI coherent derived unit		
	Name	Symbol	Expressed in terms of SI base units
dynamic viscosity	pascal second	Pa s	m^{-1} kg s^{-1}
moment of force	newton meter	N m	m^2 kg s^{-2}
surface tension	newton per meter	N/m	kg s^{-2}
angular velocity	radian per second	rad/s	m m^{-1} s^{-1} = s^{-1}
angular acceleration	radian per second squared	rad/s^2	m m^{-1} s^{-2}= s^{-2}
heat flux density, irradiance	watt per square meter	W/m^2	kg s^{-3}
heat capacity, Entropy	joule per kelvin	J/K	m2 kg s^{-2} K^{-1}
specific heat capacity, specific entropy	joule per kilogram kelvin	J/(kg K)	m^2 s^{-2} K^{-1}
specific energy	joule per kilogram	J/kg	$m^2 s^{-2}$
thermal conductivity	watt per meter kelvin	W/(m K)	m kg s^{-3} K^{-1}

energy density	joule per cubic meter	J/m^3	m^{-1} kg s^{-2}
electric field strength	volt per meter	V/m	m kg s^{-3} A^{-1}
electric charge density	coulomb per cubic meter	C/m^3	m^{-3} s A
surface charge density	coulomb per square meter	C/m^2	m^{-2} s A
electric flux density, electric displacement	coulomb per square meter	C/m^2	m^{-2} s A
radiant intensity	watt per steradian	W/sr	m^4 m^{-2}kg s^{-3}= m^2kg s^{-3}
radiance	watt per square meter steradian	W/(m^2sr)	m^2m^{-2}kg s^{-3}= kg s^{-3}

Source: THE INTERNATIONAL SYSTEM OF UNITS (SI) (2008).NIST Special Publication 330.

Table A-5. SI prefixes

Factor	Name	Symbol	Factor	Name	Symbol
10^1	deka	da	10^{-1}	deci	d
10^2	hecto	h	10^{-2}	centi	c
10^3	kilo	k	10^{-3}	milli	m
10^6	mega	M	10^{-6}	micro	μ
10^9	giga	G	10^{-9}	nano	n
10^{12}	tera	T	10^{-12}	pico	p
10^{15}	peta	P	10^{-15}	femto	f
10^{18}	exa	E	10^{-18}	atto	a
10^{21}	zetta	Z	10^{-21}	zepto	z
10^{24}	yotta	Y	10^{-24}	yocto	y

Measurement Units and their Conversion

Length

1 inch (in)	=	2.54 cm
1 mile (mi)	=	1609.344 meter
1 foot (ft)	=	12 inches (in)
1 yard (yd)	=	3 feet
1 international nautical mile (nm)	=	1852 meters (m)
1 link (li)	=	0.66 foot
1 chain (Gunter's or Surveyors Chain)	=	66 foot 20.1168 meter 100 links
1 rod (rd), pole, or perch	=	16½ feet
40 rods	=	1 furlong (fur) = 660 feet
1 furlong (fur)	=	201.168 meter
1 rope	=	20 foot
1 fathom	=	6 foot

Area

1 square foot (ft^2)	=	144 square inches (in^2)
1 square yard (yd^2)	=	9 square feet (ft^2)
1 hectare (ha)	=	100 are 10000 square meter (m^2)

Volume/Rate

1 cubic meter (m^3)	=	1000 liter
1 liter	=	1000Cubic centimeter (cc)
1 barrel (oil)	=	159 liter

1 gallon (US)	=	3.78 liter
1 gallon (UK)	=	4.55 liter
1 Cumec	=	1 cubic meter per sec ($1m^3/s$) 35.315 cusec
1 Cusec	=	1 cubic feet per sec ($1ft^3/s$) 28.32 liter/sec

Weight

1 slug	=	14.594 kilogram
1 pound	=	0.4536 kilogram
1 ton (metric)	=	1000 kilogram
1 quintal (metric)	=	100 kilogram

Velocity

1 knot	=	0.514 meter/second
1 Mach (SI standard)	=	295.0464 meter/second

Pressure

1 atmosphere	=	101325 Pa (Pascals) 101325 N/m^2 1.01329 bar 1013250 dyne/sq. cm 1.033 kgf/sq. cm 14.7 pound /sq. inch (psi) 68087.25 poundal/sq. foot 76 cm mercury 760 torr 29.92 in. mercury 33.9 ft water 325 x 10^6 $dynes/cm^2$
1 pascal	=	1 newton/square meter
1 bar	=	100000 pascal
1 bar	=	14.5 psi

Energy

1 Calorie	=	4.18 Joules
1 joule =	=	1 Newton-meter 1,00,00,000 erg
1 Btu (IT)	=	1055.056 joule

Power

1 watt	=	1 joules/sec
1 horsepower (hp)	=	745.7 watt
1 ton (refrigeration)	=	3.52 Kilowatt

Force

1 newton	=	100000 dyne
1 kilogram-force	=	9.8 newton
1 pound-force	=	4.448 newton
1 poundal	=	0.138254954 newton

Angle

Π radian	=	180 degree
1 degree	=	60 minute
1 revolution	=	360 degree
1 right angle	=	90 degree
1 sextant	=	60 degree

Temperature

Celsius (°C), Fahrenheit (F), Kelvin (K), Rankine (R).

1 degree Celsius	=	274.15 kelvin
(F-32)/(212-32)	=	(°C-0)/(100-0)
T(K)	=	T(°C)+273.15
T(R)	=	T(°F) +459.67
T(R)	=	$\frac{9}{5}$T(K)

Data storage

1byte 1 character	=	8 bit
1 word	=	16 bit 2 bytes
1 megabyte (MB)	=	1024 kilobyte (kB)

Appendix-B

Important Mathematical formulas

Volume and Area of Some Common Shapes

Table B-1. Volume and surface area

S N	*Geometrical shape*	*Figure*	*Volume*	*Total surface area*	*Curved surface area*	*Diagonal*
1	Cuboid	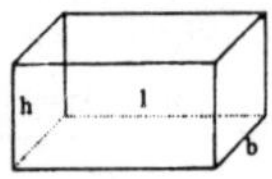	$l \times b \times h$	$2(lb + bh + lh)$	-	$(l^2+b^2+h^2)^{½}$
2	Cube	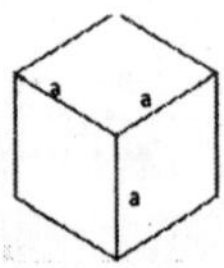	a^3	$6a^2$	-	$\sqrt{3}a$
3	Cylinder	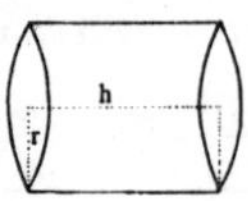	$\pi r^2 h$	$2 \pi r(h + r)$	$2 \pi r h$	-
4	Sphere	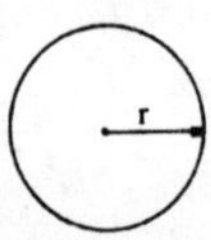	$\frac{4}{3} \pi r^3$	$4 \pi r^2$	-	-
5	Right circular cone	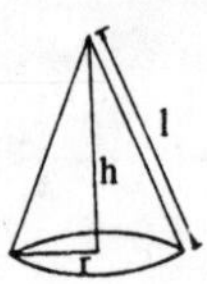	$\frac{1}{3} \pi r^2 h$	$\pi r(l+r)$	$\pi r l$	-

6	Fructum of a cone	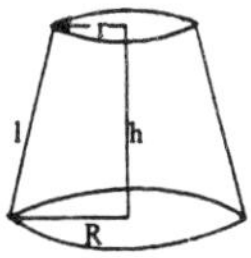	$\pi \frac{h}{3} (r^2 + R^2 + rR)$	$\pi [l(r + R) + r^2 + R^2]$	$\pi (r + R) l$	-

Table B-2. Area

Sl N	*Name of the geometrical shape*	*Figure*	*Area*	*Circum-ference/ Perimeter*
1.	Rectangle	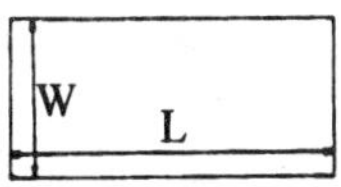	L x W	2(L+W)
2.	Square	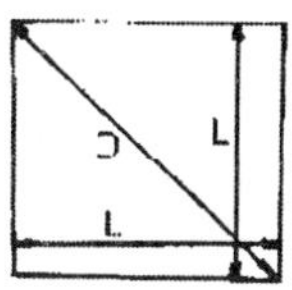	L^2 or ½ D^2	4L
3.	Parallelogram	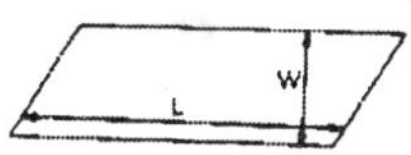	L x W	-
4.	Rhombus	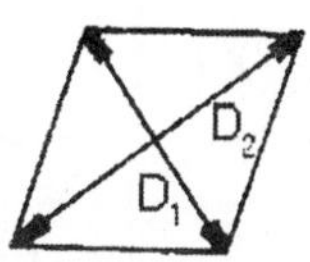	½ × (D_1 x D_2)	-
5.	Trapezium	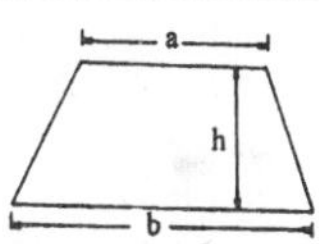	½ × (a + b) x h	-

6.	Right-angled triangle	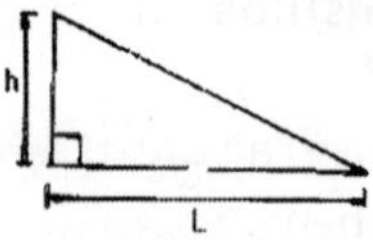	½ × L x h	-
7.	Isosceles triangle	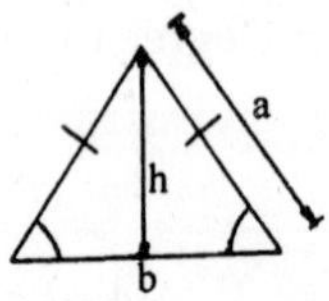	$\frac{b}{4}(4a^2-b^2)^{1/2}$	2a + b
8.	Equilateral triangle	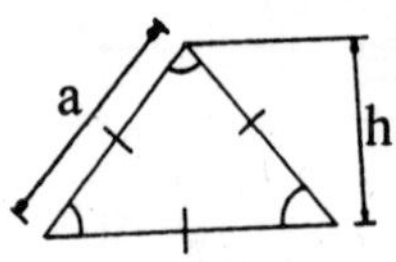	$\frac{\sqrt{3}}{4}a^2$	3 a
9.	Triangle	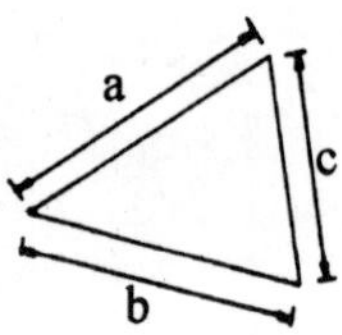	Area = $\sqrt{s(s-a)(s-b)(s-c)}$ where, $s=\frac{(a+b+c)}{2}$	a+b+c
10	Circle	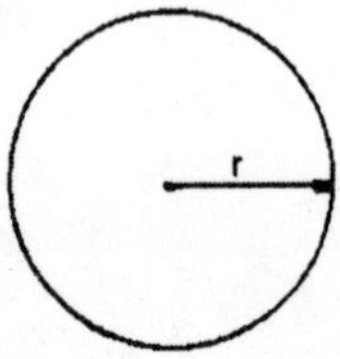	$\pi\ r^2$	$2\pi r$
11	Arc of a circle	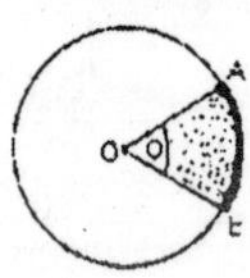	area of sector AB $=\frac{\pi r^2\theta}{360^0}$	arc AB $=\frac{2\pi r\theta}{360^0}$

Trigonometric relationships

- If in a circle of radius r, an arc of length l subtends and angle of θ radians, then
  $l = r\theta$
- Radian measure = $\frac{\pi}{180^0}$ × Degree measure
- $\cos^2 x + \sin^2 x = 1$
- $1 + \tan^2 x = \sec^2 x$
- $1 + \cot^2 x = \mathrm{cosec}^2 x$
- $\cos(2n\pi + x) = \cos x$
- $\sin(2n\pi + x) = \sin x$
- $\sin(-x) = -\sin x$
- $\cos(-x) = \cos x$
- $\cos(x + y) = \cos x \cos y - \sin x \sin y$
- $\cos(x - y) = \cos x \cos y + \sin x \sin y$
- $\cos(\frac{\pi}{2} - x) = \sin x$
- $\sin(\frac{\pi}{2} - x) = \cos x$
- $\sin(x + y) = \sin x \cos y + \cos x \sin y$
- $\sin(x - y) = \sin x \cos y - \cos x \sin y$
- $\cos(\frac{\pi}{2} + x) = -\sin x$ $\quad$ $\sin(\frac{\pi}{2} + x) = \cos x$

  $\cos(\pi - x) = -\cos x$ $\quad$ $\sin(\pi - x) = \sin x$

  $\cos(\pi + x) = -\cos x$ $\quad$ $\sin(\pi + x) = -\sin x$

  $\cos(2\pi - x) = \cos x$ $\quad$ $\sin(2\pi - x) = -\sin x$
- If none of the angles x, y and $(x \pm y)$ is an odd multiple of $\frac{\pi}{2}$, then

$$\tan(x + y) = \frac{\tan x + \tan y}{1 - \tan x \tan y}$$

$$\tan(x - y) = \frac{\tan x - \tan y}{1 + \tan x \tan y}$$

- If none of the angles x, y and $(x \pm y)$ is a multiple of π, then

$$\cot(x+y) = \frac{\cot x \cot y - 1}{\cot x + \cot y}$$

$$\cot(x-y) = \frac{\cot x \cot y + 1}{\cot x - \cot y}$$

- $\cos 2x = \cos^2 x - \sin^2 x = 2\cos^2 x - 1 = 1 - 2\sin^2 x = \frac{1-tan^2 x}{1-tan^2 x}$
- $\sin 2x = 2 \sin x \cos x = \frac{2\tan x}{1+tan^2 x}$
- $\tan 2x = \frac{2\tan x}{1-tan^2 x}$
- $\sin 3x = 3\sin x - 4\sin^3 x$
- $\cos 3x = 4\cos^3 x - 3\cos x$
- $\tan 3x = \frac{3\tan x - tan^3 x}{1-3tan^2 x}$
- $\cos x + \cos y = 2\cos\frac{x+y}{2}\cos\frac{x-y}{2}$

  $\cos x - \cos y = -2\sin\frac{x+y}{2}\sin\frac{x-y}{2}$

  $\sin x + \sin y = 2\sin\frac{x+y}{2}\cos\frac{x-y}{2}$

  $\sin x - \sin y = 2\cos\frac{x+y}{2}\sin\frac{x-y}{2}$
- $2\cos x \cos y = \cos(x+y) + \cos(x-y)$

  $-2\sin x \sin y = \cos(x+y) - \cos(x-y)$

  $2\sin x \cos y = \sin(x+y) + \sin(x-y)$

  $2\cos x \sin y = \sin(x+y) - \sin(x-y)$

Limits & Derivatives

- $10^x = e^{x\log 10}$
- $(1+x)^{1/x} = e^{(1/x)\log(1+x)}$
- $\lim_{x\to a}\frac{x^n - a^n}{x-a} = na^{n-1}$
- $\lim_{\theta\to 0} \cos\theta = 1$
- $\lim_{\theta\to 0}\frac{\sin\theta}{\theta} = 1$

- $\lim_{\theta \to 0} \frac{\theta}{\sin\theta} = 1$
- $\lim_{\theta \to 0} \frac{\tan\theta}{\theta} = 1$
- $\lim_{\theta \to 0} \frac{\theta}{\tan\theta} = 1$
- $\lim_{x \to 0} (1 + x)^{1/x} = e$
- $\lim_{\theta \to 0} \frac{\log_e(1+x)}{x} = 1$
- $\lim_{\theta \to 0} \frac{\log_a(1+x)}{x} = \log_a e$ (a>0, a≠1)
- $\lim_{\theta \to 0} \frac{a^x - 1}{x} = \log_e a$ (a>0)
- $\frac{d}{dx}\left(\frac{x^{n+1}}{n+1}\right) = x^n$
- $\frac{d}{dx}(\sin x) = \cos x$
- $\frac{d}{dx}(-\cos x) = \sin x$
- $\frac{d}{dx}(\tan x) = \sec^2 x$
- $\frac{d}{dx}(-\cot x) = \mathrm{cosec}^2 x$
- $\frac{d}{dx}(\sec x) = \sec x \tan x$
- $\frac{d}{dx}(-\mathrm{cosec}\, x) = \mathrm{cosec}\, x \cot x$
- $\frac{d}{dx}(\sin^{-1} x) = \frac{1}{\sqrt{1-x^2}}$
- $\frac{d}{dx}(-\cos^{-1} x) = \frac{1}{\sqrt{1-x^2}}$
- $\frac{d}{dx}(\tan^{-1} x) = \frac{1}{1+x^2}$
- $\frac{d}{dx}(-\cot^{-1} x) = \frac{1}{1+x^2}$
- $\frac{d}{dx}(\sec^{-1} x) = \frac{1}{x\sqrt{x^2-1}}$

- $\frac{d}{dx}(-cosec^{-1} x) = \frac{1}{x\sqrt{x^2-1}}$
- $\frac{d}{dx}(e^x) = e^x$
- $\frac{d}{dx} log|x| = \frac{1}{x}$
- $\frac{d}{dx}\left(\frac{a^x}{log\ a}\right) = a^x$

Integrals

- $\int x^n\, dx = \frac{x^{n+1}}{n+1}$
- $\int cos\ x\, dx = sin\ x + c$
- $\int sin\ x\, dx = -cos\ x + c$
- $\int sec^2 x\, dx = tan\ x + c$
- $\int cosec^2 x\, dx = -cot\ x + c$
- $\int sec\ x\ tan\ x\, dx = sec\ x + c$
- $\int cosec\ x\ cot\ x\, dx = -cosec\ x + c$
- $\int tan\ x\, dx = log|sec\ x| + c$
- $\int cot\ x\, dx = log|sin\ x| + c$
- $\int sec\ x\, dx = log|sec\ x + tan\ x| + c$
- $\int cosec\ x\, dx = log|cosec\ x - cot\ x| + c$
- $\int \frac{dx}{\sqrt{1-x^2}} = sin^{-1} x + c$
- $\int \frac{dx}{\sqrt{1-x^2}} = -cos^{-1} x + c$
- $\int \frac{dx}{1+x^2} = tan^{-1} x + c$
- $\int \frac{dx}{1+x^2} = tan^{-1} x + c$
- $\int e^x\, dx = e^x + c$
- $\int a^x\, dx = \frac{a^x}{log\ a} + c$
- $\int \frac{dx}{x\sqrt{x^2-1}} = sec^{-1} x + c$

- $\int \frac{dx}{x\sqrt{x^2-1}} = -cosec^{-1}\, x + c$
- $\int \frac{dx}{x} = log|x| + c$
- $\int \frac{dx}{x^2-a^2} = \frac{1}{2a} log \left|\frac{x-a}{x+a}\right| + c$
- $\int \frac{dx}{a^2-x^2} = \frac{1}{2a} log \left|\frac{a+x}{a-x}\right| + c$
- $\int \frac{dx}{x^2+a^2} = \frac{1}{a} tan^{-1} \frac{x}{a} + c$
- $\int \frac{dx}{\sqrt{x^2-a^2}} = log\left|x + \sqrt{x^2 - a^2}\right| + c$
- $\int \frac{dx}{\sqrt{a^2-x^2}} = sin^{-1} \frac{x}{a} + c$
- $\int \frac{dx}{\sqrt{x^2+a^2}} = log\left|x + \sqrt{x^2 + a^2}\right| + c$
- $\int f_1(x).f_2(x)\ dx =$
  $f_1(x) \int f_2(x) - \int \left[\frac{d}{dx} f_1(x). \int f_2(x)\ dx\right] dx$
- $\int e^x[f(x) + f'(x)]\ dx = \int e^x f(x)\ dx + c$

Matrices

A *matrix* is an ordered rectangular array of numbers or functions. The numbers or functions are called the elements or the entries of the matrix

- **Column matrix**

  A matrix is said to be a *column matrix* if it has only one column.

  For example, $A = \begin{bmatrix} 5 \\ 3 \\ 9 \end{bmatrix}$ is a column matrix of order 3× 1.

- **Row matrix**

  A matrix is said to be a *row matrix* if it has only one row.

- **Square matrix**

  A matrix in which the number of rows are equal to the number of columns, is said to be a *square matrix*.

- **Diagonal matrix**

  A square matrix B = $[bij]\ m \times m$ is said to be a *diagonal matrix* if all its non diagonal elements are zero, that is a matrix B = $[b_{ij}]$ $m \times m$ is said to be a diagonal matrix if $b_{ij} = 0$, when $i \neq j$.

For example, A=[5], B=$\begin{bmatrix} 2 & 0 \\ 0 & 9 \end{bmatrix}$, C=$\begin{bmatrix} 1 & 0 & 0 \\ 0 & 8 & 0 \\ 0 & 0 & 7 \end{bmatrix}$.

- **Scalar matrix**

  A diagonal matrix is said to be a *scalar matrix* if its diagonal elements are equal.

  For example, A= $\begin{bmatrix} 3 & 0 & 0 \\ 0 & 3 & 0 \\ 0 & 0 & 3 \end{bmatrix}$

- **Identity matrix**

  A square matrix in which elements in the diagonal are all 1 and rest are all zero is called an *identity matrix*.

  For example, A=[1], B=$\begin{bmatrix} 1 & 0 \\ 0 & 1 \end{bmatrix}$, C=$\begin{bmatrix} 1 & 0 & 0 \\ 0 & 1 & 0 \\ 0 & 0 & 1 \end{bmatrix}$.

- **Transpose of a Matrix**

  If A = $[a_{ij}]_{m \times n}$ be an m × n matrix then the matrix obtained by interchanging the rows and columns of A is called the transpose of the matrix. Transpose of A is denoted by A′ or A^T.

  Properties of the transpose of a matrix.

  (i) (A′)′ = A (ii) (A + B)′ = A′ + B′ (iii) (KA)′ = KA′, K is a scalar (iv) (AB)′ = B′A′

- **Non-Singular Matrix**

  An n × n matrix A is called non-singular or invertible if there exists an n × n matrix B such that

  $$AB = I_n = BA$$

  Or

  A square matrix that is not singular,i.e., one that has a matrix inverse. Non-singular matrices are sometimes also called regular matrices. A square matrix is non-singular if its determinant is **non zero**.

For example: $\begin{bmatrix}1 & 0\\0 & 1\end{bmatrix}, \begin{bmatrix}0 & 1\\1 & 1\end{bmatrix}$

- **Singular matrices**
  A square matrix that does not have a matrix inverse. A matrix is singular if its determinant is 0.
  For example: $\begin{bmatrix}0 & 0\\0 & 1\end{bmatrix}, \begin{bmatrix}0 & 1\\0 & 1\end{bmatrix}$

- **Symmetric matrix**
  A square matrix A = $[a_{ij}]$ is symmetric if $a_{ij} = a_{ji}\ \forall i, j$. Also a square matrix A is symmetric if A′ = A

- **Skew Symmetric Matrix**
  A square matrix A = $[a_{ij}]$ is skew-symmetric, if $a_{ij} = -a_{ji} \forall i, j$. Also a square matrix A is skew - symmetric, if A′ = – A.
- **Determinant**
  To every square matrix A = $[a_{ij}]$ of order n × n, we can associate a number (real or complex) called determinant of A. It is denoted by det. A or |A|.

Sequence and series

- Arithmetic progression (A.P.) is a sequence in which terms increase or decrease regularly by the same constant. This constant is called common difference of the A.P. Usually, we denote the first term of A.P. by **a**, the common difference by **d** and the last term by ***l***. The general term or the n th term of the A.P. is given by $\mathbf{a_n = a + (n-1)\,d}$.
  The sum S_n of the first n terms of an A.P. is given by:

  $$S_n = \frac{n}{2}[2a + (n-1)d]$$
  $$= \frac{n}{2}[a + l]$$

  Where $l=a+(n-1)d$
- A sequence is said to be a geometric progression or G.P., if the ratio of any term to its preceding term is same throughout. This constant factor is called the common

ratio. Usually, we denote the first term of a G.P. by a and its common ratio by r. The general or the nth term of G.P. is given by $a_n = ar^{(n-1)}$. The sum S_n of the first n terms of G.P. is given by

$$S_n = \frac{a(r^n - 1)}{r-1} = \frac{a(1-r^n)}{1-r}$$

Sum of natural numbers

- The sum of the first n natural numbers, S_n, is:

$$S_n = \frac{n(n+1)}{2}$$

- The sum of the squares of the first n natural numbers is:

$$S_n = \frac{n(n+1)(2n+1)}{6}$$

- The sum of the square of first n natural numbers, is:

$$S_n = \left\{\frac{n(n+1)}{2}\right\}^2$$

Infinite series

- **Expansion by binomial theorem**

$$(a+b)^n = {}^nC_0 a^n + {}^nC_1 a^{n-1} b + {}^nC_2 a^{n-2} b^2 \dots\dots\dots {}^nC_{n-1} a b^{n-1} + {}^nC_n b^n$$

- **Binomial series**

$$(1+x)^n = {}^nC_0 + {}^nC_1 x + {}^nC_2 x^2 \dots\dots\dots {}^nC_n x^n$$

- **Taylor and Maclaurin series**

  Taylor expansion of a function $f(x)$ valid for values of x near to a:

$$f(x) = f(a) + (x-a)f'(a) + \frac{(x-a)^2}{2!}f''(a) + \frac{(x-a)^3}{3!}f'''(a) + \dots\dots\dots$$

A Maclaurin series is a Taylor series with a = 0,

$$f(x) = f(0) + xf'(a) + \frac{x^2}{2!}f''(0) + \frac{x^3}{3!}f'''(0) + \dots\dots\dots\dots\dots\dots$$

- Power series with real variables

$$e^x = 1 + \frac{x}{1!} + \frac{x^2}{2!} + \frac{x^3}{3!} + \dots\dots\dots\dots \frac{x^n}{n!} + \dots\dots\dots\dots$$

valid for all x

$$\log_e(1+x) = x - \frac{x^2}{2} + \frac{x^3}{3} + \dots\dots\dots\dots(-1)^{n+1}\frac{x^n}{n}\dots\dots$$

valid for -1<x<1

$$\sin x = \frac{e^{ix} - e^{-ix}}{2i} = x - \frac{x^3}{3!} + \frac{x^5}{5!} + \cdots \dots\dots\dots\dots \text{ valid for all x}$$

$$\cos x = \frac{e^{ix} + e^{-ix}}{2i} = 1 - \frac{x^2}{2!} + \frac{x^4}{4!} - \frac{x^6}{6!} \dots\dots\dots\dots \text{valid for all x}$$

$$\sinh x = \frac{e^{x} - e^{-x}}{2} = x + \frac{x^3}{3!} + \frac{x^5}{5!} + \cdots \dots\dots\dots\dots \text{valid for all x}$$

$$\cos x = \frac{e^{x} + e^{-x}}{2} = 1 + \frac{x^2}{2!} + \frac{x^4}{4!} + \frac{x^6}{6!} \dots\dots\dots\dots\dots \text{ valid for all x}$$

Complex number

- A number of the form a + ib, where a and b are real numbers, is called a complex number, a is called the real part and b is called the imaginary part of the complex number.
- Let $z_1 = a + ib$ and $z_2 = c + id$. Then

  (i) $z_1 + z_2 = (a + c) + i\,(b + d)$

  (ii) $z_1 z_2 = (ac - bd) + i\,(ad + bc)$
- For any integer k, $i^{4k} = 1$, $i^{4k+1} = i$, $i^{4k+2} = -1$, $i^{4k+3} = -i$
- The conjugate of the complex number $z = a + ib$, denoted by $\bar{z}$, is given by $\bar{z} = a - ib$.
- The polar form of the complex number z = x + iy is r (cosθ + i sinθ), where $r = \sqrt{x^2 + y^2}$

(The modulus of z) and $\cos\theta = \frac{x}{r}$, $\sin\theta = \frac{y}{r}$. θis known as the argument of z. The value of θ such that $-\pi<\theta<\pi$, is called the principal argument of z.

- The solution of the quadratic equation $ax^2 + bx + c = 0$, where a, b, c ∈R, a≠0, $b^2-4ac<0$, are given by

$$x = \frac{-b\pm\sqrt{4ac-b^2}i}{2a}$$

Permutations and combinations

- If an event can occur in m different ways, following which another event can occur in n different ways, then the total number of occurrence of the events in the given order is m × n.

- The number of permutations of n different things taken r at a time, where repetition is not allowed, is denoted by $^nPr = \frac{n!}{(n-r)!}$, where $0 \le r \le n$.

- The number of combinations of n different things taken r at a time, denoted by

$$^nCr = \frac{n!}{n!(n-r)!}, \text{ where } 0 \le r \le n.$$

Vectors

- The scalar product of two given vectors $\vec{a}$ and $\vec{b}$having angle θ between them is defined as

$$\vec{a}.\vec{b} = |\vec{a}||\vec{b}| \cos\theta$$

- If θis the angle between two vectors $\vec{a}$ and $\vec{b}$, then their cross product is given as

$$\vec{a} x \vec{b} = |\vec{a}||\vec{b}| \sin\theta \cdot \hat{n}$$

Where, $\hat{n}$ is a unit vector perpendicular to the plane containing $\vec{a}$ and $\vec{b}$. Such that, $\vec{a}$, $\vec{b}$ and $\hat{n}$ form right handed system of coordinate axes.

- If we have two vectors $\vec{a}$ and $\vec{b}$, given in component form as

- $\vec{a} = a_1\hat{\imath} + a_2\hat{\jmath} + a_3\hat{k}$and $\vec{b} = b_1\hat{\imath} + b_2\hat{\jmath} + b_3\hat{k}$ and λ be any scalar,

Then

$\vec{a} + \vec{b} = (\boldsymbol{a_1} + \boldsymbol{b_1})\hat{\imath} + (\boldsymbol{a_2} + \boldsymbol{b_2})\hat{\jmath} + (\boldsymbol{a_3} + \boldsymbol{b_3})\hat{k}$

$\lambda\vec{a} = (\lambda a_1)\hat{\imath} + (\lambda a_2)\hat{\jmath} + (\lambda a_3)\hat{k}$

$\vec{a}\,.\,\vec{b} = a_1 b_1 + a_2 b_2 + a_3 b_3$

$$\vec{a} \times \overrightarrow{b} = \begin{vmatrix} \hat{\imath} & \hat{\jmath} & \hat{k} \\ a_1 & a_2 & a_3 \\ b_1 & b_2 & b_3 \end{vmatrix}$$

$- (a_2 b_3 - a_3 b_2)\hat{\imath}\ (a_1 b_3 - a_3 b_1)\hat{\jmath} + (a_1 b_2 - a_3 h_1)\hat{k}$

$\hat{\imath} \times \hat{\jmath} = \hat{k},\qquad \hat{\jmath} \times \hat{\imath} = -\hat{k}$

$\hat{\jmath} \times \hat{k} = \hat{\imath}\qquad \hat{k} \times \hat{\jmath} = -\hat{\imath}$

$\hat{k} \times \hat{\imath} = \hat{\jmath}\qquad \hat{\imath} \times \hat{k} = -\hat{\jmath}$

$\hat{\imath} \times \hat{\imath} = \hat{\jmath} \times \hat{\jmath} = \hat{k} \times \hat{k} = 0$

Basics of co-ordinate geometry

Straight lines

- *Slope* (m) of a non-vertical line passing through the points (x_1, y_1) and (x_2, y_2) is given by

  $m = \frac{y_2 - y_1}{x_2 - x_1} = \frac{y_1 - y_2}{x_1 - x_2},\ x_1 \neq x_2.$
- If a line makes an angle α with the positive direction of x-axis, then the slope of the line is given by m = tan α, $\alpha \neq 90°$.
- An acute angle (say θ) between lines L1 and L2 with slopes m_1 and m_2 is given by

  $\tan\theta = \left|\frac{m_2 - m_1}{1 + m_1 m_2}\right|,\ 1 + m_1 m_2 \neq 0.$

- Two lines are parallel if and only if their slopes are equal.
- Two lines are perpendicular if and only if product of their slopes is –1.
- Equation of a line making intercepts a and b on the x-and y-axis, respectively, is $\frac{x}{a}+\frac{y}{b}=1$
- The perpendicular distance (d) of a line Ax + By+ C = 0 from a point (x_1, y_1) is given by

$$d=\frac{|Ax_1+By_1+C|}{\sqrt{A^2+B^2}}$$

Circles

- The equation of a circle with centre (h, k) and the radius r is

  $(x-h)^2+(y-k)^2=r^2$

- The general equation of a circle is $x^2+y^2+2gx+2fy+c=0$, where the centre is given by (–g, –f) and the radius by $r=\sqrt{g^2+f^2-c}$

  Intercept of x axis is $2\sqrt{g^2-c}$

  Intercept of y axis is $2\sqrt{f^2-c}$

  If the circle touches both the axis then $g^2=f^2=c$

- Equation of circle if given end point of diameter (x_1, y_1) and (x_2, y_2) is

$$(x-x_1)(x-x_2)+(y-y_1)(y-y_2)=0$$

Parabola

- Standard equation of parabola $y^2=4ax$

  The focus is (a,0)

  The vertices is (0,0)

  The equation of axis is y=0

  The equation of directrix is x=-a

Appendix-C

Important Dimensionless Numbers

i. Cauchy Number (Ca)

The Cauchy number is used in compressible fluid flow characterization; it is the ratio of ***inertial to compression forces***. The Cauchy number is defined as

$$Ca = \frac{\rho v^2}{\beta}$$

Where ρ= density of fluid, kg/m^3

v = speed of fluid, m/s

β = bulk modulus of fluid, kg/(m·s^2)

The number was named after Baron Augustin Louis Cauchy, French mathematician and physicist.

ii. Cowling Number (Co)

The Cowling number is used in magneto-hydrodynamics; it is defined as

$$Co = \frac{B^2}{\mu \rho v^2}$$

Where B = magnetic flux density, kg/(s^2·A) (tesla)

μ = permeability, (m·kg)/(A^2·s^2)

ρ= density, kg/m^3

v = fluid velocity, m/s

The number was named after Prof. T. Cowling of the University of Leeds, who was a pioneer in the study of magneto-hydrodynamics.

iii. Euler Number (Eu)

This number is used in fluid dynamics, especially in the analysis of fluids flowing in a conduit. The Euler number is defined as ratio of ***pressure force to inertial force***.

$$Eu = \frac{p}{\rho v^2}$$

Where p = pressure, kg/(m·s^2)

ρ= density, kg/m^3

v = velocity, m/s

This number was named after Leonhard Euler, a Swiss mathematician, astronomer and engineering physicist. He introduced natural logarithm (the base of which is ("*e*"), *i* for $\sqrt{-1}$and the notation *f*( ) for functions.

iv. Fourier Number (Fo)

There are two Fourier numbers: one for *heat transfer* (*Fo*), and one for *mass transfer* (*Fo**). The former is defined as ratio of ***heat conduction rate to the rate of thermal energy storage in a solid.***

$$Fo = \frac{k\Delta t}{\rho c r^2},$$

where k = thermal conductivity; dimension, (m·kg)/(s^3·°C)

Δt= time interval, s

ρ= density, kg/m^3

c = the fluid's specific heat capacity, m^2/(s^2·°C)

r = radius, m

The Fourier number for *mass transfer* is defined as ratio of ***diffusion rate to rate of storage.***

$$Fo^* = \frac{D\Delta t}{L^2}$$

where D = diffusion coefficient (diffusivity), m^2/s

Δt = time interval, s

L = representative linear size, m

Joseph Fourier was a French mathematician and scientist who did pioneering work on the theory of heat and numerical analysis.

v. **Froude Number (Fr)**

This dimensionless variable is used to characterize fluid motion in open channels. It is defined as ratio of ***inertial force to gravitational force.***

$$Fr = \frac{v}{\sqrt{gL}}$$

Where, v = velocity of fluid, m/s

g = gravitational acceleration, m/s²

L = representative linear size, m

This number was named after William Froude, an English engineer and naval architect.

vi. **Grash of Number (Gr)**

This number is used in fluid mechanics to characterize free convection by *gravitational* and *inertial* effects; it is defined as ratio of ***buoyancy to viscous force.***

$$Gr = \frac{L^3 \rho^2 g \beta \Delta t}{\mu^2}$$

Where, L = characteristic linear size, m

ρ= density of liquid (fluid or gas), kg/m³

g = gravitational acceleration, m/s²

β = volume expansion coefficient, °C⁻¹

Δt = temperature difference, °C

μ = dynamic viscosity of fluid, kg/(m·s)

The number is named after Franz Grashof, a German applied mathematician and engineer.

vii. **Grätz Number (Gz)**

This number is used for heat transfer expressions for laminar flow in pipes. The number is defined as ratio of ***thermal capacity to convective heat transfer.***

$$Gz = \frac{wC}{kL}$$

Where, w = mass flow rate of fluid, kg/s

c = specific heat capacity of fluid, $m^2/(s^2 \cdot °C)$

k = heat conductivity of fluid, $(m \cdot kg)/(s^3 \cdot °C)$

L = representative linear size, m

L. Grätz was a German investigator in the field of fluid mechanics.

viii. **Hartmann Number (Ha)**

This number is used in magneto-hydrodynamics to characterize the flow of a conducting fluid in transverse magnetic field. The Hartmann number is defined as

$$Ha = BL\sqrt{\frac{k_e}{\mu}}$$

Where, B = magnetic flux density, $kg/(s^2 \cdot A)$

L = representative linear size, m

k_e = electric conductivity, $(A^2 \cdot s^3)/(m^3 \cdot kg)$

μ = dynamic viscosity, $kg/(m \cdot s)$

ix. **Knudsen Number (Kn)**

This number is used in the study of a very low pressure gas. In this circumstance the mean free path of a molecule is comparable with the size of the vessel in which the gas is contained. The Knudsen number is defined as

$$Kn = \frac{\lambda}{L}$$

Where, λ = free mean path of the molecule, m

L = linear size of the vessel, m

The number was named after M. Knudsen, the inventor of the pressure gauge for very low pressures.

x. **Mach Number (Ma)**

This dimensionless number is used in aerodynamics to characterize the speed of an object with respect to the velocity of sound in the same medium and under the same conditions (temperature, pressure). The Mach number is defined as

$$Ma = \frac{v_1}{v_2}$$

Where,

$v1$ = the velocity of the object (e.g., airplane), m/s

$v2$ = the velocity of sound in the same medium, m/s

The number was named after Ernst Mach, an Austrian physicist.

xi. **Nusselt Number (Nu)**

This is also called the Biot number. There are actually two Nusselt numbers: Nusselt number for heat transfer, and Nusselt number for mass transfer. The Nusselt number for *heat transfer* characterizes the heat energy transferred between a moving liquid and a solid surface (e.g., pipe wall). It is defined as

$$Nu = \frac{hD}{K}$$

Where, h = heat transfer coefficient between the liquid and the pipe, kg/(s³ °C)

D = diameter of the pipe (or some other representative linear size), m

k = thermal conductivity, (m·kg)/(s³ °C)

The Nusselt number for *mass transfer* is defined as

$$Nu^* = \frac{mL}{tA\rho D}$$

Where, m = mass transferred

L = representative linear size

t = time elapsed

ρ = representative density

D = diffusion coefficient

A = area affected

H. Nusselt was a German engineer who derived the Nusselt number; B. Biot was a French physicist who was an early worker on the mathematical theories of convective heat transfer.

xii. Peclet Number (Pe)

The Peclet number has a role in characterizing forced heat convection and mass transfer. The former is defined as

$$Pe = \frac{\rho c v L}{k}$$

Where, ρ = density of fluid (or gas), kg/m^3

c = specific heat capacity of fluid, m^2/(s^2·°C)

v = velocity of fluid, m/s

L = characteristic linear size, m

k = thermal conductivity of liquid, (m·kg)/(s^3·°C)

Note that the Peclet number for heat transfer is the product of the Prandtl and Reynolds numbers, i.e., $Pe = Pr \cdot Re$.

The Peclet number for *mass transfer* is defined as

$$Pe^* = \frac{Lv}{D}$$

Where, D is the diffusion coefficient (diffusivity), m^2/s

Symbols L and v are as defined for Pe above.

J. Peclet was the first to apply Fourier's heat theories to solve engineering problems.

xiii. Prandtl Number (Pr)

The Prandtl number is used in fluid mechanics; it is defined as ratio of ***momentum and thermal diffusivity.***

$$Pr = \frac{c\mu}{k}$$

Where, c = specific heat capacity of the fluid, m^2/(s^2·°C)

μ = dynamic viscosity of fluid, kg/m·s

k = thermal conductivity of fluid, (m·kg)/(s^3·°C)

This number was named after Ludwig Prandtl, a German physicist. However, it was H. Nusselt, a German engineer, who first derived this number in 1910. To his credit, Prandtl acknowledged Nusselt's priority in his book in 1952.

xiv. Rayleigh Number (Ra)

This number is used in problems of heat transfer by free convection. It is defined as

$$Ra = \frac{L^3 \beta g \rho^2 c_p \Delta t}{\mu k}$$

Where, L = representative linear size, m

β = cubic expansion coefficient, 1/°C

g = gravitational acceleration, m/s^2

ρ= density of fluid, kg/m^3

c_p= specific heat capacity of fluid (at constant pressure),m^2/(s^2·°C)

Δt= temperature difference, °C

μ = dynamic viscosity of fluid, kg/m·s

k = thermal conductivity of fluid, (m·kg)/(s^3·°C)

The Rayleigh number is the product of the Grashof and Prandtl numbers. The Rayleigh number is named after Lord Rayleigh (John William Strutt), an English physicist.

xv. Reynolds Number (Re)

This is one of the more important dimensionless *named* variables; it is used to characterize the laminar or turbulent nature of a fluid flow. If $Re < 2000$, then the flow is laminar, otherwise it is turbulent. The Reynolds number is defined as ratio of ***inertial and viscous forces.***

$$Re = \frac{\rho v L}{\mu}$$

Where, v = velocity of fluid flow, m/s

L = representative linear size (e.g., inner diameter of a pipe, m

ρ = density of fluid, kg/m^3

μ = dynamic viscosity of fluid, kg/(m·s)

The Reynolds number is named after Osborne Reynolds, an English physicist and engineer.

xvi. Schmidt Number (Sc)

The Schmidt number is used to characterize diffusive mass transports. It is defined as ratio of ***momentum and mass diffusivities.***

$$Sc = \frac{\mu}{\rho D}$$

Where, μ = dynamic viscosity of fluid, kg/(m·s)

ρ = density of fluid, kg/m^3

D = diffusion coefficient (diffusity), m^2/s

The number was named after the German engineer E. Schmidt.

xvii. Stanton Number (St)

There are two Stanton numbers: one for heat transfer, and one for mass transport. The heat transfer Stanton number (St) is used to characterize forced heat convection and is defined as

$$St = \frac{h}{\rho v c_p}$$

Where, h = heat transfer coefficient, kg/(s^3·°C)

v = velocity, m/s

c_p = specific heat capacity of the fluidic medium at constant pressure, m^2/(s^2·°C)

ρ = density of the fluidic medium, kg/m^3

The heat transfer Stanton number is equivalent to the Nusselt number divided by the product of the Prandtl and Reynolds numbers. Thus

$$St = \frac{Nu}{Pr.Re}$$

The mass transfer Stanton number (St^*) is defined as

$$St^* = \frac{M}{\Delta t A \rho v}$$

Where, M = mass transferred, kg

Δt= time interval, s

A = area, m^2

ρ and v are as defined above

The Stanton numbers were named after the British scientist Sir Thomas Stanton.

xviii. Weber Number (We)

This dimensionless variable is used in the study of ***surface tension and inertial forces*** in liquids (e.g., bubble formations). The number is defined as

$$We = \frac{\rho v^2 L}{\sigma}$$

Where, ρ = density of fluid, kg/m^3

v = velocity of fluid, m/s

L = representative linear, m

σ = surface tension, kg/s^2

The number is named after the brothers Ernst and Wilhelm Weber. Ernst was a physiologist and Wilhelm a physicist, but together they studied the behaviour of flowing liquids.

Appendix-D

Some Important Equations

- **Manning's formula**

The Manning's equation is an empirical equation that applies to uniform flow in open channels and is a function of the channel velocity, flow area and channel slope.

$$V = 1 / n\, R^{2/3} S^{1/2}$$

$$Q = A \times V$$

Where;

Q = Flow Rate, [m^3/s]

V = Velocity, [m/s]

A = Flow Area, [m^2]

n = Manning's Roughness Coefficient (i.e. represents the roughness or friction applied to the flow by the channel)

R = Hydraulic Radius (area/wetted perimeter), [m]

S = Channel Slope, [m/m or dimensionless]

- **Chezy's formula**

In fluid dynamics the Chezy's formula describes the mean flow velocity of steady, turbulent open channel flow.

$$V = C\sqrt{R.S}$$

Where,

V = the mean velocity [m/s],

C = is the Chezy coefficient [$m^{1/2}/s$],

R = the hydraulic radius [m], and

S = the bottom slope [m/m].

This formula can also be used with Manning's Roughness Coefficient, instead of Chezy's coefficient. Manning derived the following relation to C based upon experiments.

$C = \frac{1}{n} R^{1/6}$, where n= Manning's roughness coefficient.

- **Darcy's weisbach formula**

When the water is flowing in a pipe, it experiences some resistance to its motion, whose effect is to reduce the velocity and ultimately the head of water available. An empirical formula for the loss of head due to friction was derived by Henry Darcy.

The loss of head due to friction according to Darcy is,

$$h_f = \frac{4flv^2}{2gd}$$

Where,

h_f = head loss [m]

f = friction factor

l = length of pipe work [m]

d = inner diameter of pipe work [m]

v = velocity of fluid [m/s]

g = acceleration due to gravity [m/s²]

- **Rational formula**

The rational method is appropriate for estimating peak discharges for small drainage areas of up to about 200 acres (80 hectares) with no significant flood storage. The method provides the designer with a peak discharge value, but does not provide a time series of flow nor flow volume.

The Rational Formula is defined as

$$Qp= 0.28 \times C \times I \times A$$

Where;

Qp = Peak runoff rate [m^3/sec]

C = Runoff coefficient [dimensionless]

I = Rainfall intensity [mm/hr]

A = Drainage area [km^2]

The Rational Formula follows the assumption that:

- The predicted peak discharge has the same probability of occurrence (return period) as the used rainfall intensity (I),
- The runoff coefficient (C) is constant during the rain storm, and
- The recession time is equal to the time of rise.
- The assumption that rainfall is uniformly distributed over the drainage area.

- **Modified Rational Formula**

A Modified rational method, actually an extension of the conventional Rational Method, has been used in the past for preliminary sizing of detention basins. The method is restricted to drainage areas of less than 20 acres.

In the Modified Rational Formula, a storage coefficient is included to account for a recession time larger than the time the hydrograph takes to rise.

The Modified Rational Formula is defined as:

$$Q_P = 0.28 \times C_S \times C \times I \times A$$

Where;

Cs	= Storage coefficient	[dimensionless]
Qp	= Peak runoff rate	[m^3/sec]
C	= Runoff coefficient	[dimensionless]
I	= Rainfall intensity	[mm/hr]
A	= Drainage area	[km^2]

- **SCS Curve Number Method**

  The runoff curve number (also called a curve number or simply CN) is an empirical parameter used in hydrology for predicting direct runoff or infiltration from rainfall excess. The curve number method was developed by the USDA Natural Resources Conservation Service, which was formerly called the Soil Conservation Service or SCS popularly known as a "SCS runoff curve number".

- **Affinity laws of pumps or fans**

  The Affinity Laws of centrifugal pumps or fans indicates the influence on volume capacity, head (pressure) and/or power consumption of a pump or fan due to

  - ✓ change in speed of wheel - revolutions per minute (rpm)
  - ✓ geometrically similarity - change in impeller diameter

a) **Change in speed of wheel (RPM) :**

When the impeller diameter of a centrifugal pump is held constant the effect of changing the speed (RPM) of the pump is in accordance with the following:

- ✓ Capacity : $Q1/Q2 = (N1/N2)$
- ✓ Head : $H1/H2 = (N1/N2)^2$
- ✓ Break Horse Power : $BHP1/BHP2 = (N1/N2)^3$

b) **Changing the Impeller Diameter:**

When the speed (RPM) of a centrifugal pump is held constant the effect of changing the impeller diameter (D) is as follows :

- ✓ Capacity : $Q1/Q2 = (D1/D2)$
- ✓ Head : $H1/H2 = (D1/D2)^2$
- ✓ Break Horse Power: $BHP1/BHP2 = (D1/D2)^3$

- **Hagen Poisuellie's equation**

The equation is also known as the Hagen–Poiseuille law, Poiseuille law and Poiseuille equation. It gives the pressure drop in a fluid flowing through a long cylindrical pipe. The assumptions of the equation are that the flow is laminar viscous and incompressible and the flow is through a constant circular cross-section that is significantly longer than its diameter.

The volumetric flow rate (V) through the pipe is given by

$$V = \frac{\Delta p \pi R^4}{8 \eta L}$$

Where;

Δp = pressure loss (P[pa)

L = length of pipe (m)

η = dynamic viscosity (Pa·s)

V = volumetric flow rate (m3/s)

R = radius of pipe (m)

- **Kirpich's formula**

This formula is used for estimating the time of concentration (Tc) in the watershed. The Tc is defined as the time required for a particle of water to travel from the most hydrologically remote point in the watershed to the point of collection.

It is defined as

$$Tc = 0.0192\ L^{0.77}(S)^{-0.385}$$

Where;

Tc = time of concentration (in minutes)

L = maximum hydraulic flow length (in meter), and

S = slope of watershed [ratio of the difference in elevation (meter) between the outlet of the watershed and the hydraulically most remote point in the watershed (H) to the maximum hydraulic flow length (meter) or simply H/L]

- **Specific speed of pump**

Specific Speed is a number characterizing the type of impeller in pump in a unique and coherent manner. It identifies the geometrically similarity of pumps.

It is defined numerically as

$$Ns = (N \times Q^{1/2}) / H^{3/4}$$

Where;

Ns = specific speed [dimensionless]

N = pump rotational speed [rpm]

Q = flow [cumec or m^3/s]

H = head [m]

- **USLE equation**

Universal Soil Loss Equation (USLE) : Wischmeier and Smith's (1960) established an empirical model for predicting annual soil loss on a cultivated field so that erosion control specialists could choose the kind of measures needed in order to keep erosion within acceptable limits given the climate, slope and production factors.

This erosion prediction equation is composed of five sub-equations :

$$E = R \times K \times LS \times C \times P$$

Where;

A = Estimated average soil loss (in tons per acre per year)

R = rainfall-runoff erosivity factor, equals E, the kinetic energy of rainfall, multiplied by I_{30} (maximum intensity of rain in 30 minutes expressed in cm per hour).

K = soil erodibility factor, depends on the organic matter and texture of the soil, its permeability and profile structure. It is measured on bare reference plots 22.2 m long on 9% slopes.

LS = topographical factor, depends on both the length and gradient of the slope.

C = cover management factor, is a simple relation between erosion on bare soil and erosion observed under a cropping system. The C factor combines plant cover, its production level and the associated cropping techniques. It varies from 0 to 1.

P = support practice factor such as contour tilling or mounding, or contour ridging. It varies from 0 to 1.

❖ **Limitations**

- ✓ It predicts average annual soil loss.
- ✓ The model applies only to sheet and rill erosion since the source of energy is rain; so it never applies to linear or mass erosion.
- ✓ The model has been tested and verified in the plain and hilly country with 1-20% slopes.
- ✓ The model applies only for average data over 20 years and is not valid for individual storms.

- **Modified USLE**

The Modified Universal Soil Loss Equation (MUSLE), developed by Williams and Berndt (1976) can be used to calculate sediment yields from drainage basins to specific locations for selected storm events which take into account not rainfall erosivity but the volume of runoff.

The formula is given as:

$$T = 95 (V \times Q_P)^{0.56} \times K \times LS \times C \times P$$

Where;

T = sediment yield per storm event [tons]

V = volume of runoff per storm event [acre-feet]

Q_P = peak flow per storm event [cubic feet per second]

K, LS, C, and P are USLE factors

Values for V and Q_P are determined from the sites drainage analysis

- **Revised USLE**

The Revised Universal Soil Loss Equation (RUSLE) was developed by Renard (1992). It has improved the effects of soil roughness and the effects of local weather on the prediction of soil loss and sediment delivery. RUSLE is a computation method which may be used for site evaluation and planning purposes and to aid in the decision process of selecting erosion control measures. It provides an estimate of the severity of erosion. It will also provide quantifiable results to substantiate the benefits of planned erosion control measures, such as the advantage of adding a diversion ditch or mulch. For example, a diversion may shorten the length of slope used in calculating a LS factor.

RUSLE has the same formula as USLE, but has several improvements in determining factors. These include some new and revised isoerodent maps; a time-varying approach for soil erodibility factor; a subfactor approach for evaluating the cover-management factor; a new equation to reflect slope length and steepness; and new conservation-practice values.

- **Weir formula**
  - A weir is an opening in the sidewall of a tank at top. The stream of liquid coming out the weir is known as a nappe, sheet, or vein. A weir is generally an overflow structure, with a broad crest, built across an open channel. A weir or notch is generally used for measuring the flow of liquids.
  - The top of weir wall over which the liquid flows is known as the sill or crest.
  - The head under which the weir is discharging is measured from the crest to the free surface.
  - **Rectangular Weir**

    The flow rate measurement in a rectangular weir is based on the Bernoulli Equation principles and can be expressed as:

    $$Q = 2/3 \times C_d \times b \times (2\,g)^{1/2} \times h^{3/2}$$

    Where;

    Q = flow rate (m^3/s)

    h = head on the weir (m)

    b = width of the weir (m)

    g = acceleration due to gravity (9.81 m/s^2)

    C_d = discharge constant for the weir

    Note:

    ✓ *If the height of water above the weir crest is greater than two times of the width of the crest of weir, the weir is called a Narrow Crested weir. A narrow crested weir is hydraulically similar to an ordinary weir or to a rectangular weir.*

    ✓ *The discharge equation for an ogee weir remains the same as that of a rectangular weir.*

- **Triangular or V-Notch Weir**

For a triangular or v-notch weir the flow rate can be expressed as:

$$Q = 8/15 \times C_d \times (2\ g)^{1/2} \times \tan(\theta/2) \times h^{5/2}$$

Where:

θ = v-notch angle

- **Cippoletti weir:**

It is a trapezoidal weir with side slopes 1 in 4 (1H: 4V). The formula for the discharge over a cippoletti weir is the as that for a rectangular weir without end contractions.

$$Q = 2/3 \times C_d \times b \times (2\ g)^{1/2} \times h^{3/2}$$

- **Broad-crested rectangular weir:**

If the height of water above the weir crest is not greater than two times of the width of the crest of weir, the weir is called a Broad Crested weir. The head over a crest on the u/s is H and d/s edge is h.

$$Q = C_d \times b \times 2g^{1/2} \times (H\ h^2 - h^3)^{1/2}$$

$$\text{Here } H = h + (V_a^2/2g)$$

- **Sutro Weir (linear Proportional Weir)**

The linear proportional weir, with its linear head-discharge characteristic is used as a control for dosing services, as a flow measuring device and as an outlet for grit chambers. The linear proportional Weir was devised by Stout (1897). This is of theoretical interest only as its width at base is infinite. This was modified by Sutro (1908) to develop a practical linear Proportional Weir and is known as the Sutro Weir. A designed shape is fitted for the Sutro Weir which has a rectangular base. It is to be noted that for flows above the base of the weir, the discharge is proportional to the head measured above a reference plane located at one third of the depths of the crest of the base weir.

The discharge over the rectangular weir for a depth of flow h above the origin is

$q_w = \frac{4}{3} W C_d \sqrt{2g}\left[(h+s)^{\frac{3}{2}} - h^{\frac{3}{2}}\right]$

- **Darcy's formula:**

The flow of ground water or any other fluid moving through rock or any media isgoverned by an empirical law, one derived from experimental observation, not from theory. This expression for ground water flow is known as Darcy's Law. Henry Darcy formulated this law in the 1850's and published his observations in1856.

$$Q = -kA\frac{dH}{dL}$$

The negative sign is used by convention to note that water is flowing from highest to lowest hydraulic head.

Where,

Q = Flow rate; A = cross section Area

dH/dL = Hydraulic gradient i.e. Head loss per unit length

k = the permeability of the medium. It depends on the size, shape, packing and orientation of the material.

Darcy's Law is only applicable to laminar flow with small Reynolds numbers (<1-10) Groundwater behaves as laminar flow under most circumstances.

- Water horse power

$$WHP\ (hp) = \frac{flow\ rate\ \left(\frac{m^3}{s}\right) \times Head\ (m) \times Density\ of\ liquid\ \left(\frac{kg}{m^3}\frac{kg}{m^3}\right)}{75}$$

Institutes working on Soil Water Engineering Aspect

Institutes Abbreviations	Full name	Location
International Institutes		
IWMI (Formerly IIMI)	International Water Management Institute (International Irrigation Management Institute)	Colombo, Sri Lanka.
IILRI	International Institute for Land Reclamation and Improvement	Netherland.
NRCS (formerly SCS)	Natural Resources Conservation Service (Soil Conservation Service).	Washing-ton, D.C., USA
National Institutes		
WALMI	Water and Land Management Institute	Aurangabad Maharashtra
CAZRI	Central Arid Zone Research Institute	Jodhpur, Rajasthan
NBSS&LUP	National Bureau of Soil Survey and Land Use Planning	Nagpur, Maharashtra
CSSRI	Central Soil Salinity Research Institute	Karnal, Haryana
NGFRI	Indian Grassland and Fodder Research Institute	Jhansi, UP.
IISWC (formerly CSWCRTI)	Indian Institute of Soil and Water Conservation (Central Soil & Water Conservation Research Training Institute)	Dehradun, Uttarakhand
IIWM (formerly DWM)	Indian Institute of Water Management (Directorate of Water Management)	Bhubaneswar, Orissa
CWPC	Central Water and Power Commission	Pune, Maharashtra
CWC	Central Water Commission	New Delhi
WQAA	Water Quality Assessment Authority	New Delhi
CGWB	Central Ground Water Board,	New Delhi

NWDA	National Water Development Agency	New Delhi
RGNGWTRI	Rajiv Gandhi National Ground Water Training & Research Institute	Raipur, Chhattisgarh

Abbreviations :

- **NCIWRD:** National Commission on Integrated Water Resources Development
- **PIM:** Participatory Irrigation Management
- **CADA:** Command Area Development Authority
- **PRA**: Participatory Rural Appraisal
- **NMMI:** National Mission on Micro Irrigation
- **NCPAH:** National Committee on Plasticulture Agriculture with Horticulture
- **WUA:** Water User Association
- **NWP:** National Water Policy

Miscellaneous

FACTS AND FIGURES

- According to the UN estimates, the total amount of water on earth is about **1400 million cubic kilometer** which is enough to cover the earth with a layer of 3000 metres depth.
- In global water resources, the salt water occupies: **97.3 %**
- About **2.7** per cent of the total water available on the earth is fresh water of which about **75.2** per cent lies frozen in Polar Regions and another **22.6** per cent is present as ground water.
- The stage of Ground Water Development in the Country is **61%**.
- The ground water resources of the Country have been estimated for freshwater based on the guidelines and recommendations of the **Groundwater Resource Estimation committee-1997 (GEC-97).**
- The total Annual Replenishable ground water resources of the Country have been estimated as **431 billion cubic meter (BCM)**. Keeping 35 BCM for natural discharge, the net annual ground water availability for the entire Country is 396 BCM. The Annual ground water draft is 243 BCM out of which 221 BCM is for irrigation use and 22 BCM is for domestic & industrial use.
- Under the CAD programme, initially 60 major and medium irrigation projects were taken up, covering a Culturable Command Area (CCA) of about 15 million hectare.
- **RRR**: Repair, Renovation & Restoration
- **DRIP**: Dam Rehabilitation and Improvement Project (started in 2012)

- The North Eastern Regional Institute of Water and Land Management (NERIWALM) is a registered society established on 23rd December, 1989 at Tezpur, Assam, India under the aegis of North Eastern Council (NEC), Shillong, Ministry of Development of North Eastern Region (DoNER), Government of India.
- The Centrally Sponsored Command Area Development (CAD) programme was launched in **1974-75** for development of adequate delivery system of irrigation water up to farmers' field with an objective to enhance water use efficiency and production and productivity of crops per unit of land and water for improving socio-economic condition of farmers.
- Central Ground Water Board was established in 1970 by renaming the **Exploratory Tube wells Organization** under the Ministry of Agriculture, Government of India. It was merged with the Ground Water Wing of the Geological Survey of India during 1972.

Various Iso term

- **Isohyet:** It is an imaginary line on a map connecting points having the same amount of rainfall in a given period.
- **Isobath:** It is an imaginary line on a map connecting points of equal groundwater depth.
- **Isopleth:** It is an imaginary line on a map connecting points having equal depth of evapotranspiration.
- **Isobar:** It is an imaginary line connecting points of equal atmospheric pressure.
- **Isotherm:** It is an imaginary line connecting points of equal temperature.
- **Isochor:** It is an imaginary line connecting points of equal volume.

- **Isochrone:** It is an imaginary line connecting points of equal traveling time from a point.
- **Isohel:** It is an imaginary line on a map connecting points having the same duration of sunshine.
- **Isohaline:** It is an imaginary line drawn on a map or chart to indicate connecting points of equal salinity in the ocean.
- **Isoneph:** It is an imaginary line representing points of equal amounts of cloud cover.
- **Isotachs:** It is an imaginary line representing points of equal wind speed.
- **Isoline:** it is also called as contour line or isarithm or isogram. It is an imaginary line representing points of equal value.
- **Isosine:** It is an imaginary line representing points of equal slope.
- **Isocline:** It is a curve through points at which the parent function's slope will always be the same, regardless of initial conditions.
- **Contour line:** It is an imaginary line representing points of equal elevation (height) above a given level, such as mean sea level.
- **Isentropic:** It is an imaginary line connecting points of equal entropy
- **Isobathytherm**: It is an imaginary line connecting points of equal temperature and depth underground
- **Isobront**: It is an imaginary line connecting points of simultaneous storm development
- **Isochar line:** It is an imaginary connecting points of similar distinguishing characteristics of plant life
- **Isocheim:** It is an imaginary line connecting points of same average winter temperature

- **Isodose:** It is an imaginary line connecting points that receive equal doses of radiation
- **Isodrosotherm:** It is an imaginary line connecting points of equal dew point
- **Isogon line**: It is an imaginary connecting points of same specified angle or same wind direction.
- **Isometric:** It is an imaginary line connecting points of equal variations of pressure.
- **Isopach:** It is an imaginary line connecting points of equal thickness of geological strata.
- **Isophene:** It is an imaginary line connecting points of the same phenotype or seasonal variation.
- **Isoseismal:** It is an imaginary line connecting points of same earthquake intensity.
- **Isothere**: It is an imaginary line connecting points of equal summer temperature.
- **Isotherombrose:** It is an imaginary line connecting points of equal ratio of summer rainfall to annual rainfall.
- **Isoerodent :** It is an imaginary line connecting points areas of equal erosion potentials.

OOOOO